Classic Art

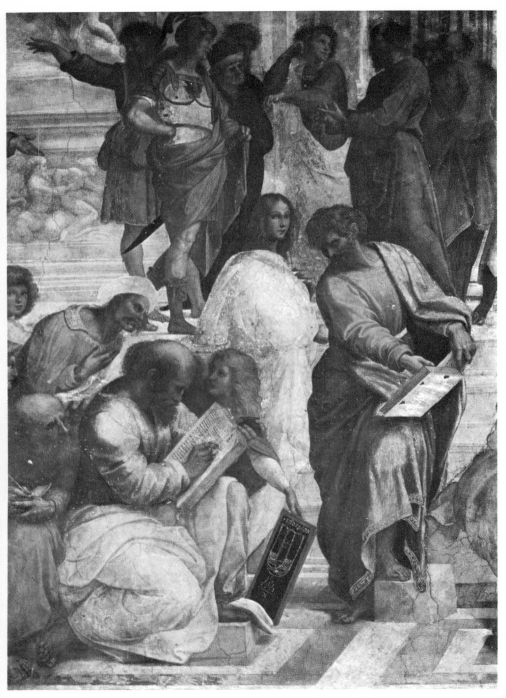

RAPHAEL: Detail from the *School of Athens*. Vatican

Classic Art

An Introduction to the
Italian Renaissance

Heinrich Wölfflin

Phaidon · Oxford

Phaidon Press Limited, Littlegate House,
St Ebbe's Street, Oxford, OX1 1SQ

First published 1952
Fourth edition (photographically reprinted)
1980
All rights reserved

Translated by Peter and Linda Murray from the
eighth German edition published by Benno
Schwabe and Co., Basle

British Library Cataloguing in Publication Data
Wölfflin, Heinrich
　　Classic art. – 4th ed. – (Landmarks in art
　　history).
　　1. Art, Italian
　　2. Art, Renaissance – Italy
　　I. Title　　　　II. Series
　　709′.45　　　　　N6915

ISBN 0-7148-2101-2

Printed in Great Britain at The Pitman Press, Bath

CONTENTS

INTRODUCTION

by HERBERT READ

W HEN HEINRICH WÖLFFLIN died in 1945 at the age of eighty-one, it could be said of him that he had found art criticism a subjective chaos and left it a science. In 1893 he had succeeded Jacob Burckhardt in the chair of art history in the University of Basle, and Burckhardt in his turn had been a great art historian. But genial as were his intuitions, convincing as were his generalisations, Burckhardt had no *method* by means of which he could classify the phenomena of art, no measure to control the waywardness of his personal prejudices. Wölfflin's great distinction is that he did perfect such a scientific method in art-historical criticism, and there is no art critic of importance after his time who has not, consciously or unconsciously, been influenced by him.

He himself had his predecessors, from whom he took fruitful suggestions. Burckhardt himself was certainly the most important of these, but even more decisive was the famous German sculptor, Adolf Hildebrand, whose short treatise on *The Problem of Form* (published in 1893) Wölfflin describes in the Preface to this volume as "a refreshing shower upon parched earth". Hildebrand in his turn had been influenced by Conrad Fiedler (1841–95), a brilliant but fragmentary philosopher whose aphorisms on painting, sculpture and architecture were original and penetrating. This amounts to saying that Wölfflin was the culmination of a certain development in the science of art, which in its turn was part of the general historical development of thought between 1850 and 1950. We may call it the scientific temper of the age, and it begins, of course, long before 1850. But it was only very slowly and tentatively that the phenomena of art were submitted to intellectual analysis—it was felt, even by such a dispassionate observer as Burckhardt, that mysterious personal factors were involved, and these were beyond analysis. It was Wölfflin's distinction that he, first of all, kept his eye steadily fixed on the work of art, and began to analyse what he saw, and to classify the results of such visual analysis.

His first book (apart from a doctrinal thesis on the psychology of architecture) was *Renaissance und Barock*, published in 1888. It was followed ten years later by the present volume, dealing with the art of what we call the High Renaissance, and in 1915 came the first edition of *Kunstgeschichtliche Grundbegriffe* (translated in 1932 as *Principles of Art History*), in which the emphasis shifts to the Baroque period. The series—for there is a certain continuity between all the volumes— was completed by *Italien und das deutsche Formgefühl* in 1931. This by no means represents all Wölfflin's publications—there is a book on Albrecht Dürer (1905), a collection of essays (*Gedanken zur Kunstgeschichte*, 1941) and a volume of posthumous papers (*Kleine Schriften*, 1946). Throughout Wölfflin is concerned with what he calls "the problem of the development of style", which is certainly the main problem of art history, objectively considered. In order to solve this problem, Wölfflin invented a morphology of form with special terminology, and although this terminology was only perfected with the publication of *Kunstgeschichtliche Grundbegriffe*, it makes a tentative appearance in the second part of this volume and it is therefore desirable that the reader should have some knowledge of it.

Wölfflin posited a law of development *within* the formative imagination, a cyclic theory to account for the parallelism to be discerned between the visual arts of any self-contained period, as well as for the alternation of certain generally distinctive characteristics from one period to another. He formulated five pairs of contrary concepts—the opposite poles, as it were, between which the artistic spirit oscillates:

(1) From *linear* to *painterly*.
(2) From *plane* to *recession*.
(3) From *closed form* to *open form*.
(4) From *multiplicity* to *unity*.
(5) *Absolute clarity* and *relative clarity* of the subject.

We must not elaborate these concepts here—the reader not familiar with them should refer to *Principles of Art History*. One word, however, calls for comment—the word "painterly", which has been invented to convey the meaning of the German word *malerisch*. It is a word absolutely essential to the discussion of stylistic problems in art, and purists must admit it into our language, for no other word is exact enough. It stands for that depreciation and gradual obliteration of line (outline and tangible surface) and for the merging of these in a "shifting semblance" of things—it is an attempt to represent the vague and impalpable essence of things. English readers who are familiar with the distinction which Blake made between "the hard and wiry line of rectitude" and the "broken lines, broken masses, and broken colours" which he denounced as "bungling" will have already seized the full meaning of the word.

With these concepts Wölfflin found that he could unravel the intricate developments of style within any period of western art, and could clearly indicate the transitions from one style to another. It was almost too easy, and critics were not lacking to point out that "form" was not everything in a work of art—the content was also significant, and *what* the artist painted at any given time might be of more importance than the formal conventions he had accepted as a matter of course. Besides, how account, formally, for the kaleidoscopic changes of a modern artist like Picasso, who seemed to take all Wölfflin's contrary concepts in his stride? Wölfflin was not insensitive to these criticisms, and in his later work made full allowance for the symbolic image as distinct from the structural form in the work of art. Not that Wölfflin was ever intransigently formalistic. What will immediately strike the reader hitherto unfamiliar with his work is the extraordinary acuteness of his visual sensibility, but a sensibility it is, and not a calculating machine. He misses nothing in a painting or a piece of sculpture, and accounts for everything. The multiplicity that he reveals is always related to a total impression of unity, and that impression could only be intuitive. He is particularly eager to discover unity where to the superficial view it might seem not to exist, as in the ceiling of the Sistine Chapel (pp. 52–3). I emphasise this point because the usual complaint directed against formal criticism such as Wölfflin's is that it is destructive of aesthetic pleasure—"we murder to dissect". That may be true of the method of some of Wölfflin's followers, but in this volume at any rate, Wölfflin is by our present standards almost embarrassingly effusive. A perfect example of his method is his description of a portrait by Andrea del Sarto (pp. 180–2). Although he gives a very precise geometrical analysis of the composition (vertical and horizontal axes, etc.), he does not hesitate to use phrases like "mysterious charm", "*noblesse*", "subtle", "spiritual"—all unanalysable qualities. Like all good critics of art, Wölfflin is a master of words—only a master of words has the equipment necessary to express adequately in the literary medium the qualities of a plastic medium like painting: there is a wide area of "poesy" common to both arts. In this respect nothing Wölfflin ever wrote can match Pater's two or three masterpieces of evocation—nothing ever written about works of art, not even by Ruskin, has quite that breathless delicacy. But Pater and Ruskin wrote what we call dubiously "prose-poetry", which is poetry all the same. Wölfflin is essentially a prose-artist, but still an artist.

In his descriptions of general tendencies (as in the chapters here on "The New Ideals" and "The New Beauty") Wölfflin rivals his predecessor Burckhardt. There is perhaps more precision in his method, but hardly so wide a vision— Burckhardt, after all, had profound historical insight of almost unlimited scope. It is in his final chapter, foreshadowing the *Grundbegriffe*, that Wölfflin displays his originality. Here he broaches those generic characteristics of a period which defy minute formalistic analysis, but which determine the method of presentation, or pictorial form (the way of seeing), in any given period. Certain concepts— of repose and grandeur, of simplicity and lucidity, of complexity, of unity and inevitability—are seen as the underlying causes of a new way of seeing the world, and as present whatever the subject and whoever the artist. We do not explain them by calling them expressions of the Zeitgeist, etc., and it may be that Wölfflin does not go very far in basic explanation—for that we had to wait for the concept of the archetype which we owe to another Swiss scholar, C. G. Jung. But Wölfflin does put us in possession of some of the dimensions of the archetypes in art, and this last chapter is infinitely suggestive. His "conclusion" shows him searching for a conception of art-history which would avoid on the one hand the superficiality of a subjective interpretation of art (art as an expression of the spirit of the age) and on the other hand the aridity of a purely formalistic type of art criticism. In his later works he is still searching for this new conception of art-history, and approaching ever nearer to it.

Wölfflin has had a great influence on art-historical criticism in every part of the world. In England one should mention Roger Fry, who reviewed this book as long ago as 1903 (in *The Athenaeum,* No. 3974, pp. 862–3). Some years later, in reviewing *Kunstgeschichtliche Grundbegriffe* in *The Burlington Magazine* (Vol. xxxix, September, 1921, pp. 145–8) he characterized Wölfflin in the following terms: *Unlike so many art historians, Dr. Wölfflin looks on art with some under-standing of the problems of the creator. He does not merely see what there is in the work of art, but he knows what mental conditions in the artist's mind are implied by that configuration. In fact, he begins where most art-historians leave off. They are content to show that a picture was produced by such an artist at such a date. He tries to show why at such a date and in such surroundings the picture has the form that we see.*

There is no doubt that Fry himself was profoundly influenced in his views on art (as well as in his method of art criticism) by Wölfflin. The influence of Wölfflin on Bernard Berenson is equally obvious, and has been acknowledged.

That formalistic criticism has developed to excess in our time must perhaps be ascribed to the fact that critics (at any rate in the English-speaking countries) have so often absorbed Wölfflin's conceptions at second-hand. Now that his two main works are available in excellent translations, we may see a return to Wölfflin's own more generous and philosophic conception of the critic's task. The translation of further works by this master of enlightenment is most earnestly to be desired.

TRANSLATORS' NOTE

THE present translation has been made from the eighth German edition (Basel, 1948), which is textually a reprint of the sixth edition, the last one supervised by Wölfflin himself. 'Die klassische Kunst' first appeared in 1899 and was translated into English in 1903 when much of Wölfflin's terminology was still unknown in England. In the half-century since its first publication the book has become one of the classics of art-history and much of the terminology has been familiarised; for example, by the appearance of an English translation of 'Kunstgeschichtliche Grundbegriffe' (Principles of Art History). Inevitably, however, certain passages have been to some extent invalidated by later research and this brings us to the thorny question of notes. Above all, the present translators have desired to retain as much of Wölfflin as possible and all his notes are, therefore, translated in full; on the other hand, they have wished to avoid the defect of presuming to 'improve' upon their author by 'bringing him up-to-date', that is, thrusting forward their own views in the guise of translators' notes. It is, nevertheless, undeniable that much of the information given in Wölfflin's notes is of little use to modern English readers—there is little point in referring the reader of a translation to, for example, the *Jahrbuch der preussischen Kunstsammlungen* for 1894 when he may get the same information from a book in English which is readily available. Re-arrangement of galleries has also led to some works being moved from the places in which Wölfflin saw them—*e.g.* from the Academy in Florence to the Uffizi. So far as possible these changes have been noted, but under present conditions it is impossible to hope for completeness. For these reasons the translators have added some notes, enclosed in square brackets, whenever they have felt it necessary or helpful, yet as rarely as possible. Such a compromise may be distasteful to purists, and scholars will certainly find them inadequate, but scholars will refer to Wölfflin's own citations. It is hoped that these notes may be of service to those who read no German: nothing else is claimed for them.

The publishers have added a considerable number of new illustrations so that all the works discussed in any detail are here reproduced. This is perhaps the best service that can be given to one of the most important and influential art-historical books ever written.

Finally, the translators would like to thank Dr. L. D. Ettlinger, of the Warburg Institute, and Mrs. Ettlinger, for the immense care with which they have weighed the English version against the original so that as many as possible of the nuances of Wölfflin's thought have been incorporated; and they would also like to thank Mr. A. F. Bramley for his timely and much-appreciated help in preparing a typescript from a somewhat obscure draft.

Peter Murray

London, December 1950   *Linda Murray*

POSTSCRIPT

This book was first published more than 80 years ago, so it is hardly surprising if it seems to reflect the ideas and tastes of the Victorian era rather than our own. The emphasis given to the work of Andrea del Sarto, and especially the splendidly buxom women in the *Birth of the Virgin* (Fig. 106), is, indeed, Edwardian rather than Victorian; and, perhaps, German-Swiss rather than Anglo-Saxon. A book published so long ago must necessarily reflect not only its author's ideas and predilections, but also those of Vasari. This is because Vasari was still the major source of information, both primary and secondary, on the art of the Cinquecento, since few of the modern classics of art history had then been published—Berenson's famous *Lists* began with the publication, in 1894, of his *Venetian Painters of the Renaissance*, followed by the *Florentine Painters* . . . in 1896.

In his own admirable book on the High Renaissance (1975), Michael Levey takes exception to Wölfflin's neglect of the Venetians and his following of Vasari in emphasizing the primacy of *disegno*: 'Wölfflin's over-praised and deplorably influential *Classic Art*, the English edition of which provides nearly forty illustrations of Raphael's work and only four by Titian . . .' Nevertheless, it is legitimate to prefer drawing to colour (as did Michelangelo), and, while it is fair to draw attention to the bias introduced by Vasari's Florentine *campanilismo*, Vasari may have been right. In any case, Winckelmann wrote a classic of art history without having seen many Greek statues, and Wölfflin's book is now a classic in its own right.

P.M. and L.M., 1980

PREFACE TO THE FIRST EDITION

CONTEMPORARY public interest, in so far as it is in touch with the visual arts, seems nowadays to desire a return to specifically artistic questions. The reader no longer expects an art-historical book to give mere biographical anecdotes or a description of the circumstances of the time; he wants to be told something of those things which constitute the value and the essence of a work of art, and he reaches out eagerly for new concepts—for the old words will no longer serve—and once again, he is beginning to pay attention to aesthetics, which had been entirely shelved. A book like Adolf Hildebrand's 'Problem der Form' fell like a refreshing shower upon parched earth: at last there was a new method of approach to art, a point of view which was not only expanded in breadth by new material, but which also made a deep study of detail.

The artist who wrote this now much-quoted book twisted, in it, a prickly garland with which to crown our art-historical efforts. The historical point of view, he says, has led to the differences between, and changes in, artistic manifestations being brought more and more into the foreground; it is a point of view which treats art as the emanation of various individuals considered as personalities, or as a product of differing historical circumstances and national peculiarities. From this there develops the false notion that art is primarily a matter relating to the personal and non-artistic side of human beings; every standard of judgement of art, as such, is then lost. The minor relationships are made the chief things, and the artistic content, which follows its own inner laws, unaffected by all temporal changes, is ignored.

It seems to me, continues Hildebrand, like a gardener growing plants under cloches of varying shapes in order to make his shrubs grow in different shapes, after which people concerned themselves only with these different shapes, quite forgetting, in their interest in these differences, that they were dealing with plants with an inner growth and natural laws of their own.

This criticism is one-sided and harsh, but perhaps it is salutary.[1] The characterization of artistic personalities, or the style of an individual or an age, will always remain a task for art history and will always arouse a strong interest among men, but historical learning has, in fact, almost abandoned the greater theme of 'art' and has passed it over to a separate study—the philosophy of art— to which it has already frequently denied the right to exist. The natural thing would be for every art-historical monograph to contain some aesthetics as well.

---

[1] The real analogy with the reprehensible conduct of the art historian is not to be found in this story of the gardener, but rather in a kind of botany which should seek to be nothing more than a study of the geographical distribution of plants.

The author of this book has had such a goal before his eyes: his intention was to emphasise the artistic content of Italian classic art, an art which reached its maturity in the Cinquecento. Anyone who wishes to understand it will do well to take the bull by the horns, that is, to make himself acquainted with the fully developed phenomenon, for it is only there that the full essence of this art expresses itself, and there, too, that standards of criticism can first be achieved.

This enquiry is confined to the great masters of Central Italy—Venice developed along similar lines, but it would have confused the issue to have dealt with the special conditions obtaining there. It goes without saying that only masterpieces are mentioned, and even here the author must be permitted a certain freedom in the choice and treatment of them, in so far as his plan did not aim at the portrayal of individual artists, but at the comprehension of general features and of the style as a whole. In order to be more sure of reaching his goal, the first—historical—section has a systematic one as its counterpart, which is arranged according to concepts and not according to personalities, and this second part is supposed to give, at the same time, an explanation of the phenomenon.

The book is not intended to be an academic treatise, but it is probable that a certain schoolmasterly quality will be observed in it, and the author gladly confesses that his experiences in the interchange of ideas with young art-lovers at the University, the joy of teaching people to see, and learning to see, in the course of teaching art-history have been the principal factors in encouraging him to the rash decision to make public his opinions on so eminently artistic a theme as the classic style, when he himself is not an artist.

Basel, Autumn 1898   *Heinrich Wölfflin*

EXTRACTS FROM THE PREFACES TO THE
SECOND AND FOURTH EDITIONS

. . . . A more ample treatment or more extensive discussion of examples may well seem desirable, here and there; but the author's main purpose would gain but little, his purpose being to treat and to elucidate the art of a whole period in the round. Doubtless, in order to come to grips with the phenomenon, the questions should have been formulated more comprehensively and acutely—the whole subject of colour is entirely left out—but for the time being our efforts must be directed towards bringing order into the separate observations. The concepts of 'Ideals', 'Beauty', 'Pictorial Form' state the main trends, and I confess that it is scarcely possible to misunderstand me more grievously than by proposing to do away with the division between the chapters on 'Beauty' and 'Pictorial Form'. Art-history must now call to mind its own formal problems, problems which are not settled by defining one ideal of beauty as against another; that is, by making sharp distinctions between styles, for these formal problems begin much further back and are fundamental to the concept of representation as such. There is still a great deal of work to be done here. Comprehensive and connected researches must be made into the development of draughtsmanship, the treatment of chiaroscuro, perspective and the representation of space, and so on, if art-history is to be not only illustrative of the history of civilization, but is to stand on its own feet as well. At present, such researches appear somewhat threadbare, but, if the signs are not deceptive, this is the moment to take up these important supplementary studies, as contributions towards a general 'History of artistic vision'.

. . . . The author would have been inclined towards sweeping revision, although his views remain unchanged, for he could wish for additional argument and description: yet it soon became clear that mere patchwork would not attain the desired result. For this reason he plans, so far as he is able, to fill the gap of which he is conscious by writing a special book, containing detailed analyses, which to some extent may serve as a second volume to the present book.

H. W.

INTRODUCTION

THE word 'classic' has, for us, a rather chilly sound. We feel that it drags us away from the bright, living world into airless rooms inhabited not by warm, red-blooded human beings but only by shadows. 'Classic Art' seems to be the eternally-dead, the eternally-old, the fruit of the Academies, the result of learning and not of life, and in us the desire for the living, the actual, the tangible, is so urgent. What the modern man wants above all is an art with a strong smell of earth about it, and so the Quattrocento, not the Cinquecento, is the darling of our age, because of its vivid sense of reality, and the naive quality of its vision and perception. We accept some archaisms of expression as part of the bargain for we are so eager to admire and to be amused at the same time.

The old masters tell their stories with such simplicity and truth that the visitor to Florence gazes with inexhaustible enjoyment at their pictures, feeling himself drawn into the pleasant rooms of the Florentines, where the woman in bed receives her visitors after her child is born, and into the streets and squares of the old city, where people stand about and where someone looks out of the picture at us with a casual yet disconcerting directness. Everyone knows Ghirlandaio's paintings in the church of Santa Maria Novella. With what zest he tells the stories of the Virgin and St. John, bourgeois—but not petty bourgeois —life, seen in festival splendour, with a frank pleasure in opulence and bright colour, rich clothes, ornament, furnishings and elaborate architecture! Can anything be more charming than Filippino's picture in the Badia, where the Virgin appears to St. Bernard and lays her small, delicate hand on his book? How graceful and natural are the exquisite girl-angels who accompany Mary and, with hands folded only mechanically in prayer, press forward behind her mantle to stare with shy curiosity at the strange and extraordinary man. And is not even Raphael overshadowed by the magic of Botticelli, and can he who has once discovered the melancholy sensuousness of his eyes still find the *Madonna della Sedia* interesting?

For us the Early Renaissance evokes a vision of slight and lovely girls in gaily coloured dresses, of fluttering veils, flowering meadows, and open airy halls where slender columns support the wide arches; it means all the infinite variety of youth and strength, unaffectedly natural yet with a touch of fairytale splendour about it. Reluctantly and grudgingly we step out of this bright, gay world into the high, still halls of classic art. What sort of men are these? The strangeness of their gestures disturbs us and we miss the simple, naive unselfconsciousness of the earlier art. No one here looks at us with the intimate glance of an old friend; there are no more comfortable, homely rooms littered with household goods, only blank walls and massive architecture.

In fact, the modern Northerner comes up against works of art like the *School of Athens,* or similar representations, so completely unprepared, that his bewilderment is natural. The spectator cannot be blamed if he secretly wonders why Raphael did not rather paint a Roman flower market, or the lively scene on a Sunday morning in Piazza Montanara when the peasants come in to be shaved. These classic works set out to solve formal problems which are outside the range of modern taste in art, and our predilection for the quaint and the picturesque handicaps us, from the start, in our effort to appreciate the form of these works of art. We like the primitive simplicity of language, we like the hard, childish, clumsy composition, the rough-hewn, breathless style, while the carefully constructed Augustan periods are neither valued nor understood.

But even where the ideas are more familiar to us, where the Cinquecento deals with the old, simple, Christian themes, our reluctance is understandable. We lack confidence and are not sure if we can accept as genuine the gestures and ideas of classic art for we have had to swallow so much false classicism that our gorge rises at it and we long for simpler, purer fare. We have lost faith in inflated gestures, we have become weak and suspicious, and everywhere we detect theatrical effect and empty rhetoric. And, finally, our faith has been undermined by the oft-repeated innuendo that this art is not really original, that it is borrowed from the antique, and that the marble world of long-dead antiquity has laid its numbing, ghostly hand blightingly on the radiant life of the Renaissance.

Yet classic art is nothing more than the natural continuation of the Quattrocento, and a completely spontaneous expression of the Italian people. It was not an imitation of a foreign prototype,—the Antique,—it is no spindly hot-house plant but one grown in the open fields in the full strength of vigorous life. This close relationship is obscured for us because—and this is the only possible ground for prejudice against Italian classicism—a purely national feature has been taken for a general thing, and an attempt has been made to imitate, under quite different conditions, forms which have life and significance only on a specific soil and under a specific sky. The art of the Italian High Renaissance remains an Italian art, and if the 'ideal' was used to heighten reality, this reality had not only already been very thoroughly studied, but the idealizing was the heightening of an essentially Italian reality.

* * * * *

Vasari himself made the division, beginning a new epoch with the sixteenth century—an epoch to which the earlier period was made to seem only a preliminary stage and a preparation—when he began the third part of his history of artists with Leonardo, whose *Last Supper*, painted in the last decade of the fifteenth century, was the first great work of the new art. At the same same time, Michelangelo, almost twenty-five years younger than Leonardo, was already saying entirely new things in his first great works. Fra Bartolommeo was his contemporary, Raphael followed about ten years later, and, close to him, came Andrea del Sarto. In round figures, it is the twenty-five years from 1500 to 1525 which are the most important in the development of the classic style in Florentine-Roman art.

It is not easy to obtain a general view of this period. However well-known to us from youth onwards these masterpieces may be, through engravings and reproductions of every kind, only slowly does a consistent and living picture form itself of the world which bore these fruits. It is different with the Quattrocento. In Florence, the fifteenth century still stands before our eyes like a living thing. True, much of it is lost, many things have been taken from their natural setting and put into the prison-like custody of museums, but there still remain enough places to recreate for us a vivid impression of the life of those days. The Cinquecento is preserved more fragmentarily and, moreover, did not reach a complete development. In Florence one has the feeling that the broad substructure of the Quattrocento lacks the crown of final achievement because one cannot properly see the completion of the development. I do not mean that this is because of the export of panel pictures out of the country, so that, for example, there is practically nothing by Leonardo left in Italy, but because, from the beginning, the forces squander themselves. Leonardo's *Last Supper*, which is an essentially Florentine work, is in Milan; Michelangelo became half Roman and Raphael entirely so. Of their great Roman works, the Sistine ceiling is an absurdity, a torment to the artist and the spectator alike, and Raphael had to paint some of his Vatican pictures in sections on walls where one can never see them properly. So one is left wondering how much ever came to anything, how much out of those short, few, peak years remained only as a project or fell victim to early destruction. Leonardo's *Last Supper* itself is only a wreck; his great battle-piece, commissioned for Florence, was never finished and even the cartoon is lost. Michelangelo's *Bathing Soldiers* shared the same fate, while the Julius Tomb remained unexecuted, save for a few single figures, and the façade of San Lorenzo, which was to have displayed the full splendour of Tuscan architecture and sculpture, remained no more than a project on paper. The Medici Chapel only counts as a partial substitute, for it already stands on the verge of Baroque. Classic art has left no monument in the great style, where architecture and sculpture are blended together for the full expression of the artist's concept, and the greatest architectural commission on which all the artistic forces of the age were concentrated—St. Peter's in Rome—was, finally, not allowed to become a monument of the High Renaissance.

One can compare classic art with the ruins of a building, nearly, but never quite, finished, the original form of which must be reconstructed from far-scattered fragments and incomplete accounts, and it is perhaps not wrong to say that in the whole history of Italian art no epoch is less known than the Golden Age.

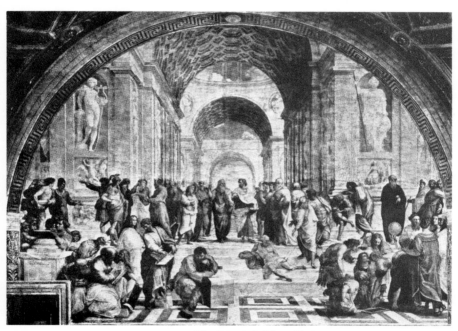

I. RAPHAEL: *The School of Athens.* Vatican

PART ONE

Chapter I : ANTECEDENTS

AT the beginning of Italian painting stands Giotto; he it was who loosened the tongue of art. What he painted speaks, and his stories live in the memory as experiences. He concerns himself with the whole range of human life, he tells the stories of the Bible and the legends of the Saints, and everywhere he makes them into living, convincing narratives. He goes direct to the heart of the event and brings the incident before us in its natural setting, just as it must have happened. The spirited way of setting out the holy stories and embellishing them with intimate, individual traits, he took over from the preachers and poets of the Franciscan school, who had accustomed the people to this kind of approach, only, the essence of his power lies, not in poetic invention, but in pictorial representation, for he made visible things which no one before had ever been able to render in pictures. He had an eye for the most telling dramatic moment of the event and he, perhaps, did more than anybody else to enlarge the boundaries of expression in painting. One must not think of Giotto as a sort of Christian Romantic, as if he carried in his pocket the 'outpourings from the heart of a Franciscan friar'[1], as if his art had blossomed under the pure breath of inspiration from that great love with which the Saint of Assisi brought Heaven down to Earth and made Earth into a Heaven. He was no fanatic, but a man of fact, no lyricist, but an observer, an artist who never allowed himself to be carried away by passion, but who always spoke clearly and expressively. In spiritual depth of invention and in the power of sympathy, others surpassed him. The sculptor Giovanni Pisano expresses in his unyielding material greater depth of emotion than Giotto the painter: the story of the Annunciation is nowhere more tenderly told in the spirit of the century than where Giovanni tells it in his relief on the Pistoia pulpit, and in its fervid imagery one feels something of the warmth of Dante. But just that was his undoing. He over-reached himself and his power of expressing sensibility destroyed his feeling for form, so that his art ran wild in over-emotionalism.

Giotto is more calm, more detached, more equable, and always more popular, because everyone can understand him. The heartiness of the peasant comes more easily to him than the delicate or refined, and his earnest concentration on the significant makes him seek his effects in clarity instead of in beauty of line. It is very striking, too, to notice that he has practically no trace of what then constituted style—that melodious flow of line in draperies, the rhythmic swing in movement and pose. Beside Giovanni Pisano he is heavy, and beside Andrea

---

[1][A punning reference to G. W. Wackenroder, *Herzensergieszungen eines kunstliebenden Klosterbruders*, Berlin, 1797, a classic of the German Romantic Revival.—*Trans.*]

Pisano, the master of the bronze doors of the Baptistery in Florence, he is simply ugly. In the *Visitation*, where Andrea makes the two women embrace while a serving-girl stands nearby, the grouping and the line have all the quality of a song; Giotto, with his clear-cut lineaments, is very hard—but extraordinarily expressive. One does not easily forget the line of his Elizabeth (Padua, Arena Chapel) bending to look into Mary's eyes, while of Andrea Pisano's group the only memory is of a beautiful and harmonious unison of curves.

The highest point of Giotto's art lies in the paintings in Santa Croce. In the clarity with which he sets out his narrative he goes far beyond his earlier works and in composition he strives for effects which, in their intention, set him on a level with sixteenth century masters. His immediate followers could no longer understand him. Simplification and concentration were again abandoned in the quest for richness and variety of effect and in the effort to force more depth and subtleties of meaning into the picture, which, as a result, became confused and overloaded with inessentials. Then, at the beginning of the fifteenth century, there came a new painter, Masaccio, who was able, by the force and clarity of his intelligence, to bring order into the confusion, and to establish the pictorial equivalents of the visual world.

In Florence, one should see Giotto and Masaccio immediately after each other, so as to appreciate the difference in all its sharpness. The disparity is enormous.

Vasari has a phrase about Masaccio which sounds trivial: 'He recognized,' he says, 'that painting is naught else but the imitation of things as they are.'[1] One may ask why as much could not have been said equally of Giotto. There is, in fact, a deeper meaning in the sentence. What seems to us so natural now —that painting should give the impression of reality—was not always so. There was a time when this requirement never entered anyone's mind because it was believed to be impossible to reproduce spatial reality in depth on a flat surface. The whole Middle Ages thought thus and were content with a system of representation which merely contained references to objects and their spatial relation, but made no attempt to compete with Nature. It is wrong to believe that a medieval picture was ever looked at with our concepts of illusionistic effects. It was certainly one of the greatest advances made by man when these limitations began to be regarded as prejudices and people conceived the idea that, in spite of entirely different means of effect, it would yet be possible to approach nearer to the impression of Nature. One man alone could not complete such a reversal of ideas, nor even one generation. Giotto did much, but Masaccio added so much more that one may well say that he first broke through to 'the imitation of things as they are'.

---

[1]Vasari, Milanesi Edition, II, p. 288.

To begin with, we are amazed by his complete mastery of spatial problems. For the first time, the picture becomes a stage, constructed by establishing a unified point of vision; a space in which people, trees, houses, have their specific place, which can be geometrically calculated. In Giotto everything is still glued together; he superimposes head upon head, without allowing himself sufficient space for all the bodies, and the architecture of the background is only an uncertain, wavering stage-set without any real relation in scale to the figures. Masaccio shows not only possible, habitable houses, but the space in the picture is clear to the last lines of the landscape. He places the point of sight at the height of the heads, so that the figures on the flat stage are all of the same height to the crowns of their heads, a device which gives substance and solidity to a row of three profile heads one behind the other, closed, perhaps, by a fourth head seen full face. Step by step we are drawn into the depth of the space, where everything is clearly set out in layers one behind the other, and the new art may be seen in all its glory in Santa Maria Novella in the fresco of the *Trinity* where four zones are developed in depth, with the strongest spatial effect, by the use of architecture and overlapping planes. Beside this Giotto looks completely flat and his frescoes in Santa Croce have the same effect as a tapestry, for the even blue of the sky links together the various pictures of the cycle, painted one above the other, so that they offer one flat surface. It would seem that the idea of an accurate representation of reality was still a long way off: the area is at best filled up to the top, as though it were only a question of covering it with a decorative ornament.[1] Around the pictures run bands of mosaic-pattern ornament, and when these same patterns are repeated in the picture itself the imagination ceases to make any distinction between framing and framed, and the sense of a flat wall decoration inevitably obtrudes itself. Masaccio frames his pictures in painted pilasters so that he gives one the illusion of the picture going on behind them.

Giotto used only quite weak shadow on his forms and generally ignored cast shadows, not because he did not see them, but because it seemed to him superfluous to go into the matter deeply. He regarded them as a disturbing accident in the picture, which could add nothing to the significance of the matter. In Masaccio light and shadow are elements of primary importance for the way he sought to render the essence, the corporeality, in the full strength of natural effect. The decisive thing here is not just his feeling for body and mass, not the power with which he establishes his figures, nor the compactness of his crowds of people; it is the way in which he gives an entirely new impression

---

[1] It is a sign of an advance in the modern appreciation of pictures, that the decorative, flat style of Giotto is now recognised as something of cardinal importance. Yet one must guard against the bias which would make this quality the most important thing in art.

in dealing merely with the detail of a head, marking the limits of the form by a few massive strokes, so that the volume is rendered with unheard-of force. And so with all other forms, and, as a consequence, the bright colour of earlier pictures, with their unsubstantial appearance, was replaced by a colour scheme conveying greater solidity. The whole appearance of the picture is strengthened and the aptness of Vasari's observation, that in Masaccio people stood firmly on their feet for the first time, is clear.

Yet still more is to come, in the sharpened feeling for personality and, the emphasis on the individual. For though Giotto differentiated his figures yet they are only general distinctions; in Masaccio we come up against clearly marked individual characters. The new age is spoken of as the century of 'realism'. This word has been put to so many uses that it no longer has any real meaning. Something proletarian clings to it, a taint of embittered opposition as if brutal ugliness would force its way in and assert its right to be seen, since it, too, exists in the world. Quattrocento realism, however, is of an essentially joyous kind, since the new elements are due to the increased perception of values. The interest is now not only in the 'character' head, but the full range of individual pose and movement is included in the province of pictorial subjects and the artist can concentrate on the texture and the wayward fall of the folds in a piece of drapery and rejoice in the play of a line with a vitality of its own. The old formulas of beauty seemed to do violence to nature; the tilted posture, the rich undulations of the draperies came to be regarded as fine, empty phrases, boring and meaningless. A craving for the real appearance of things is something which must be satisfied, and if proof is needed of the pure faith with which the newly grasped vision was held, it is to be found in the fact that the supernatural was now for the first time envisaged in an earthly guise, with individualised features and with no trace of idealization in the forms.

It is not a painter but a sculptor who is the first full and true exponent of the new spirit. Masaccio's early death cut short what he had to say, but Donatello's long career spread over the whole first half of the fifteenth century. He was immensely productive and he is, indeed, the most significant figure of the Quattrocento. Although he seized on the new ideas of his time and exploited them with unequalled energy, he never degenerates into an unbridled realism. He is a sculptor who looks at humanity, searching for the characteristic form even in the depths of ugliness, and who then, suddenly pure and serene, is able to express his vision of a beauty, calm, noble and almost magical. Some figures by him push the quest for the bizarrely individual to an extreme limit, and beside them stands such a figure as the bronze *David* (*Fig.* 2), where the High Renaissance feeling for beauty is already clearly to be seen. He is always a storyteller of unsurpassable liveliness and full of dramatic effect, qualities which make the *Salome* relief in Siena, for example, the best narrative of the century. Later, at Padua, in the *Miracles of St. Anthony*, he deals with problems which approximate to those of the Cinquecento, in that he introduces into the composition excited crowds, strong in emotive effect, in complete and unexpected contrast to the placid rows of spectators in contemporary pictures.

The counterpart to Donatello in the second half of the Quattrocento is Verrocchio (1435–1488), not comparable to him in personal greatness but clearly representative of the new ideals of a new generation.

From the mid-century, a growing desire for the refined, the graceful, the elegant, is noticeable. Bodies lose their lumpishness, limbs become more slender and slim in the joints, and the simplicity of line is broken up by petty movement and decoration. Precision of modelling and the most subtle nuances of relief are admired and sought for, and interest shifts from calm and passive figures to ones full of tense, mannered movement, with fingers spread in conscious elegance and heads turned or bent with sweet smiles, or gazing upwards with sentimental expressions. Against this kind of preciousness a natural and unaffected perception and approach is often unable to hold its own.

The contrast can readily be appreciated if Verrocchio's bronze *David* (*Fig.* 3) is compared with the same figure by Donatello. The sturdy youth has become a fine-limbed boy, yet lean enough to display the precise form, with a pointed elbow deliberately set akimbo so that it is included in the main silhouette.[1] All the limbs are in tension: the leg outstretched, the knee straightened, the sword-arm taut. How strongly this contrasts with the calm arrangement of Donatello's figure! The whole motive is developed so as to create an impression of movement, and movement is now sought for even in the expression of the head, for a smile flickers over the features of the youthful victor. The taste for ornament is gratified by the details of the armour, which, subtly, both follows and interrupts the graceful lines of the body and, if one examines the treatment of the nude, Donatello's summary handling seems almost empty compared with the wealth of detailed forms in the Verrocchio.

Much the same comparisons can be made between the two equestrian statues, the *Gattamelata* in Padua and the *Colleoni* in Venice. Verrocchio keys up the tension in his handling of the seat of the rider and the movement of the horse. The pose of his Colleoni, riding with stiff legs, with his horse pressing forward to give the impression of pulling, the grasp of the baton, the twist of the head, all show the same trend in taste. Donatello, by comparison, seems infinitely simple and unassuming, for he keeps his large surfaces unbroken and smooth, where Verrocchio splits them up into minute detail, using the trappings of the

---

[1] On the taking of photographs in full frontal view, *cf.* Wölfflin, *Wie man Skulpturen aufnehmen soll*, in the *Zeitschrift für bildende Kunst*, 1894 and 1895.

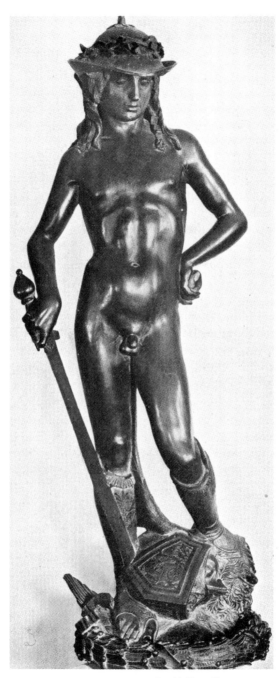

2. DONATELLO: *David*. Bargello

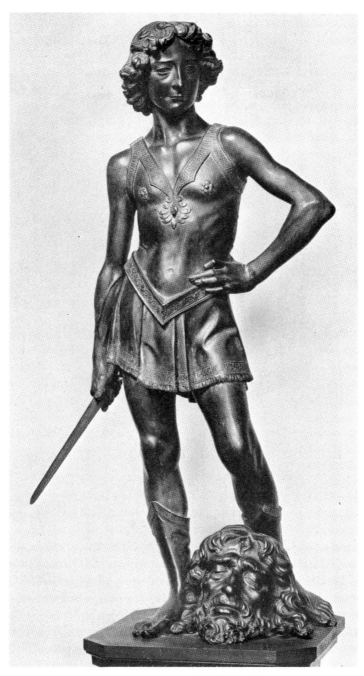

3. VERROCCHIO: *David*. Bargello

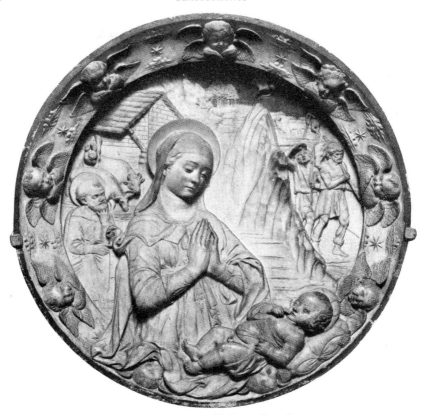

4. ROSSELLINO: *Madonna*. Bargello

horse to break up the planes. His treatment of the armour and of the horse's
mane is a most instructive example of late Quattrocento decorative art. But in his
working of the muscles of the charger the artist went so far that the criticism
was soon levelled at it that Verrocchio had made a flayed horse.[1] The danger
of degenerating into niggling was clearly an urgent one.

Verrocchio's chief fame is as a bronze-worker. The real characteristics of the
material were then being developed; the aim of the artist was to break up the
masses, to separate the figures and to give an elegant silhouette, while the beauty
of bronze from the picturesque point of view was recognized and exploited. In
the luxuriant richness of folds of drapery, like, for example, those in the group
of the *Incredulity of St. Thomas* on Orsanmichele, not only the linear effect but
also the play of sparkling, glancing lights, dark shadows and flickering reflections
are taken into account.

---

[1]Pomponius Gauricus, *De Sculptura* (ed. Brockhaus), p. 220. [1st ed., Florence, 1504.—*Trans.*]

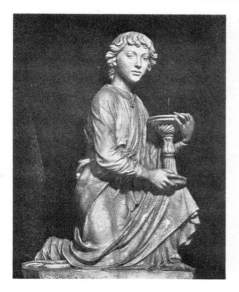
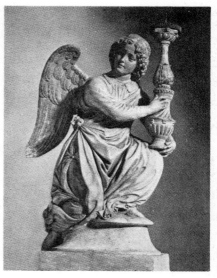

5. LUCA DELLA ROBBIA: *Angel with Candlestick*. Florence, Cathedral

6. BENEDETTO DA MAIANO: *Angel with Candlestick*. Siena, S. Domenico

The marble workers, too, found that the new taste was to their benefit. The eye had become sensitive to the slightest nuances of modelling, and stone was now handled with unheard-of delicacy. Desiderio carved his exquisite fruit-garlands and the lovely, laughing heads of young Florentine women; Antonio Rossellino, and the somewhat broader Benedetto da Maiano, rival painting by the richness of their handling. The chisel is now able to render the soft flesh of children and the fine veils of head-dresses, and, if one looks more closely, here and there the breeze has lifted an end of drapery and blown it into a graceful cluster of folds. In architectural or landscape perspectives, the ground of the relief is deepened inwards; in fact, everywhere in the treatment of the surfaces the artist strives to give the impression of something living, trembling and quivering (*Fig.* 4).

The familiar subjects for sculpture were, wherever possible, transformed stylistically to give full scope to the new feeling for movement. The kneeling angel with the candlestick, simple and beautiful, as Luca della Robbia had made him, is no longer enough; he, too, must now rush tempestuously forward, like Benedetto's angel with a candelabrum in Siena (*Figs.* 5, 6). With a smiling face and a merry tilt of the head, the little acolyte makes a hasty bob while his full robe flutters round his pretty ankles. These running figures are further developed into the flying angels, which, with powerful surging movements, seem to cut through the air in their thin garments, and which, worked as reliefs and applied to the wall, have the effect of free-standing figures (Antonio Rossellino, Tomb of the Cardinal of Portugal in S. Miniato, Florence, *Fig.* 45).

Parallel with the group of sculptors working in this delicate style are the painters of the second half of the century who, naturally, are even more indicative of the taste of the time. From them is formed our picture of Quattrocento Florence, for when speaking of the early Renaissance it is of Botticelli, Filippino and the festive pictures of Ghirlandaio that we think. Fra Filippo Lippi, who formed himself on the frescoes in the Brancacci Chapel, is an example of an immediate follower of Masaccio, and, about the middle of the century, he carried out an admirable work in the paintings in the choir of Prato Cathedral. His handling was not lacking in breadth, and as a painter, in the special sense of the word, he has peculiar power. His panel pictures treat of subjects, such as the twilight interior of a wood, which occur again only with Correggio, and in his frescoes he excels all the Florentines of his century in charm of colour. Whoever has seen the apse of Spoleto Cathedral where, in the *Coronation of the Virgin*, he tried to portray in marvellous colour the splendour of Heaven itself, will agree that there is nothing to be compared with it anywhere. Yet, with all this, his pictures are badly constructed, they suffer from a cramped and unclear rendering of space and from such a diffusion of interest that one cannot but regret how little he was able to make use of Masaccio's great discoveries. Much still remained for the coming generation to improve on: and they did it. If, after a visit to Prato, one goes to see the frescoes by Ghirlandaio in Santa Maria Novella in Florence, one is immediately struck by the clear and calm effect which he creates, by the way the space explains itself and by the assured appearance of the whole, transparent yet tangible. And similar traits are discernible in analogous comparisons with a Filippino or a Botticelli, whose blood ran much less calmly in their veins than Ghirlandaio's.

Botticelli (1446–1510) was a pupil of Fra Filippo, but that is perceptible only in his very first works. They were of two quite different temperaments: the Frate with his broad laughter and equable, good-humoured pleasure in the things of this world, and Botticelli, impetuous, passionate, always inwardly exalted, an artist to whom the painterly qualities of a surface meant little, who found his ideal in linear rhythms and who endowed his heads with a wealth of character and expression. Consider his Madonna with her narrow face, mute mouth, and heavy, troubled eyes; it is quite a different picture from the contented twinkle of Filippo. His Saints are never healthy people with whom all is well, his St. Jerome is consumed with inner fire and in the young St. John he searches for the expression of fanaticism and asceticism. He takes the holy stories seriously, and this seriousness increases with the years until he abandons all charm of external appearance. His beauty has something afflicted, and even when he smiles it seems only a transitory lighting-up. How little real joy there is in the dance of the Graces in his *Primavera (Fig. 7)*, and look what kind of bodies they have! The austere leanness of immaturity has become the ideal of the age; in movement, tension and angularity are sought for rather than the saturated curve, and in every form the stress is on the fine-drawn and pointed, not on the full and rounded. The representation of grasses, of the little flowers on the ground, of the draperies and the highly-wrought ornament, is given a decorative quality verging sometimes on the fantastic. Nevertheless, contemplative lingering over details was certainly not Botticelli's way; even in the nude

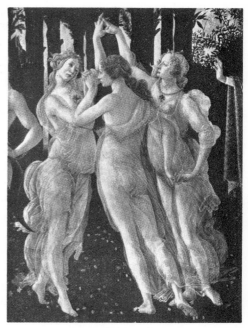

7. BOTTICELLI: *The Three Graces*. Detail from the *Primavera*. Uffizi

he soon wearied of minutely-rendered detail and sought, in sweeping line, a simplified presentation. That he was an eminent draughtsman, even Vasari recognized in spite of his Michelangelesque upbringing. His line is always emotionally moving and spirited with something passionate and impetuous about it, and in the representation of hurried movement he is incomparably effective. He even succeeds in imparting this flowing line to his large masses, and where he orders his picture in a unified composition around one centre something specifically new is created, the consequences of which are of great importance. It is in this sense that his compositions of the *Adoration of the Magi* are to be considered.

Filippino Lippi (*c.* 1459–1504) may be mentioned in the same breath as Botticelli, for the same atmosphere gives a similar appearance to these two different personalities. From his father, Filippino inherited a gift for colour which Botticelli never had. The surface, the skin of things, charms him; he treats his flesh tones more delicately than anyone else and he gives softness and gleam to hair; what for Botticelli was only a play of lines was to him a painterly problem; he is very fastidious in his choice of colour, especially in blue and violet tones; his line is gentler, more undulating, and one can even say that he is somewhat feminine in feeling. There are early pictures by Filippino of enchanting tenderness of perception and execution; often, however, he seems almost too soft. The St. John of the *Madonna and Four Saints* of 1486 (Uffizi) is not the austere preacher of the wilderness, but a sentimental enthusiast. The Dominican, in the same picture, does not grasp his book with his hand but balances it on the ball of his thumb with a piece of drapery between them, and the slender, flexible fingers wave like highly sensitive antennae. His later development does not match these beginnings: the inner vibration is transformed into an irregular, external agitation, the pictures become unquiet and chaotic, and the painter who knew how to finish Masaccio's chapel in the Carmine conscientiously and restrainedly, is, in the later frescoes in Santa Maria Novella, only with difficulty recognized as the same man. In external decorativeness he is unendingly inventive and what in Botticelli is only hinted at—the fantastic and exaggerated—is in him a strongly marked trait. He seizes upon this quality of agitation and often gets splendid effects through an abundance of movement—the *Assumption of the Virgin* in Santa Maria sopra Minerva, Rome, with the ecstatic, Bacchante-like angels is a perfect rendering of exultation—then he drops back into mere unrest and even becomes coarse and trivial. When he paints the martyrdom of St. Philip, he has to choose the moment when the cross, pulled up by ropes, waves about in the air, to say nothing of the grotesque tatterdemalions with which he peoples the picture. One has the feeling that a very great talent has run to seed through lack of inner discipline, and it is understandable that men with much less sensitive temperaments—Ghirlandaio, for example—outstripped him. In Santa Maria Novella, where the two stand together, in chapels side by side, one soon tires of Filippino's fidgety stories, while Ghirlandaio, with fine and honest craftsmanship, fills the spectator with a true and lasting contentment.

Ghirlandaio (1449–94) never suffered from excessive sensibility. His was an equable temperament, and his open, cheerful nature and his joy in pageantry compel our liking. He is very entertaining and it is from him that one gains the most insight into Florentine life. He treats the content of his stories very lightly: in the choir of Santa Maria Novella he had to recount the lives of the Virgin and of the Baptist, and he has done so, but anyone who did not already know the stories would scarcely be able to grasp them from him. What did not Giotto make of Mary in the Temple! How penetratingly he brings the scene before us: the little Mary climbing the Temple steps of her own accord, the priest bending towards her, the parents accompanying the child with look and gesture. In Ghirlandaio, we find a dressed-up schoolgirl, glancing coquettishly sideways in spite of the haste of her movements, the priest scarcely visible, hidden from view behind a pillar, and the parents indifferently watching the scene. In the *Marriage*, Mary comes in undignified haste to the exchange of rings, and the *Visitation* is merely a pretty, but quite secular, greeting between two ladies out walking. It did not seem to worry Ghirlandaio that, in the picture of the angel appearing to Zacharias, the real action is completely eclipsed by the numerous portrait figures in the foreground of spectators without parts in the story.

He is a picture-maker, not a story-teller. He enjoys things for their own sake. He paints lifelike heads, but when Vasari praises him for the expression of passing emotions, the judgement is well beside the point. He is more successful in peaceful than in agitated scenes: in scenes such as the *Massacre of the Innocents* Botticelli is far better than he is. Generally he sticks to a simple, calm presentation and pays his due to the contemporary taste for movement only in a hurrying servant-girl, or some similar figure. His observation is never acute. While many other painters in Florence were studying, with the greatest penetration, problems of modelling and anatomy, colour technique and aerial perspective, he did not venture beyond general and accepted advances of knowledge. He was no experimenter, no discoverer of new pictorial effects, but an artist who possessed an average understanding of the technical knowledge of his age, and who used it to attempt new monumental effects. In style, he turns from petty detail to greater effects of mass; he is rich, yet clear, gay and often great. The group of five women in the *Birth of the Virgin* has no equal in the fifteenth century. What he attempts in motives of composition, in the centralising of the story and the treatment of the corner figures, is of a kind that links him directly with the Cinquecento masters. One must be careful, however, not to overestimate the value of his performance. Ghirlandaio's paintings in Santa Maria Novella were finished about 1490; Leonardo's *Last Supper* was created in the years immediately following. Were this available for comparison in Florence the 'monumental' Ghirlandaio would at once seem quite poverty-stricken and limited. The *Last Supper* is a picture infinitely greater in formal conception and in it form and content are completely fused.

What is often wrongly said of Ghirlandaio—that he united in his art the inventions and innovations of the Florentine Quattrocento—is true in the highest degree of Leonardo (born 1452). He is sensitive in his observation of detail and broad in his grasp of the whole; he is an eminent draughtsman and an equally great painter; there is no artist who has not found his own special problems dealt with by him, and developed further; and he surpasses all in the depth and fullness of his personality.

Since Leonardo is usually spoken of along with the Cinquecentisti one easily forgets that he was very little younger than Ghirlandaio and actually older than Filippino. He worked in Verrocchio's shop and had Perugino and Lorenzo di Credi as fellow apprentices. The latter is a star who shines, not with his own light, but with the reflected radiance of another sun: his pictures look like diligent school performances of a set task. Perugino, on the other hand, brought

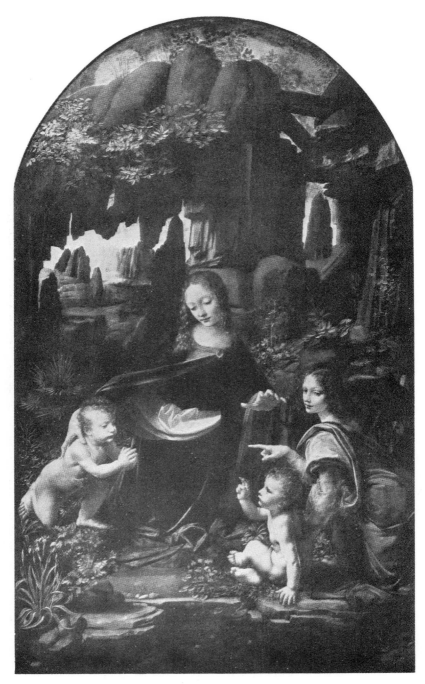

8. LEONARDO: *The Madonna of the Rocks*. Louvre

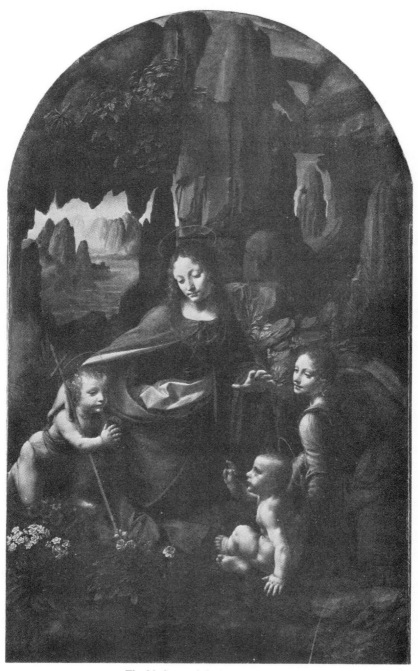

9. LEONARDO: *The Madonna of the Rocks*. London, National Gallery

something of his own which was of great significance in the context of Florentine art: more will be said of this later. Verrocchio's instruction was made famous by his pupils and it was clearly the most versatile workshop in Florence. The combination of painting and sculpture was the more beneficial in that the sculptors were accustomed to a thoroughly methodical study of nature, which meant that they were in less danger of falling into the blind alley of an arbitrary, personal style. But between Leonardo and Verrocchio there seems also to have existed an inner relationship. From Vasari, we know how many interests they had in common and how many threads Leonardo took up which Verrocchio had originally spun. And yet the youthful works of the pupil still come as a surprise. If the angel in Verrocchio's *Baptism* (*Fig.* 155; Florence, Academy)[1] strikes us like a voice from another world, how entirely unique is a picture like the *Madonna of the Rocks* (*Fig.* 8) in a company of Florentine Quattrocento Madonnas! Mary is kneeling, bending forward, not in profile but seen from the front. She puts her right hand about the little St. John, who, close to her, presses forward in ardent prayer towards the Christ Child, while her left hand accompanies the movement with a flat sweep forward, in characteristic foreshortening. The Christ Child, seated on the ground and held by a large and beautiful kneeling angel, answers with a gesture of blessing. The angel is the only figure in the picture to look outwards at the spectator, and his pointing right hand significantly directs one's attention—a hand in pure profile, simple and clear as a signpost. The whole scene is set in a lonely, secret, rocky wilderness, with occasional glimpses into the open air and the light.

Here, everything is new and significant—in motive as well as in treatment: the freedom of movement in details, and the orderly disposition of masses in the whole[2]; the infinitely subtle animation of the forms; the new, painterly, use of light clearly intended to give the figures a strongly plastic effect against the dark ground and, at the same time, to lead the imagination into depth in an unexpected way. The over-riding impression, at a distance, is the sense of solidity in the bodies, and the clear intention of an effect of order achieved by the triangular grouping. The picture has an architectonic backbone, which is quite a different thing from mere symmetry, as it is found in the earlier masters. Here

---

[1][Now in the Uffizi.—*Trans.*]

[2]The Louvre version of the *Madonna of the Rocks* is so superior to the London one (*Fig.* 9) that it seems inconceivable that its originality could ever have been doubted. Certainly, the pointing finger of the angel is, for us, rather unpleasing, and the omission of the hand in the London picture is understandable in the light of the later appreciation of beauty. Yet, had Leonardo supervised the new version he would have known how to fill in the resultant gap: there is now a hole in the picture in spite of the moving forward of the angel's shoulder. Drawing and modelling have been strengthened and simplified in the Cinquecento manner, so that many nuances are lost, and this in spite of the more spiritual expression given to the angel's head.

[For some new aspects in the controversy over the London–Paris versions, see Martin Davies, *The Virgin of the Rocks*, London, National Gallery, 1947.—*Trans.*]

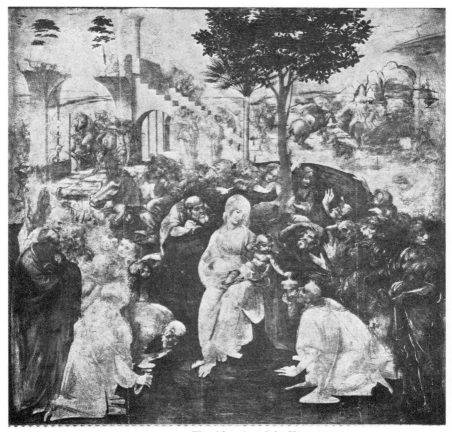

10. LEONARDO: *The Adoration of the Kings.* Uffizi

there is more freedom and yet more order, and the particular is subordinated into essential relation with the whole: in other words, it is the Cinquecento style. Leonardo early shows signs of it. In the Vatican is a kneeling *St. Jerome with the lion,* by him. The figure is noteworthy as an example of movement and it has been admired as such, but one may well ask who, except Leonardo, could have so related the lines of the saint to those of the lion. I can think of no one.

The most influential of Leonardo's early pictures is the under-painting for an *Adoration of the Kings* (Uffizi; *Fig.* 10). Painted about 1480, it has a somewhat old-fashioned look, due to the multiplicity of incidents. This displays the Quattro-cento delight in variety, but a new inventiveness is to be seen in the way in which the principal subject is emphasised. Botticelli and Ghirlandaio also painted the *Adoration of the Kings* with the Virgin seated in the centre of a group of people, but she seems always to be too unimportant. Leonardo was the first to understand how to make the principal motive the dominating one. The arrangement of the outer figures, set against the edges as strong, closing coulisses, is again a motive of importance for later works, and the contrast between the crowding of the spectators and the easy pose of the Madonna, sitting quite free, is of that far-reaching kind which is peculiar to Leonardo. Even if we had only the outline of the Madonna herself, we should have to rank him as an original creator, so unprecedentedly fine is her sitting pose and the correlation of Madonna and Child. Others placed Mary as if she straddled the throne: he gives her a more subtle, feminine pose with her knees drawn close together. All the later men borrowed this from him, and the enchanting motive of the twist of the body, combined with the sideways movement of the Child, is repeated almost literally in Raphael's *Madonna di Foligno* (*Fig.* 84).

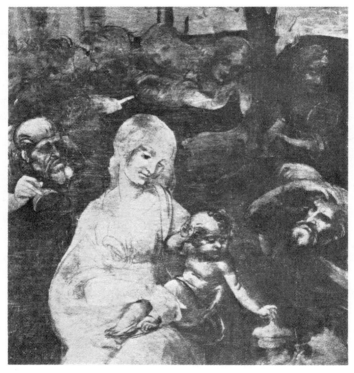

Detail from Fig. 10

CHAPTER II : LEONARDO (1452–1519)

O F all Renaissance artists, Leonardo was the one who most enjoyed the world. All phenomena captivated him—physical life and human emotions, the forms of plants and animals, the sight of the crystal-clear stream with the pebbles in its bed. To him, the one-sidedness of the mere figure-painter was incomprehensible.

"Do you not see how many and how varied are the actions which are performed by men alone? Do you not see how many different kinds of animals there are, and also of trees and plants and flowers? What variety of hilly and level places, of springs, rivers, cities, public and private buildings; of instruments fitted for man's use; of divers costumes, ornaments and arts?"[1]

He is a born aristocrat among painters, sensitive to delicacy, with a feeling for fine hands, for the charm of transparent stuffs, for smooth skin, and above all, he loves beautiful, soft, rippling hair. In Verrocchio's *Baptism* (*Fig.* 155) he painted a few tufts of grasses, and one sees at once that they were painted by him, for no one else had quite this feeling for the natural grace of growing things. The strong and the soft are equally his province. If he paints a battle, he surpasses all others in the expression of unchained passions and tumultuous movement, yet he can catch the most tender emotion and fix the most fleeting expression. In single 'character' heads he shows himself the most uncompromising of realists, and then suddenly he flings all that aside and loses himself in visions of ideal faces of almost unearthly beauty, dreaming of sweet, soft smiles, which seem reflections of an inner radiance. He discovered the painterly charm of the surfaces of things and yet he can think as a physicist and an anatomist. Qualities which seem mutually exclusive are combined in him: the tireless observation and collection of data of the scientist, and the most subtle artistic perception. As a painter, he is never content to accept things merely by their outward appearance: he throws himself into investigating, with the same passionate interest, inner structure and the factors governing the life of every created thing. He was the first artist to make a systematic study of proportion in men and animals and to investigate the mechanics of movements like walking, lifting, climbing, pulling, and it was he, too, who made the most comprehensive physiognomical studies and thought out a coherent system for the expression of emotions.

For him, the painter is like a clear eye which surveys the world and takes all visible things for its domain. Suddenly the world revealed itself in all its

---

[1]Leonardo, *Trattato della Pittura*, Ludwig's Italian-German ed., No. 73. [English translation in McCurdy, *Notebooks of Leonardo da Vinci*, II, p. 256.—*Trans.*]

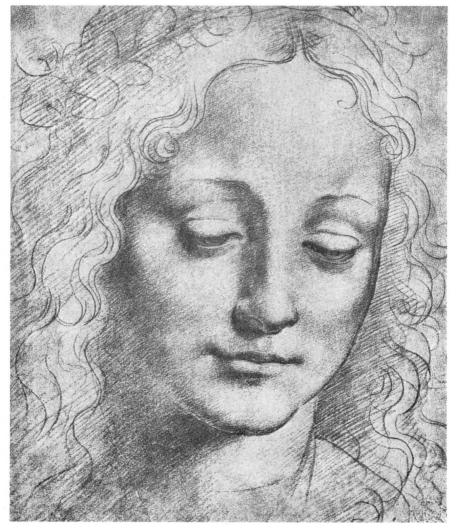

11. Manner of LEONARDO: *Head of a Girl*. Silverpoint drawing. Uffizi

inexhaustible riches and Leonardo seems to have felt himself united by a great love to all living things. Vasari tells a story which reveals this: he was sometimes seen in the market-place, buying caged birds that he might give them back their freedom. This incident seems to have impressed the Florentines.

In so universal an art there are no major and minor problems; the ultimate subtleties of light and shade are not more interesting than the most elementary task—the rendering of a three-dimensional object in apparent solidity on a flat surface—and the artist who, more than any other, made the human face a mirror of the soul can still say, 'Relief is the principal aim and the soul of painting'. Leonardo was so sensitive to so many more aspects of things that he was forced to seek new technical methods. He became an experimenter who could scarcely satisfy himself. He is said to have allowed the *Mona Lisa* to leave his studio before he considered it to be finished. Technically, she is a mystery, but even where the medium is obvious, as in the simple silver-point drawings, he is no less astounding (*Fig.* 11). He is perhaps the first to use line with expressive sensibility and there are almost no parallels for the way in which his contours are made up of touches of varying firmness. He models with simple, parallel, even strokes; it is as if he needed only to stroke the surface to bring out the roundness of the form. Never have simpler means been used to greater effect, and the parallel lines, like those which occur in older Italian engravings, give an inestimable unity of effect to the drawings.[1]

We have but few completed works by Leonardo. He was untiring in observation and insatiable in his search for knowledge, he continually set himself fresh problems, yet it seems as if he wished to solve them only for himself. He could never bring himself to a definite conclusion or to finish off a picture, and the problems which he set himself were so far-reaching that he may well have felt that his solutions were only provisional.

1. The *Last Supper*

AFTER Raphael's *Sistine Madonna*, Leonardo's *Last Supper* (Fig. 12, 12a) is the most popular picture in the whole of Italian art. It is so simple and expressive that it impresses itself upon everyone. Christ is at the centre of a long table, with the Disciples disposed equally on either side of Him. He has said, 'One of you shall betray me', and the unexpected words have thrown the gathering into an uproar. He alone remains calm, His eyes downcast, and in His silence lies the repeated, 'Verily I say unto you, that one of you shall betray me'. One feels that there is no other possible way of depicting the event, and yet *everything* in Leonardo's picture is new, and the very simplicity is a triumph of the highest art. If we look around for Quattrocento prototypes, we find a good example in Ghirlandaio's *Last Supper* in Ognissanti, dated 1480 and, therefore, about fifteen years earlier (*Fig.* 13). This picture, one of the master's best works, retains the typical older elements of the composition, the scheme which was handed down to Leonardo: the table with projecting ends, Judas isolated on the near side, the other twelve in a row on the far side, with St. John asleep beside the Lord, one arm on the table. Christ's right hand is raised, and He

---

[1] *Trattato* No. 70 [McCurdy, *op. cit.*, p. 262] on light and shade melting into one another, 'like smoke' (an earlier expression). The same passage has the injunction to observe where lines 'are heavy and where they are fine'.

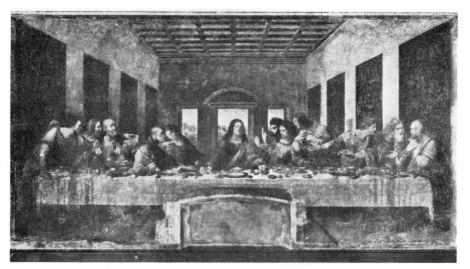

12. LEONARDO: *The Last Supper*. Milan, S. Maria delle Grazie

speaks, but the announcement of treachery must already have been made, for the Disciples are grief-stricken. Some protest their innocence, and Peter challenges Judas.

To begin with, Leonardo has broken with tradition in two ways. He takes Judas from his isolated position and places him in the same row as the others, and then he emancipates himself from the traditional motive of St. John lying on the Lord's breast—where he is usually shown asleep—a pose which is bound to become awkward when combined with the 'modern' seated position at table. In this way, he obtains greater unity in the scene, and the Disciples can be

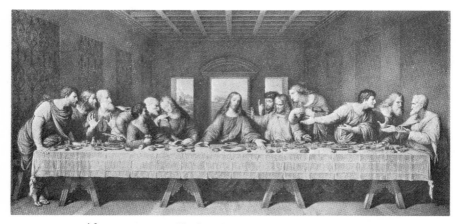

12a. After LEONARDO: *The Last Supper*. Engraving by Raphael Morghen

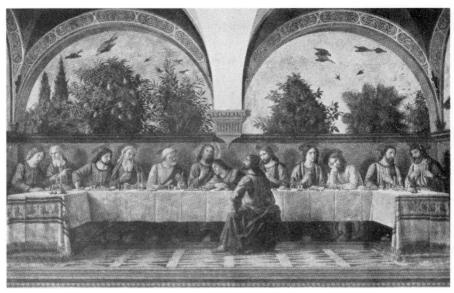

13. GHIRLANDAIO *The Last Supper*. Florence, Ognissanti

split into two symmetrical groups on either side of the Saviour; in this he is governed by the need for an architectonic arrangement. He goes still further, and forms smaller groups—two groups of three on each side, left and right—and thus Christ becomes the dominating central figure, unlike any of the others. Ghirlandaio's picture is a gathering without centre, with more or less independent half-length figures set one beside another, confined between the two great horizontals of table and wall, with its cornice hard above their heads. Unfortunately, a console supporting the roof projects in the centre of the wall. What does Ghirlandaio do? Without allowing it to embarrass him, he calmly moves his Christ to one side. Leonardo, to whom the emphasis on the central figure was of cardinal importance, would never have tolerated such a console. On the contrary, he uses the background to help him towards his goal, and it is through no coincidence that Christ sits framed in the light opening of the door at the back. Next, he breaks away from the limitations of the two horizontal lines; naturally, he retains the table, but above it the silhouettes of the groups must be allowed free play, so that quite new emotional effects are created. The perspective of the room, the shape and decoration of the walls are harnessed to the effect of the figures, everything is subordinated to their plasticity and scale—hence the depth of the room, and the dividing up of the walls by single hangings. The overlapping forms increase the plastic illusion and the repeated verticals accentuate the diverging movements. It is noticeable that these surfaces and lines are all small so that they cannot seriously compete with the figures, while a painter of the older generation, such as Ghirlandaio, sets a scale, with his great arches in the background, which is bound to make the figures look small.[1]

As we saw, Leonardo retained only one great line, the indispensable one of the table, yet even here there is something new. I do not mean the omission of the projecting ends—he is not the first to do that; the innovation lies in having the courage to depict a physical impossibility in order to obtain a heightened effect. The table is far too small. If the covers are counted it is clear that all the people there could not have sat down. Leonardo wishes to avoid the effect of the Disciples lost behind a long table, and the impression made by the figures is so strong that no one notices the lack of space. Only thus was it possible to arrange the figures in closed groups and yet keep them in contact with the principal figure. And what groups, what gestures these are! The words of Our Lord have struck like a thunderbolt and a storm of emotion has broken out: the Apostles comport themselves, not without dignity, but like men who are about to be deprived of their most treasured possession. An immense fund of new expression is added to art, and although Leonardo does not lose touch with his predecessors, it is the unheard-of intensity of expression which makes his figures appear to have no parallels. When such forces are brought into play, it is obvious that many of the subordinate interests of earlier art must be omitted. Ghirlandaio had to deal with a public which would examine every detail with attention, which had to be regaled with rare plants, birds and other animals, and he paid particular attention to the setting of the table, even counting out so many cherries to each of the company. Leonardo contents himself with the essentials. He may reasonably expect that the dramatic content of the picture will distract the spectator from such minor curiosities. Later, others carried this simplification even further.

This is not the place to describe the motives of each figure in detail, but something must be said of the economy which governed the distribution of the roles. The end figures are calm: two profiles enclosing the whole scene, and both quite vertical. Their tranquillity extends to the second members of the groups, and then the movement begins, increasing within the groups at either side of Christ, whose left-hand neighbour throws his arms wide apart 'as if he saw the earth opening at his feet', and at His right hand, quite close to Him, Judas draws sharply back.[2] The sharpest contrasts are juxtaposed: Judas sits in the same group as St. John.

---

[1] The edges of Leonardo's picture do not coincide with the limits of the room depicted; there is a considerable amount of space imagined above the upper edge of the picture. This division of space is one of the means by which it is possible to compose large scale figures in a small space without their appearing confined. The Quattrocentisti were in the habit of rendering interiors with side-walls and the whole of the ceiling—*cf.* Ghirlandaio's *Birth of St. John* or Castagno's *Last Supper*.
[2] Goethe's error, widely repeated since his day, must here be corrected. He thought St. Peter had struck Judas in the side with a knife, which could explain the sudden movement.

The contrasted arrangement of the groups, as well as the relationship subsisting between them—on the one side, the connecting links approach the front plane, on the other they are developed in depth—involve the kind of analysis which will continually occupy the student, and all the more so, as the calculations underlying them are concealed by the apparent simplicity of the arrangement. Indeed, they are of only secondary importance, compared to the one great effect reserved for the main figure. In the centre of all the tumult, Christ is quite still, His hands spread listlessly out as one who has said all there is to say. Unlike the older pictures, He is not represented as speaking, He does not even look up, but the silence is more eloquent than any words. It is the fearful silence which leaves no room for hope. In the face and gesture of Christ there is a calmness and greatness which may be called aristocratic, in so far as aristocratic has the meaning of noble; a word which cannot be applied to any painter of the Quattrocento. It would almost seem that Leonardo had made his studies from a different type of humanity, did we not know that he created the type himself. He has here drawn on the best in his own nature, and in any case, this air of greatness was to become the common property of the Italians of the sixteenth century. From Holbein onwards, what trouble the Germans took to acquire the magic of such a bearing! Yet, it must be insisted, that which makes the figure of Christ appear so different from all earlier representations is not to be explained solely by His face and gesture, but, even more essentially, by His role within the composition as a whole. In the earlier masters, the unity of the scene is lacking: the Apostles converse among themselves while Christ is speaking, and it is not always clear whether the scene depicted is the announcement of treachery or the Institution of the Eucharist. In any case, it was quite beyond the horizon of Quattrocento thought to make the silence following speech the motive of the principal figure. Leonardo was the first to venture this, and, by doing so, he reaps the infinite advantage that he can sustain the keynote for as long as he wishes: the original impulse to the emotional excitement continues to echo, and the action is at once momentary, eternal and complete.

Only Raphael understood Leonardo in this. There is a *Last Supper* from his School, engraved by Marcantonio[1], where Christ is depicted at a psychologically similar moment, staring, motionless, into space, His eyes wide open and looking out of the picture, His head a pure vertical, and the only one in the picture which is seen from the front (*Fig.* 14).

Andrea del Sarto falls below this level, in a composition (Florence, S. Salvi), which has some fine passages of painting, when he chose the moment at which

---

[1] The Albertina pen-drawing (Fischel, *Raffaels Zeichnungen*, 387) now correctly attributed to G. F. Penni, cannot be accepted as a preparatory drawing for this Marcantonio engraving as it is quite different in composition.

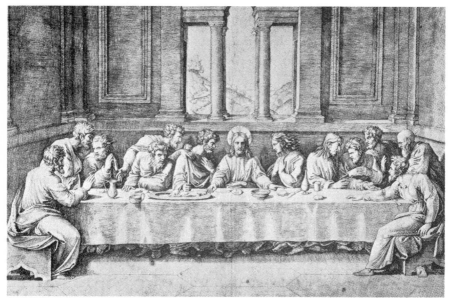

14. After RAPHAEL: *The Last Supper*. Engraving by Marcantonio Raimondi

the traitor is made known by the dipping of the sop, while Christ turns to St. John and consolingly takes his hand—a charming idea, but one which destroys the domination of the principal figure and the unity of feeling. Maybe Andrea said to himself that it was no use competing with Leonardo.

Other artists introduced trivialities, thinking to contribute something new. In Baroccio's large *Institution of the Eucharist* (Urbino), while the Lord is speaking, some of the Disciples call to the landlord to fetch more wine, as though they were going to drink a toast.

Finally, there is an observation to be made about the relationship between Leonardo's picture and the room where it is painted. It is well known that it decorates the end wall of a long, narrow refectory, which is lit from one side only, and Leonardo took the actual source of light as the source for his picture, which was not an unusual idea. The light comes from high up on the left, so that the opposite wall in the picture is only partly illuminated and the variety of tones between light and dark is so considerable that, by comparison, Ghirlandaio seems all one tone and flat. The brightly lit tablecloth stands out and the play of light on the heads gives them a strongly plastic effect against the dark wall, and there is still another effect gained by this use of the actual source of light: Judas, who has been taken out of his usual isolation and set among the other Disciples, still remains an isolated figure, for he is the only one to sit with his back completely turned to the light, so that his face, therefore, is entirely in shadow. This simple and effective means of characterization was, perhaps, recollected by the young Rubens when he painted his *Last Supper*, now in the Brera.

2. The *Mona Lisa*

IN the Quattrocento, occasional attempts had already been made to go beyond the mere representation of the sitter in portraits; more was wanted than that sum of features which gives the likeness, more than the permanent forms of the head, which give the character. Something was sought for which should mirror the mood of the hour, and record the passage across the face of momentary emotions. Some of Desiderio's busts of girls have just this quality: they smile, and the smile is not a stereotyped one, but the genuine reflection of a happy moment (*Fig.* 15). Everyone knows these young Florentine women with joyous mouths and brows arched over eyes which, even in marble, seem to sparkle. There is a smile, too, on the face of the *Mona Lisa* (*Fig.* 16), but only a very faint smile, in the corners of the mouth and almost imperceptibly trembling across the features. Like a breath of wind rippling the water, the soft planes of the face are moved, and the light and shadow play across it in whispered dialogue, to which we never tire of listening. Poliziano says somewhere, 'She flashed with a sweet, fond smile'.[1] I doubt if the conception and expression recur in the Cinquecento itself, when smiling no longer was in vogue, or, rather, only the subdued smile that we see in Sebastiano del Piombo's *Dorothea* (*Fig.* 81).

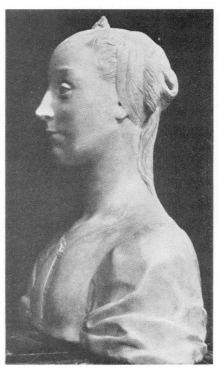

The brown eyes look out from under the narrow lids, not Quattrocento eyes with a forthright sparkle, but a veiled glance. The lower lids are almost hori-zontal—reminding one of the Gothic form of eye where the same motive is used to give a moist and liquid effect—and all the part below the eyes speaks of great sensibility, of fine nerves be-neath the skin.

The absence of eyebrows is striking.

---

[1] Poliziano, *Giostra*, I, p. 50, '*lampeggiò d'un dolce e vago riso.*'

15. DESIDERIO DA SETTIGNANO:
Bust of a Girl. Bargello

The curved surface of the eye-sockets runs, without transition, into the exceedingly high forehead, but this is not an individual peculiarity, for a passage in the 'Cortegiano' tells us that it was fashionable for women to pluck their eyebrows.[1] A wide extent of forehead was also accounted a beauty, so that the hairs above the forehead were also sacrificed, which explains the enormous foreheads of the busts of girls by Mino and Desiderio, where the joy in modelling the white surfaces created with such tender feeling by the chisel on the white marble, outweighed all other considerations, so that the natural divisions were eliminated and the zone of the forehead extended upwards beyond reason. The *Mona Lisa* is, in this respect, an example of Quattrocento taste, for the fashion changed immediately afterwards and the line of the forehead was again lowered, and now one realizes how much better it is when eyebrows define the form. The copy of the *Mona Lisa* in Madrid has had eyebrows deliberately added.

The hair, chestnut-brown like the eyes, falls in soft waves down her cheeks, as does the loose veil which is laid over the head.

The lady sits in an armchair, and one is surprised to find so rigid and vertical a carriage of the head accompanied by such softness of execution. Obviously she bears herself according to the fashion, for an upright carriage implied distinction, as may be seen in Ghirlandaio's frescoes of the Tornabuoni ladies, bolt upright on their visits. Later, the fashion changed and the newer ideas on the subject are directly reflected in the poses of the portraits.[2]

Apart from this, the picture is not lacking in movement. For the first time, Leonardo adopted the half-length instead of the bust size, with its abrupt cutting of the body. He posed the model sitting sideways, with the upper part of the body half turned and the face seen almost directly from the front, adding the movement of the arms, one lying along the arm of the chair, the other coming forward in foreshortening with one hand laid over the other. It was not merely for decorative purposes that Leonardo added the hands, for their placid gesture adds greatly to the characterization and one feels the delicacy of touch of these sensitive fingers. In this, Verrocchio anticipated Leonardo, if, indeed, the celebrated bust in the Bargello is by him and not due to the young Leonardo himself.

The costume is simple, almost prim—to an artist of the Cinquecento the line of the bodice must have seemed hard. The pleated gown is green, of the green which was afterwards used by Luini, and the yellow-brown sleeves are not, as

[1]Baldassare Castiglione, *Il Cortegiano*, 1516. In the first Book it is stated that men imitated women in plucking the eyebrows and forehead (*pelarsi le ciglia e la fronte*).
[2]When Lucrezia Tornabuoni nei Medici, the mother of Lorenzo the Magnificent, sought a bride for her son among the Roman nobility, she wrote to her husband finding fault with the carriage of the Roman women as being less upright than that of the Florentines (Reumont, *Lorenzo magnifico*, I, 272).

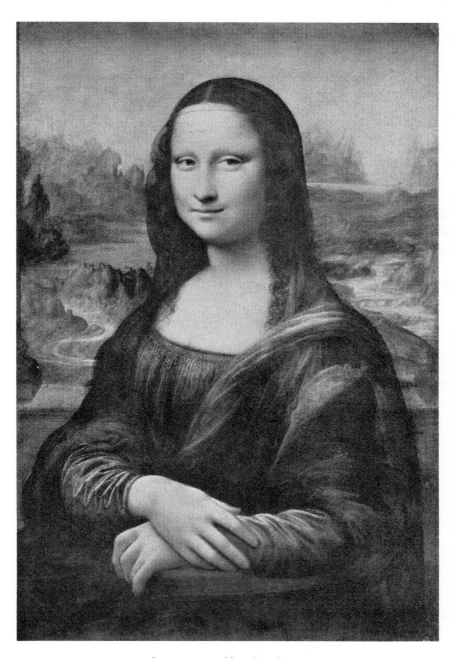

16. LEONARDO: *Mona Lisa.* Louvre

in earlier fashions, short and narrow, but reach to the wrist and are crumpled into a multitude of transverse folds so that they make an effective accompaniment to the smoothly rounded forms of the hands and the delicate fingers, untrammelled by rings; the neck, too, is unadorned.

The background is a landscape, as in some older pictures, but it does not come right up to the figure, since there is a low parapet between them and the view into the landscape is confined between columns. One must look closely to appreciate this motive, which had important consequences, since, except for their bases, the columns appear only as narrow strips. The later style did not rest content with such slight indications.[1]

The landscape itself stretches away into the distance, above the eye-level of the sitter, and it is of an unusual kind—fantastic, jagged labyrinths of mountains with lakes and streams scattered between them. What is strangest is their dream-like aspect suggested by their indeterminate execution. They are of a different order of reality from the figure and this is no caprice on the part of the artist, but a means of increasing the apparent solidity of the figure. It is an exposition of some of Leonardo's theories concerning the appearance of distant objects which he also set out in his Treatise,[2] and its success is such, that, in the Salon Carré of the Louvre where the *Mona Lisa* hangs, all the neighbouring pictures, even those of the seventeenth century, look flat. The landscape is painted in shades of brown, green-blue and blue-green passing into the blue of the sky; these are exactly the colours used by Perugino in his little *Apollo and Marsyas*, also in the Louvre.

Leonardo said that modelling was the soul of painting. If anywhere, it is in front of the *Mona Lisa* that one begins to discern the significance of these words. The delicate undulations of the surfaces become a personal experience, almost as if one had glided over them with a spirit-hand. The aim is not simplicity but complexity, and anyone who has contemplated it for a long time can confirm that it needs to be studied from close up, for it loses much of its peculiar effect if seen from a distance. This is even more true of photographs of it, which, therefore, are unsuitable as a wall-decoration. In this, it is basically different from the later portraits of the Cinquecento, and in a certain sense it marks the conclusion of a movement rooted in the fifteenth century, and is the apogee of that refined style to which the sculptors, in particular, devoted all their efforts. The next generation of Florentines did not go any further with this, and it was only in Lombardy that these delicate threads continued to be spun.[3]

---

[1] *Cf.* the Raphaelesque so-called *Drawing for the Maddalena Doni* in the Louvre.

[2] *Trattato della Pittura* (Ludwig's Italian-German ed. No. 128). [Several of these theories may be found in McCurdy's edition of the Notebooks.—*Trans.*]

[3] It has long been felt that the *Belle Ferronnière* (Louvre) has no place in Leonardo's work. This fine picture has recently been tentatively ascribed to Boltraffio, but this is not convincing.

3. The *Virgin and Child with St. Anne*

COMPARED with the *Mona Lisa*, Leonardo's other picture in the Louvre, the *Virgin and Child with St. Anne*, attracts less appreciation from the public (*Fig.* 17). The picture is probably not entirely the work of Leonardo's own hand and has suffered in its colour, while the qualities of draughtsmanship which it contains are but little prized by modern eyes, and indeed, scarcely understood. Yet the cartoon alone, in its day (1501), aroused tremendous excitement in Florence and caused a general pilgrimage to the convent of the Annunziata, where Leonardo's latest miracle could be seen.[1] The theme might well have proved arid enough; one recollects the inflexible way in which older masters arranged the three figures—one sitting on the lap of the other and all three turned to face the spectator—and yet here this dry one-on-top-of-the-other arrangement is transformed into a group of the greatest subtlety and the lifeless framework is imbued with animated movement. Mary sits sideways on her mother's lap; smiling, she bends forward and grasps the Child with both hands while He, at her feet, tries to bestride a lamb. He looks up enquiringly, still holding firmly on to the head of the unfortunate crouching animal, which tries to shrink away although the Child already has one leg over its back. Smiling, the youthful-looking grandmother watches the merry game.

The problems of grouping in the *Last Supper* are further developed here. The composition is infinitely thought-provoking, saying much in little space; all the figures have contrasting movements and the opposing directions of the main forms are resolved into a compact, closed mass which can demonstrably be contained within an equilateral triangle. All this is the fruit of strivings, perceptible as early as the *Madonna of the Rocks* (*Fig.* 8), to subordinate the whole composition to simple geometric forms; but how diffuse the earlier work looks beside the compressed riches of the *St. Anne*! It was not love of the artificial, the over-wrought, which led Leonardo to attempt more and more movement within an ever-diminishing space, for the strength of the effect is increased in proportion. The difficulty lay in preserving the clarity and calm of the total effect, and that was the rock on which his feebler imitators foundered. Leonardo attained complete lucidity and his principal motive—the bending forward of the Virgin—is of enchanting beauty and warmth, with all the minor beauties, which so often led the Quattrocento astray, subordinated to it with an unsurpassed mastery of expression. Consider the way in which the lines of shoulder and head, light on dark, stand out in relief, yet retain their wonderful softness. How calm, yet how full of movement! The restraint of St. Anne

---

[1] The cartoon is lost and the picture may have been executed considerably later; *cf.* Cook, *Gazette des Beaux-Arts*, 1897.

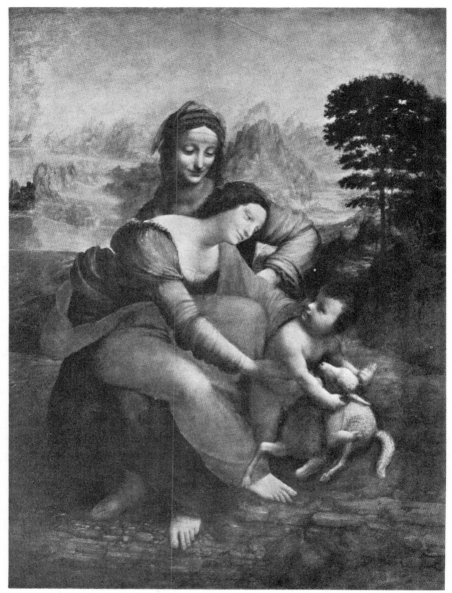

17. LEONARDO: *The Virgin and Child with St. Anne.* Louvre

provides a most telling contrast, and the group is closed below, in the happiest way, by the Child glancing upwards, and His lamb.

A small picture by Raphael, in Madrid, reflects the impression made by this composition. As a young man in Florence, he attempted a similar problem, substituting St. Joseph for St. Anne, but with much less success. The lamb alone is very wooden, for Raphael was never successful as an animal painter, while Leonardo could succeed in anything he undertook. But a more formidable competitor than Raphael now entered the lists against Leonardo—Michelangelo. More will be said of this later.

The *St. Anne* contains none of the grasses, flowers and reflecting pools of water of the *Madonna of the Rocks*; the lifesize figures are everything. But what is more important than their actual size is their scale, the proportion of the picture-surface which they occupy. They fill the canvas more effectually than do the figures in the earlier works, or, to put it another way, the picture surface is smaller in proportion to its contents. This is the scale of proportion which became typical of the Cinquecento.[1]

4. The *Battle of Anghiari*

It is not possible to say much about this battle-piece, which was commissioned for the Great Council Chamber of Florence, since the composition no longer exists even as a cartoon, but only in the incomplete copy by a later hand; yet it cannot be passed over, since the problems raised by it are too interesting.

Leonardo studied horses very deeply—more, perhaps, than any other artist of the Cinquecento—and his interest arose from his love for the animal.[2] He was occupied for years in Milan with an equestrian statue of Duke Francesco Sforza, never cast, but for which a complete model once existed, the destruction of which is to be reckoned among the greatest losses of art. It seems to have been originally conceived as a demonstration of movement surpassing Verrocchio's *Colleoni* monument, and thus he arrived at a group of a galloping horse with a prostrate foe beneath its hoofs; the same idea as that which had already occurred to Antonio Pollaiuolo.[3] Occasionally the misgiving is expressed that Leonardo's figure might have become too much of a painter's conception, but if this has any justification it can only be with reference to sketches for this design, for the motive of the leaping horse cannot be regarded as definitive, since, in the course of the work, a development towards greater unity and simplicity took place, similar to that observable in the sketches for the *Last Supper*, and Leonardo

---

[1]The impression made on contemporaries can be clearly gauged in a report from Fra Pietro da Novellara to the Marchioness of Mantua on 3 April, 1501, where he speaks of this aspect, '*e sono queste figure grandi al naturale, ma stanno in piccolo cartone, perchè tutte o sedono o stanno curve, et una sta alquanto dinanzi all' altra.*' (*Archivio storico dell' arte*, I). [' These figures are life-size, but in quite a small cartoon, since they are all seated or bent forward and one rather in front of the other.' *cf.* also Sir Kenneth Clark, *Leonardo da Vinci*, 1940.—*Trans.*] The Cartoon in London (Royal Academy) is of a group of two women and two children, less beautiful, and may well be a somewhat earlier and less fluent composition. Its effect on Leonardo's School may be seen in Luini (Ambrosiana).

[2]Vasari (ed. Milanesi, IV, p. 21).

[3]Vasari (ed. Milanesi, III, p. 297). *Cf.* the drawing in Munich (Berenson No. 1908).

ended up with the horse simply walking, the earlier projects for a sharp contrast of direction between the heads of horse and rider being quite significantly modified. Only the backward bend of the arm with the marshal's baton remained unaltered, since Leonardo wished to enrich the silhouette and fill up the empty right-hand space behind the rider's back.[1] The only source of information left to us concerning the large battle-piece in the Florentine Council Chamber, in which Leonardo sought to turn his Milanese studies to account, is the drawing in the Louvre, ascribed to Rubens,[2] from which Edelingk engraved a well known and excellent plate. It is scarcely likely that the drawing gives everything that was in the picture, but in general it corresponds with Vasari's description.

Leonardo intended to show the Florentines, once for all, how to draw horses; for his principal motive he chose a cavalry action during the battle—the fight for the standard—with four horses and four riders in impassioned violence and the closest physical contact. The problem of composing a group with the utmost plasticity is taken here to a pitch which verges almost on the boundary of the unclear.[3] The northern engraver emphasized the pictorial, painterly aspect of the composition, so that a central dark mass is surrounded by lighter ones; an arrangement which we may well believe is Leonardo's in principle.

At that time, the specifically 'modern' task was the composition of interlocked masses and one is surprised at not coming across more battle-pieces. The School of Raphael is the only place where a major work of this kind was produced, and the *Battle of Constantine* represents the general Western conception of the classical battle-piece; in it, an advance was made from the merely episodic to the representation of a real mass action, yet although this celebrated work offers far more than Leonardo did, it is so afflicted by its imperceptive lack of clarity that one sees, already, the loss of visual sensibility and the approach of decadence. Raphael certainly had nothing to do with this composition.

*   *   *   *   *

LEONARDO left no School in Florence. Everyone learned from him, but the impression he made was superseded by that of Michelangelo. Clearly, Leonardo developed towards a conception of figures on the grand scale and, in the end, the figure became all-in-all for him. Yet Florence would have worn a different aspect had it been more Leonardesque, and the traces of Leonardo which

---

[1] On the questions of the Milanese monument and a second, later, equestrian project with a tomb below it for General Trivulzio, see Müller-Walde in the *Jahrbuch der preussischen Kunstsammlungen*, 1897 and 1899. Since then, Müntz's great book has appeared (*Léonard de Vinci*, Paris, 1899) which gives exhaustive information on all matters of fact. [The English reader is again referred to Sir Kenneth Clark's book, cited above.—*Trans.*]

[2] I do not venture an opinion on Rubens's authorship of the Louvre drawing: Rooses is emphatically in favour of it. At any rate, Rubens knew the composition—his *Lion Hunt*, in Munich, and other works attest this.

[3] [For this use of the word 'unclear', *cf.* Wölfflin, *Principles of Art History.—Trans.*]

survive in Andrea del Sarto or in Franciabigio and Bugiardini do not really signify very much. A direct continuation of his art, or, at any rate, of one side of it, is to be found only in Lombardy, but the Lombards, though gifted as painters, are utterly deficient in the architectonic sense. They never grasped the structure of the *Last Supper*, and Leonardo's grouping and involved movement offered solutions to problems outside their range. The more spirited made of movement something wild and confused, the others are of a tiresome uniformity. In Lombardy, it was the feminine side of Leonardo's art which was most influential, the passive emotions and the soft, almost smoke-like modelling of youthful bodies, particularly of feminine forms. Leonardo was extremely sensitive to the beauty of the female body; one could even say that he was the first to realise the soft texture of the skin. His Florentine contemporaries also painted female nudes, but it was just this charm that they lacked. Even those among them who were the most painterly in feeling, such as Piero di Cosimo, were primarily interested in form rather than in the quality of the surface. With the awakening of a more subtle sense of touch, manifested in the type of modelling used by Leonardo, the female body acquired a new artistic significance, and we could deduce from these psychological premises that Leonardo must have devoted much study to this theme, even if we did not happen to know that such pictures by him did once exist.

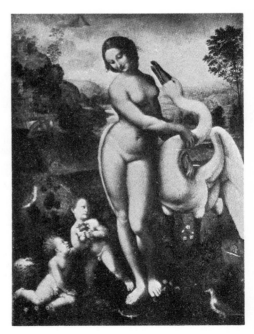

The most important seems to have been a *Leda*, which we know only from copies, principally in the form of a beautiful nude in slight movement, standing with her knees pressed together and caressing, rather than repulsing, the swan (*Fig.* 18). This figure, with twisted torso, tilted head, arm reaching across the body, and one shoulder lowered, exerted a very considerable influence. (The best known version is in the Galleria Borghese, Rome, and was at one time ascribed to Sodoma.)[1]

---

[1]*Cf.* Müller-Walde, *Beiträge zur Kenntnis des Lionardo da Vinci, Jahrbuch der preussischen Kunstsammlungen*, 1897. Müller-Walde discovered a minute pen-drawing of the figure in the Codex Atlanticus. *Cf.* Müntz, *op. cit.*, 426 ff.

18. After LEONARDO: *Leda and the Swan.* Rome, Borghese Gallery

The female nude thus became a common theme among Leonardo's Lombard followers, but as they had but little feeling for movement as something affecting the whole body, it is scarcely surprising that they abandoned whole-length figures and contented themselves with half-length schemes. Even a subject like *Susanna in the Bath,* where one might reasonably expect to find a thorough study of the plasticity of a figure, is circumscribed within this arid formula (picture by Luini in the Galleria Borromeo, Milan). As a general type of this style, the unpretentious half-length figure of *Abundance* by Gianpetrino is here reproduced (*Fig.* 19).[1]

---

[1] The picture is in the Galleria Borromeo, Milan, and should be compared with Leonardo's *Mona Lisa,* a version of which, even in his own life-time (and perhaps by Leonardo himself) was transformed into a nude. *Cf.* Müntz, *op. cit.,* p. 511.

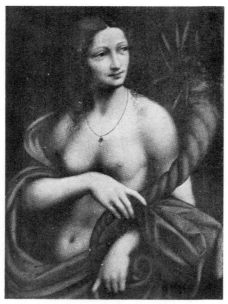

19. GIANPETRINO: *Abundantia.* Milan.
Conte Borromeo

CHAPTER III : MICHELANGELO (1475-1564)

(UP TO 1520)

THE progress of Michelangelo through Italian art was like that of a mighty mountain torrent, at once fertilising and destructive; irresistibly carrying all before him, he became a liberator to a few and a destroyer to many more. From the very beginning, Michelangelo was a complete personality, awe-inspiring in his single-mindedness, thinking of the world as a sculptor and as a sculptor only. His interest was in the definition of form, and only the human body seemed worthy of representation to him, for whom the infinite variety of created things simply did not exist. For him, the human race was not the humanity of this world, with its thousands of different individuals, but a race apart, transposed into the colossal. Compared with Leonardo's pleasure in things, Michelangelo appears as a solitary, an ascetic to whom the world, as it is, offers nothing. True, he once created an Eve, portraying indolent, soft beauty in a woman in all the splendour of a voluptuous nature; but it was only momentary. Whether he desired it or not, everything he created is steeped in bitterness.

His style aims at concentration and the creation of closed masses; a loose, sketchy contour goes against his grain, and a closely packed composition with severely restrained gesture was a temperamental necessity for him. The grasp of form and clarity of inner vision which he possessed are absolutely without parallel; there are no tentative gropings after expression; he gives everything he wants with the very first strokes, so that his drawings have a penetrative quality. They are, as it were, saturated with form.

The inner structure, the mechanics of movement, have been expressed to the very last detail, compelling the spectator to share his experience completely. Further, every turn, every bend of a limb has a latent power—quite trivial displacements have an incomprehensibly powerful effect and the impression so produced can be so great that one forgets to seek the motives behind the movement. It is characteristic of Michelangelo that he forced his means relentlessly to gain the utmost possible effect, so that he enriched art with new effects hitherto undreamed-of, but he also impoverished it by taking away all joy in simple, everyday things; it was he who brought disharmony into the Renaissance and prepared the ground for a new style—the Baroque —by his deliberate use of dissonance. This will be discussed in a later section, but the works of the first half of his life, up to 1520, still speak in another language.

1. Early Works

THE *Pietà* is the first major work from which we can deduce Michelangelo's intentions (*Fig.* 20). At present it is barbarously exhibited in a chapel of St. Peter's where neither the refinements of handling nor the charm of the movement can be realised, for the group is lost in the expanse of chapel and is

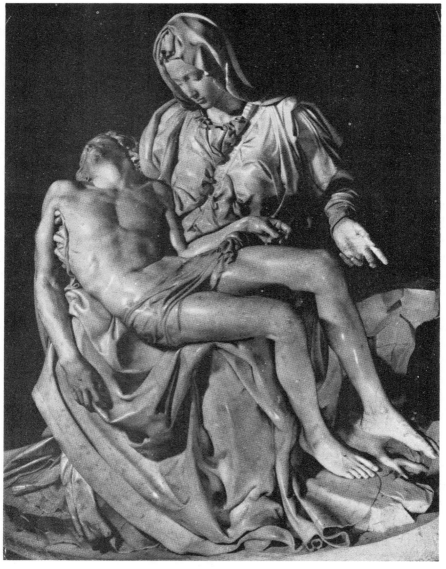

20. MICHELANGELO: *Pietà*. Rome, St. Peter's

placed so high up that it is impossible to see it from the proper point of view.

In itself, it was something novel to combine two life-size marble figures into one group, and it was also an exceedingly difficult task to place the body of a full grown man on the lap of a seated woman. We might expect to find a hard horizontal cutting through the group at sharp right angles, but Michelangelo accomplished what no one else at that time could have done, for all is twisted and turned so that the two figures combine in easy harmony: Mary grasping her burden but not overwhelmed by it, the dead Christ clearly realised from all points of view and expressive in every line. The shoulder forced upwards and the head dropped backwards give an unsurpassed pathos to the dead body. Mary's gesture is still more surprising. The weeping face distorted with grief, the swooning collapse, had been rendered by earlier masters: Michelangelo says, 'The Mother of God does not weep like an earthly mother'. Motionless, she bows her head, the features betraying no emotion, and only her drooping left hand is eloquent: half-open, it accompanies the mute monologue of anguish. Christ also shows no marks of suffering. This is the sensibility of the Cinquecento.

From the formal point of view, the Florentine origin of the work and the style of the fifteenth century are more obvious. The head of the Virgin is unlike any other, but it is of the delicate, narrow type favoured by the earlier Florentines, and the figures are similar in style. A few years later, Michelangelo would have made them broader and fuller, and even the articulation of the group he would later have felt to be too graceful, too simple, too loose; the corpse would have been more powerful and more heavily built, the outlines less diffuse, and he would have compressed the two figures into a more compact mass. The draperies are somewhat obtrusively rich, with bright ridges of folds and deep shadowy undercuttings which the sculptors of the Cinquecento gladly took for a model. The marble is highly polished, as remained the practice, creating intense reflected lights, but there is no longer any question of gilding.

Closely related to the *Pietà* is the *Bruges Madonna* (*Fig.* 21), a work which left Italy immediately on completion[1] and therefore left no significant traces there, although the completely new handling of the theme might have been expected to make a great impression. The seated Madonna and Child was not common in Florence as a plastic group, although the theme was varied in a hundred ways for altar-pieces. It is more often met with in terra-cotta than in marble, and was usually painted, since the clay was not thought pleasing in itself, but it tended to fall out of use in the sixteenth century when the increased desire for monumentality could only be satisfied in stone; where terra-cotta did

---

[1] Traces of a second, weaker, hand are observable in the subordinate parts. Michelangelo seems to have left it incomplete when he went to Rome for the second time (1505).

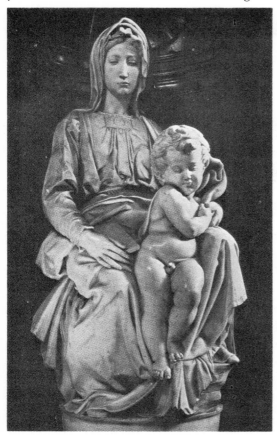

21. MICHELANGELO: *Madonna and Child*. Bruges,
Notre Dame

survive, as in Lombardy, it was preferred uncoloured. Michelangelo differs from the earlier types in taking the Child out of His mother's lap and setting Him, big and sturdily built, between her knees where He clambers about. This motive of the standing and moving Child gives a new formal content to the group, the variety of which was increased by placing the feet of the seated figure at different levels. The Child is busy with His childish games, but He is serious, much more serious than in the older representations, even those in which He is shown in the act of blessing, and the Madonna, too, is thoughtful and silent; no one would venture to speak to her. A solemn, almost hieratic, seriousness lies upon them both. This ideal of a new reverence and awe in the presence of holy things must be compared with figures embodying the sentiment of the Quattrocento, such as Benedetto da Maiano's terracotta group in the Berlin Museum (*Fig.* 22). This is the worthy Mrs. So-and-So —whom, one feels certain, one has met before, good-naturedly managing her household—and the Child is a fine, happy little urchin, who, it is true, is holding up His little hand in blessing; but nobody need take it at all seriously. The light-heartedness which shines on their faces and laughs from their eyes is banished by Michelangelo: the head of his Virgin is no more like that of a comfortable housewife than her dress is likely to lead our mind astray with thoughts of worldly wealth and splendour.

Strong and clear, in sustained chords, the spirit of a new art is manifested in the *Bruges Madonna*; indeed, one might say that the grandeur of the vertical pose of the head is in itself a motive which surpasses everything in the Quattrocento.

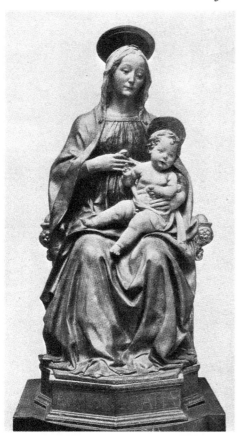

22. BENEDETTO DA MAIANO: *Madonna and Child*. Berlin, Museum

In a very early work (the small relief of the *Madonna of the Steps*) Michelangelo attempted to formulate a similar idea—that of the Madonna gazing into empty space, while the Child sleeps at her breast—and his new conception is clear even in the timidity of the drawing. In the plenitude of his power of expression he now returns to the same theme in the unfinished circular relief in the Bargello (the *Bargello Tondo*), where the Child, sleepy and solemn, leans against the mother, who, upright and seen full face, looks out from the surface of the relief like a prophetess (*Fig.* 23). From another point of view also this relief is noteworthy, for it shows the genesis of a new ideal of feminine beauty, more powerfully built, with large eyes, broad cheeks and strong chin, making a complete break with the older Florentine grace. New arrangements of the drapery accompany this, as, for example, the exposure of the neck to show its structurally important connections with the body. The impression of power is underlined by a new use of space, with the bodies coming abruptly up against the edge of the relief, and the flickering richness of an Antonio Rossellino, with its ceaseless play of light and shade from the strongest projection down to the slightest surface undulations, is given up in favour of a few strong accents which take effect at a distance. The head, with its emphatic vertical, again sets the keynote.

In London, the Florentine relief has a companion of the most charming delicacy and finished beauty, such as rarely and only momentarily flashes out in Michelangelo's work (Royal Academy).

How strange beside these, seems the joyless *Holy Family* of the Uffizi (*Fig.* 24), and how difficult to fit into the long row of Quattrocento Holy Families! The Madonna is a mannish, raw-boned woman with her arms and feet bare, who,

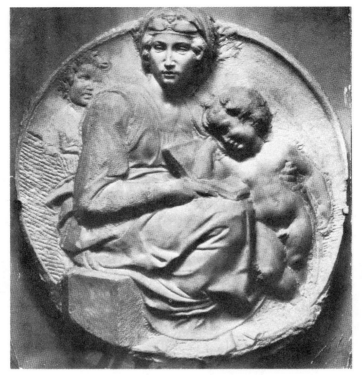

23. MICHELANGELO: *Madonna and Child*. Bargello

squatting on the ground with her legs curled under her, reaches over her shoulder for the Child, taking Him from St. Joseph sitting behind her, so that the whole group forms a tangle of figures oddly pressed together in their movement. This is no maternal Mary (there is no such thing in Michelangelo) nor is it the hieratic Virgin; it is simply the Heroine. The requirements of the subject are so brusquely contradicted that the spectator immediately senses that this is merely an exercise in interesting movement and the solution to a set problem in composition. The picture was painted for a private patron, and there may be something in Vasari's story that Angelo Doni, who commissioned it, made difficulties about accepting it; to judge from the portrait of him in the Palazzo Pitti, he may not have had much sympathy with 'art for art's sake'. Clearly, the problem here was to develop the maximum movement in the most confined space, and the real meaning of the picture lies in its concentrated plasticity. Perhaps it should be regarded as a sort of competition-piece, designed to out-do Leonardo, for it dates from the time when Leonardo's cartoon of the *Holy Family with St. Anne* was causing such excitement by its new style of closely packed figures. Michelangelo substituted St. Joseph for St. Anne, but the technical problem

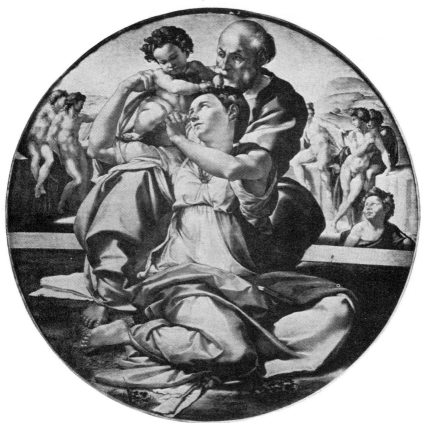

24. MICHELANGELO: *The Holy Family*. Uffizi

remained the same—to co-ordinate the figures of two adults and a child as close to each other as possible, without loss of clarity and without a cramped effect. Certainly Michelangelo surpasses Leonardo in variety of axial directions, but at what a cost! The contours and modelling are of metallic precision, so that it is no longer a picture so much as a painted relief. Plasticity has always been the strength of the Florentines—they are a race of sculptors rather than painters— but here, the national talent is raised to a pitch which opened the way to quite new interpretations of the meaning of 'good drawing'. Even Leonardo can show nothing comparable to the outstretched arm of the Virgin, full of life in every joint and muscle and of essential significance in the whole composition—not for nothing is the arm bared to the shoulder.

The impression made by this picture, with its sharply defined contours and bright shadows, never died out in Florence. Over and over again there crops up, in this home of draughtsmanship, an opposition to the exponents of chiaroscuro, and in this Bronzino and Vasari, for example, are the direct successors of Michelangelo, even though neither of them ever came anywhere near the expressive power of his sense of form.

*   *   *   *   *

AFTER the *Pietà*, the seated *Bruges Madonna*, the Madonna reliefs and the *Holy Family* tondo, one looks expectantly for those youthful works of Michelangelo which show him at his most personal—the male nudes. He began with a large nude *Hercules* which is now lost, then, in Rome, he carved a *Drunken Bacchus* (Bargello) at the same time as the *Pietà*, and shortly after that came the work which outshines them all in fame, the Florentine *David*.[1]

In the *Bacchus* and the *David* one recognises the final expression of Florentine naturalism in the fifteenth-century sense, for it was entirely in keeping with Donatello's ideas to represent Bacchus as reeling drunkenly, and Michelangelo chooses the moment when the drinker, no longer quite sure of his footing, blinks at the full up-raised goblet while supporting himself on a small companion. For his model, Michelangelo chose a plump young fellow and modelled the individual peculiarities of the soft, almost feminine, body with the greatest pleasure, a pleasure he never experienced again. Both motive and handling are characteristic of the Quattrocento. There is nothing amusing about this Bacchus and no one could laugh at it, but there is something of youthful humour in it—in so far as Michelangelo knew how to be young.

The *David* is still more striking because of the angularity of its appearance (*Fig. 25*). A David should be the portrait of a handsome young victor and it was thus that Donatello portrayed him, as a stalwart youth; so, too, did Verrocchio, reflecting a different facet of taste, as a slender, angular, fine-drawn

---

[1]The *Giovannino* of the Berlin Museum (Fig. 184) cannot be passed over in silence, as it is attributed to Michelangelo and dated c. 1495, *i.e.* before the *Bacchus*; yet I do not wish to repeat here what I have already said about this figure, which I cannot connect with Michelangelo or, indeed, with the Quattrocento at all (*cf.* Wölfflin, *Die Jugendwerke des Michelangelo*, 1891). The very artificial pose and the generalised, smooth handling of the forms lead me to place it well into the sixteenth century. The treatment of the joints comes out of the School of Michelangelo, but not the young Michelangelo; even in the master himself, the motive of the arm reaching freely forward is hardly possible before 1520, and the softness of form, which does not allow even of the indication of one of the boy's ribs or the folding of the skin in his armpit, has no analogy in even the most effeminate of the Quattrocentisti. Who, then, is the author of this puzzling figure? It has been maintained that he must have died young or it would be impossible that we should not have heard more of him. I believe he is to be sought in the person of the Neapolitan Girolamo Santacroce (born c. 1502, died 1537), whose life may be read in Vasari (*cf.* de Dominici, *Vite dei pittori, scultori ed architetti napolitani*, II, ed. of 1843). He died young and was spoiled still younger, carried away by the tide of Mannerism, some portent of which is undeniable even in the *Giovannino*. He was hailed as the second Michelangelo and the greatest hopes were entertained of him. Closely akin to the *Giovannino* is the fine altar of the Pezzo family (1524) in Montoliveto, Naples, from which one may form a sound judgement of the great gifts of this precocious artist: close to it is a similar composition by Giovanni da Nola, who is usually taken to represent Neapolitan Cinquecento sculpture but is a much inferior artist. (For a contrary view, *cf.* Bode, *Florentinische Bildhauer*, 1903). [English trans. as *Florentine Sculptors of the Renaissance*, 1908 and 1928.] Alois Grünwald has called the *Giovannino* a work by a certain Pieratti, of the early 17th century (*Münchner Jahrbuch*, 1910).

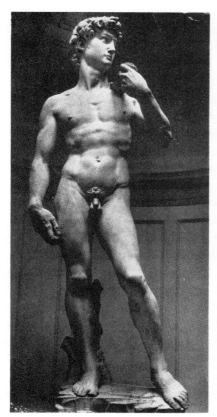

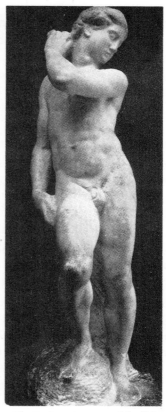

25. MICHELANGELO: *David*. Florence,
Academy

26. MICHELANGELO: '*Apollo*'
or *David*. Bargello

lad (*Figs.* 2, 3). What is Michelangelo's ideal of youthful beauty? A gigantic
hobbledehoy, neither man nor boy, a stripling at the age when the body stretches
itself and the huge hands and feet seem to have no relation to the size of the
limbs. For once, Michelangelo's sense of realism must have been thoroughly
satisfied, for he accepted the consequences of enlarging this uncouth model
to a colossal scale, making no attempt to modify the angular rhythms of the
pose and the huge, empty triangle between the legs; no concessions are made to
beauty of line. The figure is a faithful reproduction of nature, which, on this
scale, approaches the marvellous; every detail is astonishing and the feeling of
elasticity in the whole is a perpetual source of wonder. Yet, to put it bluntly, it
is thoroughly ugly.[1] Oddly enough, in spite of this, it has become the most

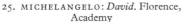

[1]Technical necessities may have played some part in the motive of the arms, so unexpected and
difficult to understand. In any case, when Leonardo treated the same subject in his well-known
drawing, he gave his David a normal sling hanging from the right hand: in Michelangelo, a broad
band runs down the back, one end being held by the right hand and the other, broadened out
into a bag shape, lies in the left hand. From the principal view-point it is of no importance at all.

popular statue in Florence, and among the Florentines, along with the specifically Tuscan grace—which is something different from Roman gravity—there is a feeling for expressive ugliness which did not die out with the Quattrocento. Some time ago, the *David* was removed from his exposed position by the Palazzo Vecchio into the shelter of a museum, but it was necessary to let the people continue to see their *gigante*, if only as a bronze cast, and a most unhappy position was chosen for this, illustrating the present-day lack of a sense of style. The bronze was set up in the middle of a large open space, so that one gets the most monstrous views of the figure before one sees him properly. In its own day, immediately after it was finished, the question of a site for the statue was referred to a committee of artists, whose memorandum still exists: they were unanimous that it must be related to a wall-surface, either in the Loggia dei Lanzi or near the door of the Palazzo della Signoria.[1] The figure requires this, for it is entirely worked in planes to be seen from the front and not from all sides: a central position is most calculated to emphasise its ugly qualities.

What would Michelangelo himself have thought of his *David* in later years? Apart from the fact that it would no longer have occurred to him to make so detailed a study from the model, he would have felt the motive itself to be empty; his mature views on the essentials of sculpture can be gathered from his so-called *Apollo* in the Bargello (*Fig.* 26) by comparison with the *David* of a quarter of a century earlier. This is a youth in the act of drawing an arrow from his quiver. Quite simple in details, the richness is reserved for the development of the action itself, in which there is neither exertion nor gesticulation, and the body is treated as a block modelled in depth, with animation and movement continued through all the planes, even those furthest away from the spectator. Beside it, the *David* appears thin and flat and the same is true of the *Bacchus*. Only in Michelangelo's youthful style does one find the expansion across the plane, the limbs treated as separate masses, the stone pierced with holes; later, he sought his effects by unification and restraint. He must have come to see the value of such a treatment quite early, for it is already present in the projected *St. Matthew* (Florence, Academy) which immediately followed the *David*.[2] Nude bodies and movement—these were the objects of Michelangelo's art. He began with them while still a boy, when he carved his *Battle of the Centaurs*, and he repeated them in his early manhood with such success that a whole generation of artists learned from him. The cartoon of the *Bathers* was undoubtedly the most important monument of his first Florentine period, the most complex demonstration of the new approach to the rendering of the human body; the

---

[1][The *David* now outside the Palazzo Vecchio is a modern marble copy.—*Trans.*]
[2]The *St. Matthew* was one of a set of the twelve Apostles ordered for Florence Cathedral, but not even this one, the first, was ever finished.

few examples, preserved by Marcantonio's engravings[1] from the lost cartoon
itself, are sufficient to give us an idea
of the concept of *gran disegno (Fig. 27)*.

It is reasonable to suppose that
Michelangelo had a share in determining
the theme. Instead of a battle-scene,
evidently projected as a pendant to
Leonardo's fresco in the Council chamber, with its accompaniment of weapons
and armour, the artist was allowed to
depict the moment when a company of
bathing soldiers was called out of the
water by the giving of an alarm, an
incident which actually happened during
the Pisan war. That such a scene could
be chosen for a monumental wall-painting
is the strongest possible testimony to
the general standard of Florentine taste;

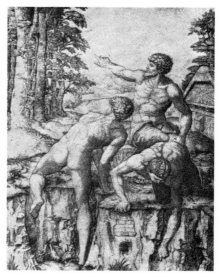

27. After MICHELANGELO:
Bathing Soldiers.
Engraving by Marcantonio Raimondi

men clambering up the steep bank, or kneeling and reaching downwards, the
erect figures arming themselves, the seated ones hastily throwing on their
clothes, the shouting and running—it all allowed a variety of different movements and naked bodies in plenty, without being unhistoric. Later painters of
ideal History would have been glad enough of the nudes, but would have felt
the theme was too low, too genre-like.

The anatomists among the Florentine artists had already depicted battles of
nude men—there are two such engravings by Antonio Pollaiuolo, and it is said
that Verrocchio made a drawing of naked warriors for transference to the façade
of a house and it is with such things that Michelangelo's work must be compared;
a comparison which would show not only that he had, as it were, rediscovered
all movements, but also that he was the first to give real coherence and unity to
the human body. However vehement the warriors are in the older representations,
it always seems that the figures are confined within invisible limits, whereas
Michelangelo first developed the human body in its entire range of action: any
two of his figures are less alike than all the figures in the entire range of the
earlier ones. It almost seems as though he were the first to discover the third
dimension and foreshortening, in spite of all the earnest researches which had
gone before. The variety of movement he was able to render is due simply to the
fact that he understood the structure of the human body inside out, and

[1]Bartsch 487, 488, 472. *Cf.* also Ag. Veneziano, B. 423.

although not the first to study anatomy, he was the first to whom the organic unity of the body was revealed, and, still more important, he knew the physical causes of the impression of movement, and could emphasize everywhere the most expressive forms, the most eloquent articulations.

2. The Ceiling of the Sistine Chapel

THE spectator may justly complain that the Sistine ceiling is a torture to him, for he is forced, with head bent back, to survey a row of episodes and a great crowd of bodies, all demanding attention and drawing him hither and thither, so that he has no choice but to capitulate to weight of numbers and renounce the exhausting sight. This was Michelangelo's own doing, for the original project was far simpler, with the twelve Apostles in the spandrels and the central field decorated only with geometric ornament. A drawing in London (British Museum) shows how this would have looked[1] and there are some critics, of good judgement, who believe that it was a pity this scheme was not adhered to, as it would have been 'more organic'. It would certainly have had the advantage of being easier to look at than the present one, for the Apostles along the sides would have been comfortably visible and the central part, with its ornamental patterns, would have given no trouble (*Fig.* 28).

Michelangelo struggled for a long time to get out of the commission. When, eventually, he undertook the task, it was by his own desire that it was so lavishly done, for it was he who represented to the Pope that the Apostles alone would make but a poor show, so that he finally got permission to paint whatever he liked. Were it not that the joy of the creator is evident in the figures of the ceiling, it might be thought that the artist was venting his spleen and revenging himself for having had to undertake the ungrateful task—the Lord of the Vatican should have his ceiling, but he would have to crick his neck to see it.

In the Sistine Chapel, Michelangelo first advanced the thesis, which became deeply significant for the whole century, that no beauty exists outside the human form. On principle, he abandons the decoration of flat surfaces with linear designs derived from vegetable forms, and where one would expect entwined foliage decoration one finds human forms and nothing but human forms, with not a trace of ornamental filling-in where the eye can rest. True, Michelangelo made distinctions and subordinated some of the categories of figures, as well as introducing variety into the colour by making some figures of stone- or bronze-colour, but this is not the same thing, and, look at it how you will, the covering of the entire surface with human bodies betrays a sort of recklessness which furnishes material for reflection.

---

[1]Published in *Jahrbuch der preussischen Kunstsammlungen*, 1892, (Wölfflin) and more recently in E. Steinmann's great work, *Die Sixtinische Kapelle*, vol. II.

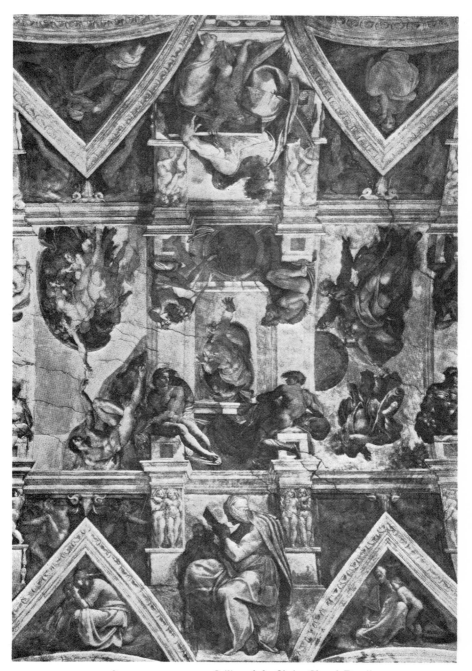

28. MICHELANGELO: *Ceiling of the Sistine Chapel.* Detail

Yet the Sistine ceiling remains a revelation which is hardly to be matched in Italy; these paintings are like the thunderous manifestations of a new force compared to the works of the preceding generation on the walls below. These Quattrocento frescoes should always be looked at first, and only after some study of them should one raise one's eyes upwards; then the surging, living power of the ceiling will have its full effect, and one will more readily appreciate the grandiose rhythm which binds and articulates these huge masses. In any case, it is to be recommended that on first entering the Chapel the visitor should ignore the *Last Judgement* on the altar wall; that is, he should turn his back on it, for in this work of his old age Michelangelo greatly damaged the effect of his own ceiling by throwing everything out of proportion with this colossal picture which sets a standard of scale that dwarfs even the ceiling.

If one seeks to analyse the causes of the effect produced by this ceiling it becomes clear that the very arrangement of parts depends upon ideas which Michelangelo was the first to conceive. In the first place, he treats the whole surface of the vault as a unity to be maintained, where any other artist would have separated the triangular spandrels from the remainder, as, for example, Raphael did in the Villa Farnesina. Michelangelo wanted to avoid a fragmentary treatment of the space, and so planned a comprehensive tectonic system with the Prophets' thrones growing out of the spandrels, so interlocked with parts of the central fields that it is impossible to think of them as separate entities. The main divisions take little account of the existing ceiling formation, for it was not the artist's intention to accept and explain the existing structure and proportions. True, he carried round the main cornice so that it corresponds roughly to the vertices of the pointed arches, but as the thrones of the Prophets in the spandrels disregard the triangular shape of these parts, a rhythm is introduced into the whole system which is entirely independent of the actual structure. The rhythm of the broad and narrow intervals in the central bays and the alternation of large and small fields between the transverse ribs, combined with the spandrel groups which coincide with the smaller fields, give so splendidly rhythmic a movement to the whole that in this alone Michelangelo surpasses all earlier achievements. He adds to it by the darker colour-scheme of the subordinate parts—the medallion fields are violet, the triangular segments near the thrones, green—so that the bright, principal parts are set off and the shifting of accent from centre to sides and back again is made more palpably evident. Again, there is a new scale of proportions and a new set of distinctions of size between the figures; the seated Prophets and Sibyls are of colossal proportions but alongside them are smaller and still smaller figures and one hardly notices the gradation of diminishing scales since one is absorbed in the apparently inexhaustible wealth of forms. A further factor in the composition as a whole is the distinction made between figures of intentionally plastic effect and the histories, which appear as pictures only. Prophets and Sibyls and all their attendant figures and accompaniments exist, as it were, in the actual room-space and possess a different degree of reality from the figures in the histories, and it even happens that the picture-plane is overlapped by the figures seated on the frame (the 'Slaves'). This distinction is linked with the contrast of axial directions, by which the figures of the spandrels are at right angles to those of the histories, so that both cannot be considered together and yet it is impossible to separate one entirely from the other; a part of one system is always included in any view of the other, so that the imagination is continually on the alert.

The wonder is that an assembly of so many forms could, in fact, be made to produce a unified impression, and it would have been impossible without the great simplicity of the strongly accentuated architectural frame-work, for the beams, cornice and thrones are all plain white; this is the first major instance of the use of monochrome. Indeed, the pretty, brightly-coloured patterns of the Quattrocento would have been meaningless, while the repeated whites and simple forms admirably attain the goal of bringing repose to the tumult.

The Histories

FROM the first, Michelangelo claims the right to tell his stories by means of nude figures. Essentially, the *Sacrifice of Noah* and the *Drunkenness of Noah* are compositions of nude figures (*Figs.* 29, 30); buildings, costumes, accessories, all the magnificent trappings which Benozzo Gozzoli provides in his Old Testament scenes, are either entirely lacking, or cut down to the barest minimum. There is no landscape, not even a blade of grass if it is not essential; here and there, tucked away in a corner, there is an indication of fern-like vegetation—this expresses the appearance of vegetation on the earth, and one tree signifies the Garden of Eden. All the means of expression are sparingly employed in these pictures; linear rhythm and spatial depth are combined to increase the expressiveness and the story is told with unparalleled conciseness, although this applies not so much to the earliest pictures, as to those where Michelangelo had got into his stride. The commentary on the frescoes follows the order in which they were developed.

The *Drunkenness of Noah* takes foremost place, in the first three pictures, on account of its concentrated composition; the *Sacrifice* stands on a lower plane, in spite of its fine motive, used to advantage by later artists, and the *Deluge* (*Fig.* 31), related in subject to the *Bathing Soldiers*, has too many important figures and appears somewhat disjointed as a whole. The spatial idea is important, with its suggestion of figures coming towards the spectator from behind the mountain, so that one does not know how many people there are and one can

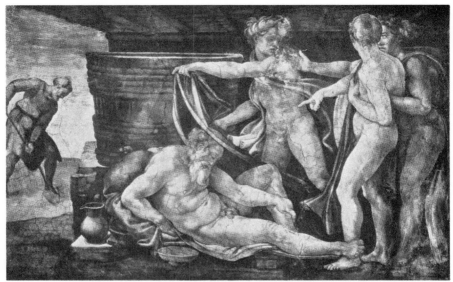

29. MICHELANGELO: *The Drunkenness of Noah*. Sistine Chapel

only imagine a vast crowd. Such insight into the means of producing a desired effect would have been desirable in many another painter, confronted with the *Crossing of the Red Sea* or similar crowd-scenes, and the Sistine Chapel itself has an example of the old, poorer, style in the frescoes along the walls.

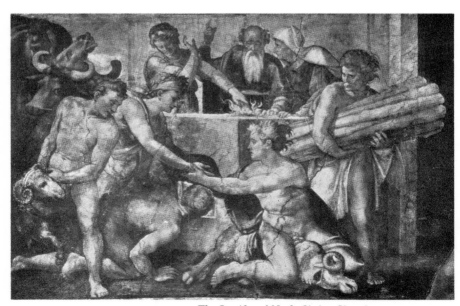

30. MICHELANGELO: *The Sacrifice of Noah*. Sistine Chapel

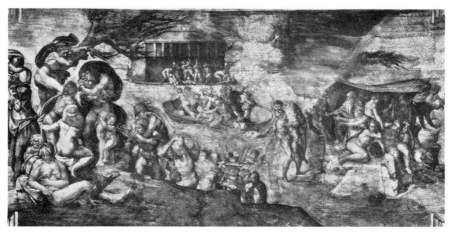

31. MICHELANGELO: *The Deluge.* Sistine Chapel

As soon as Michelangelo found himself with more space at his disposal, his powers increased, so that in the *Fall and Expulsion* (*Fig.* 32) he was able to spread his wings, now fully grown, and soar to heights which no one else has attained. In earlier art, the *Fall of Man* had been represented as a group of two standing figures, only slightly turned towards each other and only loosely related by the act of proffering the apple. In the middle stands the tree. Michelangelo creates a new configuration: his Eve reclines in an antique Roman pose expressive of indolence, with her back to the tree, turning momentarily towards the serpent and taking the apple almost indifferently. Adam, who is standing, reaches over the woman into the branches—the meaning of this gesture is not very comprehensible and the action of the limbs not altogether

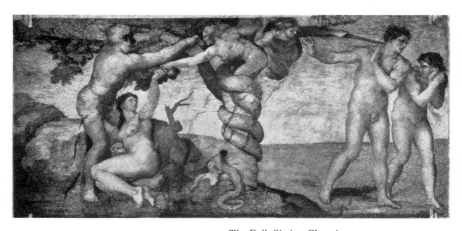

32. MICHELANGELO: *The Fall.* Sistine Chapel

clear, but the figure of Eve indicates that the story is in the hands of an artist
who has not only created new forms but is also expressing the idea that the
luxurious idleness of the woman engenders sinful thoughts. The Garden of
Eden consists merely of a few leaves. Michelangelo did not wish to characterize
the place in a material way, yet he contrives to give an effect of richness and
animation by the sweep of the lines of the ground and the spatial depth, all of
which contrast pointedly with the single, barren horizontal of the other half of
the picture where the misery of the expulsion is portrayed. The figures of the
unfortunate sinners are driven to the extreme edge of the picture, creating
between them and the tree an empty, yawning gap, as nobly grandiose as one of
Beethoven's pauses. The woman hastens her steps, her back bowed and her head
turned, lamenting as she goes, and stealing a backward glance, while Adam
moves with more dignity and calm, yet he tries to ward off the menacing sword
of the angel with a significant gesture, which had been created earlier by Jacopo
della Quercia.

In *The Creation of Eve* (*Fig.* 33), God the Father appears for the first time in
an act of creation, accomplished solely by His command, without any of the
grasping of Eve's fore-arms and more or less violent dragging of her from Adam's
side which is usual in the older masters: in fact, He does not even touch her.
Without force, with a calm gesture, He speaks: 'Arise!' and Eve does so in such

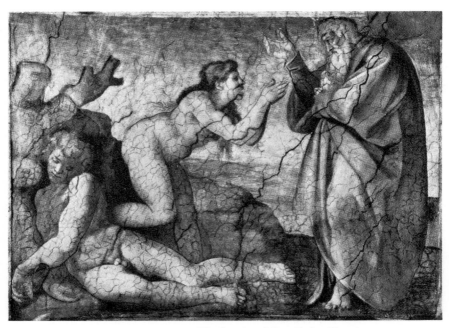

33. MICHELANGELO: *The Creation of Eve.* Sistine Chapel

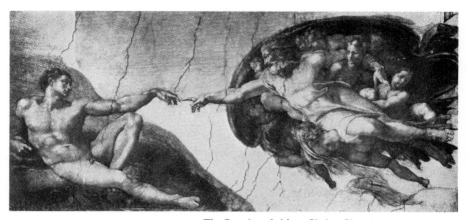

34. MICHELANGELO: *The Creation of Adam*. Sistine Chapel

a way that her complete dependence upon her Creator's movement is made manifest, while there is infinite beauty in her wondering gesture as she rises, a gesture which becomes the act of adoration. Here Michelangelo was able to portray his conception of physical beauty, and it is of Roman lineage. Adam lies sleeping against a rock, crumpled up like a corpse, with his left shoulder slumped forward, and his limbs appear the more distorted in that his hand hangs limply over a stump of wood. The outline of a hill follows the shape of his body, and encloses it, and the main direction of Eve's body is repeated by a lopped-off branch. Everything is closely packed into the space and brought so near to the edges of the picture that there is not room for God the Father to stand upright.[1] Four more times the act of creation is repeated, ever new and ever more vivid in the power of movement. First, the *Creation of Man* (*Fig.* 34), where God does not stand before the recumbent Adam, but sweeps down to him, accompanied by a choir of angels enclosed within the billowing folds of His mantle, and the act of creation is performed by contact, God just touching with the tip of His finger the outstretched hand of the man. This figure of Adam lying on the hillside is one of the most famous of all Michelangelo's inventions, with its combination of latent power and complete helplessness, for he lies in such a way that one knows he cannot rise of his own accord—the drooping fingers of his outstretched hand make that clear—he can only turn his head towards God. And yet what colossal movement there is in that motionless body, in the upraised

---

[1]The spiritual meaning of the scene has been variously interpreted and there is room for conjecture when one considers the differences of opinion advanced by the interpreters. Klaczko, *Jules II*, Paris, 1899, calls Eve '*toute ravie et ravissante . . . elle témoigne de la joie de vivre et en rend grâce à Dieu*'; Justi, *Michelangelo*, Leipzig, 1901, finds her look empty and cold as if she were posturing, 'composing herself quickly and adroitly, she knows exactly what is required of so exalted an occasion; with a gesture at once obsequious and devout, pleasing and self-assured, she performs the obligatory adoration.'

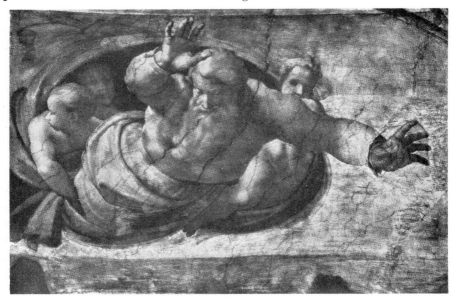

35. MICHELANGELO: *God hovering over the Waters*. Sistine Chapel

leg and the twist of the hips, in the torso seen from the front and the lower limbs in profile!

The *God hovering over the Waters* (*Fig.* 35) is the unsurpassed rendering of omnipotent and all-pervading benediction. Sweeping out of the background, the Creator extends His hands in benediction over the face of the waters, His right arm strongly foreshortened and the whole brought up sharply against the frame. Next, comes the *Creation of the Sun and Moon* (*Fig.* 36), still more dynamic, so that one recalls Goethe's words, 'A mighty crash heralds the coming of the sun.' The figure of God thunders forward, His arms outstretched, checking

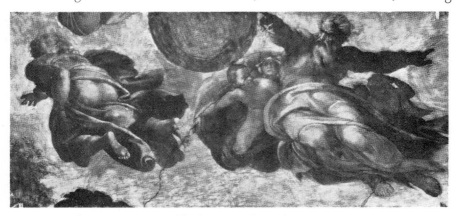

36. MICHELANGELO: *The Creation of Sun and Moon*. Sistine Chapel

Himself in His course, so that the upper part of His body is thrown backwards, and the Sun and Moon are created in this momentary pause. Both arms make gestures of creation simultaneously, but the right has the stronger accent, not only because God looks in that direction, but also on account of the sharper foreshortening, since foreshortened movement always appears more vigorous than unforeshortened. The area taken up by the figure is even greater than before and there is not a finger's breadth of superfluous space. This picture contains the curious licence of having a second figure of God, seen from behind and rushing into the depth of the picture like a cyclone.

At first, one might take this to be the retreating spirit of Darkness, but it is, in fact, the *Creation of Vegetable Life* for which Michelangelo thought a mere hasty gesture of the Creator's hand was sufficient, and His face is already directed towards a new goal. The duplication of the figure in the same picture has a somewhat old-fashioned air, but if one covers half the picture it will at once be recognised that the doubling of the figure in flight is an essential part of the general effect of movement.

In the final scene, where God the Father is borne along on sweeping clouds—the customary title, *The Division of Light from Darkness* (*Fig.* 37) is certainly

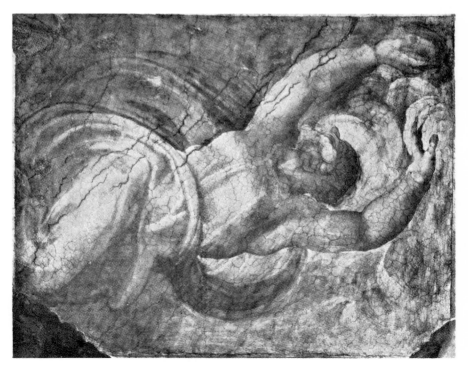

37. MICHELANGELO: *God dividing Light and Darkness.* Sistine Chapel

not correct—it is scarcely possible for us to follow the artist's intentions completely. Yet this fresco, more than any other, serves to demonstrate Michelangelo's astonishing technique, for it is clearly apparent that, at the very last moment (that is, during the actual painting) he abandoned the roughly incised preparatory outlines and tried out a different idea, and all this was done with a figure of colossal proportions, painted by a man lying on his back, so that he was unable to judge the effect of the whole.

It has been said that Michelangelo was interested only in formal motives as such, and did not think of them as the necessary symbols of expression for a programme of ideas. While this may be true of many of the single figures, where he had to tell a story he always respected the content, as one may see both in his Sistine ceiling and in the very last paintings, the Cappella Paolina frescoes. At the corners of the Sistine ceiling there are four triangular, curved spandrels which include the scene of *Judith handing the head of Holofernes to her servant*, a scene which had often been painted before, but always as a more or less indifferent act of giving and receiving. At the moment when the servant girl bends forward to take the head on her uplifted charger, Michelangelo makes his Judith glance back at the bed on which Holofernes lies; it is as if the corpse had moved. In this way, the tension of the scene is immeasurably heightened, so that even if this were the only work known by Michelangelo it would show him as a dramatic painter of the first rank.

The *Prophets* and *Sibyls*

In Florence, Michelangelo had been commissioned to carve twelve standing Apostles for the Cathedral; twelve seated Apostles were included in the first project for the Sistine ceiling but were replaced by Prophets and Sibyls. The unfinished *St. Matthew* indicated Michelangelo's intention of increasing the outward movement and inward emotion in the figure of an Apostle; what may one not expect when he creates the type of a seer! He did not feel himself bound by any prescribed iconographical ideas, and indeed, he even omitted the usual inscribed scrolls, advancing beyond a conception in which the names of the figures were the principal interest, and the figures themselves simply gesticulated to indicate that, when they were alive, they had said something of importance. He catches moments of spiritual life, inspiration itself, contemplative soliloquy and deep silent thought, calm study and excited searchings through the pages of a book, and once, a commonplace, everyday motive—that of reaching for a book on its shelf—where all the interest is concentrated on the physical action.

The series contains both old and young figures but the expression of prophetic vision is reserved for the youthful figures. This is not a yearning, ecstatic,

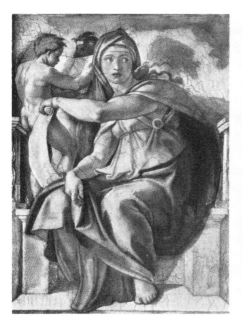
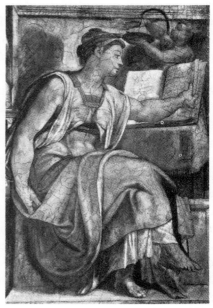

38. MICHELANGELO: *The Delphic Sibyl.*   39. MICHELANGELO: *The Erythraean Sibly.*
Sistine Chapel   Sistine Chapel

upward gaze of Peruginesque sentimentality, nor a passive receptivity, a self-surrender, as it so often is in Guido Reni, where one finds it hard to distinguish a Danae from a Sibyl; for Michelangelo it is an active state, a journey outwards from the self towards the Divine. The types have practically nothing of the individual in them and the costumes are completely idealised. What is it that distinguishes the *Delphic Sibyl* (*Fig.* 38) from all Quattrocento figures? What gives such grandeur to the action, and endows the whole with an appearance of necessary inevitability? The motive is the sudden attention of the Seer as she turns her head and momentarily pauses, holding up the scroll. The head is seen from the simplest viewpoint, not tilted, and full front, but this attitude is held only under strain, for the upper part of the torso is bent sideways and forward and the arm, reaching across, is another contradiction of the direction of the head; yet, despite the difficulties, it is just this which gives the pose with the head seen from the front its force, and the vertical axis is maintained among opposing elements. Further, the sharp conjunction of head and horizontal arm gives added energy to the twist of the head, and again, the direction of the light adds another element by putting exactly half the face in shadow, thus accentuating the central axis, a vertical which is again taken up by the peaked fold of the head-cloth. The eyes of the prophetess follow the direction of the head by their own movement to the right, and the effect of these searching, wide-open eyes carries at all distances, although they alone would not produce this effect were it not that the accompanying lines repeat and extend the movement of head and eyes. The hair is blown in the same direction and so is the great sweep of the mantle which encloses the whole figure like a sail. The handling of the drapery is an example of contrast which Michelangelo so often employs between the right and left silhouettes—one side a simple closed line, the other jagged and full of movement—and the same principle of contrast is applied to limbs, for one arm is held high and tense and the other is a dead weight. The fifteenth century thought it necessary to animate every part equally; the sixteenth found it more effective to accentuate a few isolated points only.

The *Erythraean Sibyl* (*Fig.* 39) is sitting with legs crossed and seen partly in profile, one arm reaching forward and the other hanging down, completing the closed outline. The drapery is quite exceptionally monumental. An interesting comparison can be made by glancing back at the figure of *Rhetorie* on Pollaiuolo's Tomb of Sixtus IV (St. Peter's) where a very similar motive produces a very dissimilar effect because of the caprices and artifices of the Quattrocento sculptor. Michelangelo represents the aged Sibyls as crouching with bowed backs—the *Persian Sibyl* holding her book up to her dim, bleary eyes, the *Cumaean* grasping with both hands a book which lies beside her so that a *contrapposto* effect is obtained between the upper part of the body and the legs. The *Libyan Sibyl* has a highly complicated pose, pulling down a book from the wall behind her throne without standing up, by reaching backward with both arms and at the same time looking in another direction. Much ado about nothing.

The process of development among the male figures begins with Isaiah and Joel (not with Zacharias) and goes on to the figure of the writing Daniel, already conceived on a different and grander scale, through the strikingly simple Jeremiah to Jonah, who bursts all tectonic bounds with his tremendous action. One cannot properly appreciate these figures without an exact analysis of the motives, taking into account, in every case, the pose of the figures as a whole and the movement of the limbs in detail. Our eyes are so unaccustomed to grasping these spatial and physical relationships that it is rare to be able to remember one of these motives even immediately after looking at it. Any description is bound to seem pedantic, and at the same time misleading, if it makes it seem that the limbs were arranged according to recipe, whereas the outstanding feature really consists of the union of formal qualities and the convincing expression of a moment of spiritual experience. This is not always maintained: the Libyan Sibyl, one of the latest figures of the ceiling, is exceedingly rich in formal variety but quite superficial in conception, while the same group of later figures also contains the aloof and withdrawn Jeremiah, simplest of all in form but touching our hearts the most.

The *Slaves*

ABOVE the piers of the Prophets' thrones sit nude youths, arranged in pairs facing each other with one of the bronze medallions between them, apparently engaged in encircling them with garlands of fruit. These are the so-called *Slaves* (*Figs.* 40–44). They are smaller in scale than the Prophets and their compositional function is to echo the piers in the upper zone; as finials they have the widest freedom of gesture. Thus there are twenty more seated figures, presenting new opportunities, for they are not frontal but seated in profile on very low seats; more than this—and this is the chief thing—they are nude figures. Michelangelo wanted to sate himself with the nude and he returned to the domain which he had entered with his cartoon of the *Soldiers*, so that one may well believe that here, if anywhere in the commission for the ceiling, his heart and soul were in the job. Boys with fruit garlands were by no means an unusual subject, but Michelangelo wanted more fully developed bodies, though one must not seek to enquire too closely into the individual action of the figures. The motive was chosen because it offered the greatest variety of action in pulling, dragging and carrying, and the artist is not to be bound down to a more factual explanation for his choice of motives.

There are no particularly strong muscular exertions, but this series of naked bodies has indeed the power of transfusing a current of vitality into the spectator—'a life-communicating art', as Berenson puts it. The muscular development is so powerful and the limbs make such an impression by their contrasts of direction that one feels oneself at once in the presence of a new phenomenon. What can the whole of the fifteenth century show, in the way of herculean figures, to compare with these? The variation from the normal in the structure of these bodies is insignificant by comparison with the way Michelangelo disposes the limbs, for which he discovers new and effective formal relationships; here, he brings one arm and both legs together as a series of parallels; there, he brings the downward-reaching arm across the thigh so that it forms almost a right-angle; there again, he encloses the figure from head to heels in an almost unbroken sweep of line; and these are not mathematical variations which he sets himself as an exercise, for even the most unusual action is made convincing in its effect. He has the human body in his power because he has mastered its articulations, and that is the strength of his draughtsmanship— whoever has seen the right arm of the *Delphic Sibyl* knows that there is yet more to come. He treats a simple problem, such as a supporting arm, in such way that one gets an entirely new impression from it, as may be seen by comparing the naked youth in Signorelli's *Testament of Moses* in the Sistine Chapel with Michelangelo's Slaves above the Prophet Joel, and these Slaves are

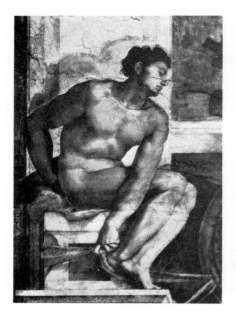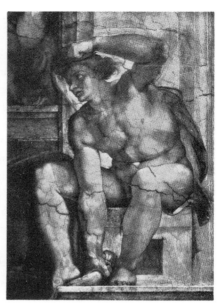

40-41. MICHELANGELO: *Two Slaves* (above Ezekiel). Sistine Chapel

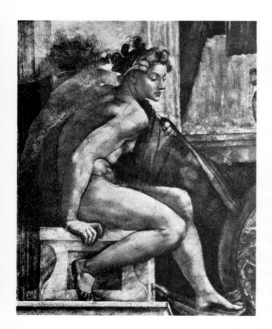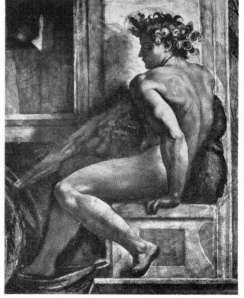

42-43. MICHELANGELO: *Two Slaves* (above Joel). Sistine Chapel

among the earliest and tamest. Later, he added stronger and stronger effects of foreshortening up to the violent *scorzi* of the final pair, the variety of action becomes even more marked, and where, at the beginning, the corresponding figures in each pair are roughly symmetrical, towards the end they present ever increasing contrasts with one another. So far from becoming tired of the tenfold repetition of the same problem, it seems clear that Michelangelo's invention was more and more stimulated. To get a clear idea of the phases of development, a comparison may be made between a pair at the beginning—the Slaves above Joel, and those above Jeremiah at the end. In the former, we see a simple, profile pose with only slight differences between the

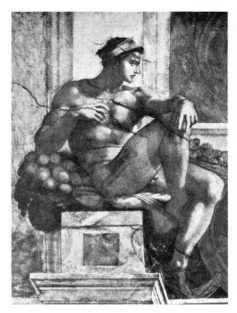

44. MICHELANGELO: *A Slave* (above Jeremiah). Sistine Chapel

limbs and almost symmetrical correspondence between the figures; in the latter, two bodies which have nothing in common, either in structure, movement or lighting, but which, by their very contrasts, increase the effect. The indolent figure in this pair may perhaps be accounted the finest of them all (*Fig. 44*), not merely on account of the nobility of his features: the figure is entirely calm, yet it contains grandiose contrasts of direction and the curious pose, with the forward tilt of the head, leaves a marvellous impression. The most abrupt foreshortening is immediately followed by the absolute clarity of planes seen in their greatest breadth. If the rich effects of light are also taken into consideration it becomes still more surprising that the figure appears so calm and still, and this would not be the case were it not for the clear relief-like development of the planes in breadth. At the same time, the whole form is grasped as a single compact mass which could almost be circumscribed by a regular, geometric figure. The centre of gravity is high up, hence the appearance of feather-lightness in spite of the herculean limbs. Later art never surpassed this example of an easy and lightly balanced seated pose and it is notable that something from the distant and foreign world of Greek art comes involuntarily to mind—the so-called *Theseus* of the Parthenon.

The remaining decorative figures on the ceiling cannot be dealt with here. The small fields with lightly indicated figures seem as if they were a sketch-book of Michelangelo's containing a number of interesting motives, including the dawning possibilities of the figures on the Medici Tombs. More important are the spandrels over the windows, where groups of resting people spread out over broad, triangular fields, such as were often used in later art, and the accompanying lunettes, doubly noteworthy in Michelangelo's work for being genre scenes and the most extraordinary subjects in such a place; and every one of them is an improvisation. The artist himself seems to have felt the need to allow the tension to die away here, after the intense physical and spiritual life of the vault. These *Ancestors of Christ* depict peaceful, everyday existence—the common destiny of humanity.[1]

By way of conclusion, a few words may be said on the progress of the work. The ceiling is not all of a piece: there are joins in it, and everyone observes that the *Deluge* and the two pictures accompanying it—the *Drunkenness of Noah* and the *Sacrifice*—are painted with figures on a far smaller scale than in the other histories, and, since this part was painted first, one may well assume that Michelangelo found the scale insufficient when seen from the ground. Yet it was a pity that the scale had to be altered, for it was clearly the original intention to diminish the size of the figures upwards, according to their category: from the Prophets to the Slaves, and from these to the histories was originally a uniform progression which gave a pleasantly restful effect. Later, the inner figures (those in the histories) grew far bigger than the Slaves and the balance was upset, while the original proportions also allowed the smaller histories to harmonise with the alternating larger ones since the scale was constant, but the alteration led to a necessary, though disadvantageous, change here as well. In the *Creation of Adam*, for example, God the Father is large, but the same figure in the *Creation of Eve* is considerably smaller.[2]

The second join is in the middle of the ceiling, where a sudden increase in scale is again noticeable, but this time it applies to all parts and the Prophets and Slaves grow so large that the architectonic system can no longer be continued on the old scale. The engravers have to some extent concealed these discrepancies, but photographs afford convincing proofs. At the same time, the colour scheme was altered, and where the earlier histories are brightly coloured, with blue sky, green fields and a range of clear, bright colours and light shadows, the later ones

---

[1]For the correlation of subject-matter between Ancestors and Prophets *cf.* P. Weber, *Geistliches Schauspiel und Kirchliche Kunst*, 1894, p. 54. A later interpretation (Steinmann and Thode) makes the spandrels depict the Jews in Exile, connected with the Lamentations of Jeremiah.

[2]Could the change of scale have led also to a change of programme and to the substitution of a new set of histories? It is unbelievable that the scenes of creation, with their few essential figures, could have filled the available space if the figures were on the scale adopted for the *Deluge*, and it seems to me unlikely that Michelangelo was resigned to discrepancies of scale from the very beginning. The idea of such a change in general plan may be supported by the fact that *Noah's Sacrifice* is obviously out of order in its present place, so that even early writers (Condivi) interpreted it as the *Sacrifice of Cain and Abel* to avoid the break in chronology; but this is untenable.

are muted, the sky greyish-white and the draperies dull, the colours less opaque and more watery, while gold disappears altogether and the shadows become darker.

From the beginning, Michelangelo worked on the full breadth of the ceiling, so that histories and Prophets were painted together, and then, at the very end and after a long interval, the lower figures—in the lunettes and spandrels—were rapidly painted in, all at the same time.[1]

3. The Julius Monument

THE Sistine ceiling is a monument of that pure High Renaissance style which did not yet know, or did not yet recognise, any dissonance, and its plastic counterpart would have been the Tomb of Pope Julius II, had this been carried out according to the original plans. However, as is well known, it was not executed until much later, much reduced in size and in a different style, incorporating only the *Moses* from among the previously executed statues, while the so-called *Dying Slaves* went their own ways and finished up in the Louvre. It is not only to be regretted, therefore, that this nobly conceived monument was spoilt, but also that we are deprived of a major example of Michelangelo's 'pure' style, since the work most nearly resembling it, although only very distantly—the chapel in S. Lorenzo—belongs to a new phase of Michelangelo's art.

This is the place in which to say something about tombs in general. The Florentines had developed a type of splendid wall-tomb, best exemplified by the Tomb of the Cardinal of Portugal in S. Miniato, by Antonio Rossellino (*Fig.* 45). The characteristic feature is the flat niche with the sarcophagus inset and the body of the dead man lying on a *lit de parade* above it. Above this, there is a circular relief of the Madonna, who smiles down on the recumbent figure, and cheerful flying angels hold the garlanded medallion. Two little naked boys sit by the bier and try to look tearful, and above them are two more angels, like finials on the pilasters, rather larger and more serious and carrying the crown and palm. The niche is framed by a drawn-back stone curtain, but in order to realise the original effect of the monument there is one important factor to be added—colour. The violet marble background, the green spaces between the pilasters and the mosaic patterns of the floor below the sarcophagus can still be seen because the colour is in the stone itself, but all painted parts have lost their colour, removed by an age that was antipathetic to it, although traces are still visible, sufficient to restore in imagination the old splendour. Everything was coloured—the Cardinal's vestments, the cushion, the brocaded bier-cloth with the pattern in slight relief; everything gleamed with gold and purple. The lid of the sarcophagus had a bright, scaly pattern and the pilaster ornaments and framing mouldings were gilt, as were the rosettes of the soffit, gold on a dark

---

[1] *Cf.* Wölfflin, *Die sixtinische Kapelle Michelangelos, Repertorium für Kunstwissenschaft*, XIII.

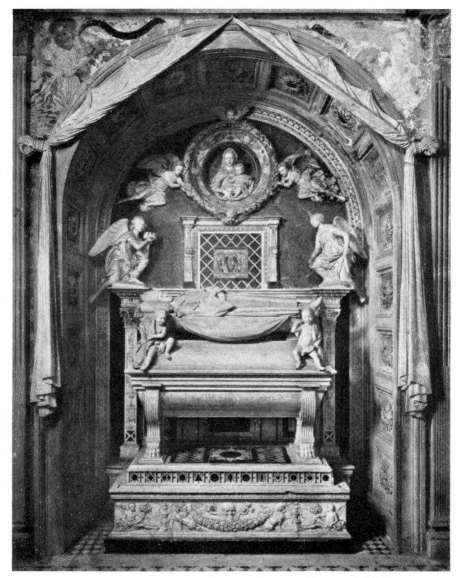

45. ROSSELLINO: *Tomb of the Cardinal of Portugal*. Florence, S. Miniato

ground. There was also gold on the garland and on the angels. The conceit of
the stone curtain is tolerable only when one thinks of it as coloured, and one can
still see clearly enough the brocade pattern of the outer side and the trellis
pattern of the lining.

With the sixteenth century this colouring ceases suddenly—the grandiloquent
Tombs by Andrea Sansovino in Santa Maria del Popolo (*Fig.* 46) have no trace

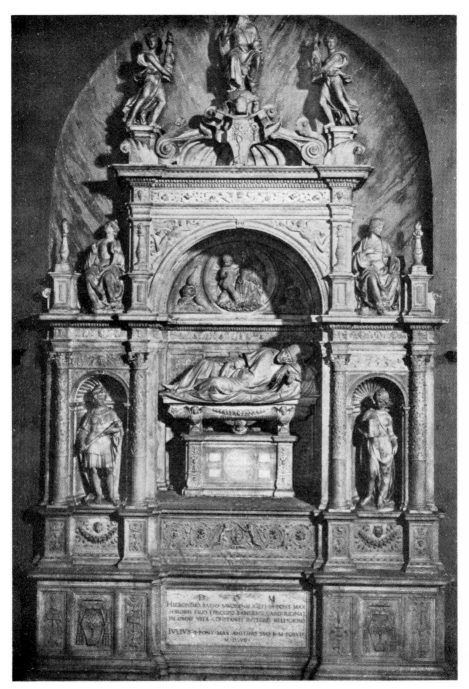

46. ANDREA SANSOVINO: *Tomb of Cardinal della Rovere*. Rome, S. Maria del Popolo

of it. Colour was superseded by chiaroscuro and the figures stand out white against deep, dark niches.

Something else, too, begins in the sixteenth century—the feeling for the architectonic. Early Renaissance buildings still have a somewhat playful quality, and the combination of figures with architecture has, for our taste, a rather accidental effect: Rossellino's Tomb is an outstanding example of this inorganic quality of the fifteenth-century style. The kneeling angels have no tectonic coherence, or, at any rate, very little, standing as they do with one foot on the tops of the pilasters and the other waving in the air. This in itself is jarring to a later taste, but still worse is the way in which the free foot trailing backwards cuts across the frame-moulding, together with the absence of any articulation between figure and wall-surface. The upper angels, too, seem to swim about in space, without form or relative position. The pilaster system inserted into the niche bears no rational relationship to the form of the whole work, and the general immaturity of the architectonic sense can be observed in the treatment of the soffit of the entrance arch, which is decorated from top to bottom with over-large cofferings and lacks any distinction between arch and impost. The idea of the stone curtain is another example of the same thing.

The leading principle in Sansovino's work is an organic use of architecture, where every figure has its inevitable place and the subdivisions form parts of a total, rational system—a larger niche with a flat rear plane and two smaller niches, one on either side, with shell half-domes; all three articulated by an order of half-columns with a complete and continuous entablature. Michelangelo's Julius Monument would have been such a combination of architecture and sculpture; not a wall-tomb but a free-standing construction of several storeys; an elaborate marble erection with a combined plastic and architectural effect something like the Santa Casa at Loreto. All existing works would have been surpassed in richness of sculptural effect, and the creator of the Sistine ceiling would have been the man to introduce a powerful unifying rhythm into the work.

The usual fifteenth-century form of effigy was recumbent with both legs outstretched and the hands folded one over the other, as if sleeping: Sansovino retained the idea of sleep, but the traditional recumbent form seemed to him to be too simple and ordinary, and so the dead man lies on his side, his legs crossed, one arm propping up the head and the hand dropping down from the cushion. Later, the figure becomes even less peaceful, as if disturbed in its sleep by bad dreams, until finally it is awakened and represented as reading or praying. Michelangelo's conception was entirely original,[1] for he attempted a group of

---

[1]*Cf.* Schmarsow, *Jahrbuch der preussischen Kunstsammlungen*, 1884, where the drawing (formerly Berlin, von Beckerath Coll.) is published which although scarcely more than a copy is our chief source of information.

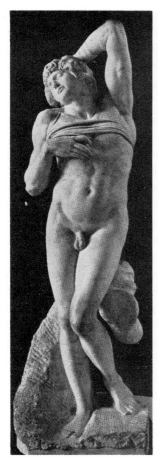

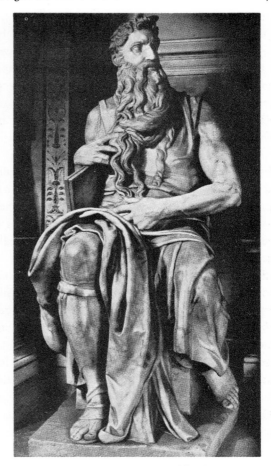

47. MICHELANGELO: *Slave.*
Louvre

48. MICHELANGELO: *Moses.*
Rome, S. Pietro in Vincoli

two angels laying the Pope to rest. He is still slightly raised, and therefore clearly visible; later, he was to be laid down, like a dead Christ. Yet this was only one incident among the projected groups of other figures, of which, as already noted, we have now only three—the two *Slaves* from the base of the monument and the *Moses* from the upper storey (*Figs.* 47, 48).

The *Slaves* are bound figures, fettered less by their actual bonds than by their architectural function, for they were to be set in front of pillars and they share the bounds of the architectural form, being so placed that they could have no movement of their own. The unfinished *St. Matthew* in Florence already showed the compact form of the entire body, as if the limbs could not move beyond certain strict limits, and this is repeated in the *Slaves*, with a more comprehensive reference to the function of the figures. Here there is an unparalleled representation of the human body just beginning a movement; the sleeping man stretches himself, his head still lolling back and his hand mechanically running up his chest, his thighs rubbing together, he draws a deep breath as he awakens, just before he reaches full consciousness. The impression of shaking himself free from something is so heightened by the piece of rough-hewn stone that its presence seems essential.

The second *Slave* has its principal view-point from the side and is not meant to be seen from the front.

The *Moses* is also cramped in his movements, but Michelangelo's reason for this confined feeling is, in this case, an act of will on Moses' own part, for it is the last moment of self-restraint before impulsive action, that is, before he leaps up. It is interesting to compare the *Moses* with the series of earlier colossal seated figures which Donatello and his contemporaries made for Florence Cathedral: even then, Donatello sought to endow the typical seated figure with momentary life, but his conception of movement is entirely different from Michelangelo's. The connection with the Prophets of the Sistine Chapel leaps to the eye, but for sculpture he sought the most compact mass possible, as opposed to his practice in painting. This is his strength, for one must go back very far to find a comparable sense of closed volumes—Quattrocento sculpture, even where it is seeking powerful effects, has a fragile look about it. Yet in Michelangelo's own work, the *Moses* still has clear traces of his early style, for he would not have tolerated the multiplicity of folds and the deep undercutting at a later period, and, as in the *Pietà*, the high polish is calculated to create effective reflected lights.

It seems to me more than doubtful if it is possible to get the full effect of the figure in its present position, even though Michelangelo himself put it there. He had no choice. The spectator may well wish to see more of the left side, where the full significance of the drawn-back leg at once becomes apparent—it is the key to the whole movement, and from a view-point partly to one side all the main axes appear with tremendous clarity for the first time: the angle of arm and leg and the stepped outline of the left side, and, dominant above it, the vertical of the swung-round head. The side turned away from the spectator is sketchily executed, and the arm with the hand grasping the beard can never make an interesting effect.

It is a difficult business now to realize the effect of the figure if seen diagonally, for the colossus is cramped in a niche, and the projected free-standing monument has shrunk to a wall-tomb, and that of more modest proportions. Forty years after it was begun the work ended in this sad compromise, and in the interval the artist's own style had altered completely. The *Moses* is placed low down and, intentionally, in surroundings which seem too narrow for him; he is set in a frame which he threatens to burst asunder. The necessary resolution of the discord can be found only through the neighbouring figures, and this is a Baroque idea.

Chapter IV : RAPHAEL (1483-1520)

RAPHAEL grew up in Umbria, distinguishing himself in the School of Perugino and so completely did he assimilate the tender style of his master that, in Vasari's judgement, it was impossible to distinguish the works of the pupil from those of the master. Probably no other pupil of genius has ever absorbed so much of his master's teaching as Raphael did. Leonardo's angel in the *Baptism* by Verrocchio strikes one immediately as having a personal quality; Michelangelo's youthful works are quite unlike anything else, but Raphael in his earliest period cannot be separated from Perugino. Then he came to Florence, at the moment when Michelangelo had produced the great works of his youth, when he had set up the *David* and was working on the *Bathing Soldiers*, and when Leonardo, who was planning his *Battle* cartoon and had already wrought the unprecedented miracle of his *Mona Lisa*, was in the prime of his years and possessor of a brilliant reputation, while Michelangelo was the recognized man of the future, on the threshold of maturity. Raphael was barely twenty. What sort of future could he hope for beside these great men?

Perugino was an esteemed master on the banks of the Arno, and the youth could expect a steady public for that kind of picture; he could cheer himself with the prospect of becoming a second, perhaps better, Perugino, and his pictures gave no promise of any greater individuality. Without a trace of the Florentine sense of reality, monotonous in his sentiments, limited to a style based on beautiful outline, he entered with the poorest prospects into competition with the great masters; yet he brought one talent which was truly his own— that of absorbing and transforming hidden possibilities. He gave the first great proof of this when he cast off his Umbrian heritage and devoted himself to Florentine studies; under the circumstances few could have done this, but if one surveys the whole short span of Raphael's life one is forced to admit that no one else has ever undergone such a process of development in so short a time. The Umbrian sentimentalist became the painter of great dramatic scenes; the youth who seemed shy of earthly reality became a painter of humanity, with a firm grip on physical appearances; Perugino's linear style became more and more painterly and the taste for calm beauty gave way to the need for bold massing—this is the Roman, adult master. Raphael had not the delicate nervous sensibility of Leonardo and even less had he Michelangelo's power; he had, as it were, the mean, that which is generally comprehensible—if the phrase is not misunderstood as a denigration—for that fortunate moderation of feeling is, nowadays, so rare that most of us find Michelangelo far more approachable than the open, serene,

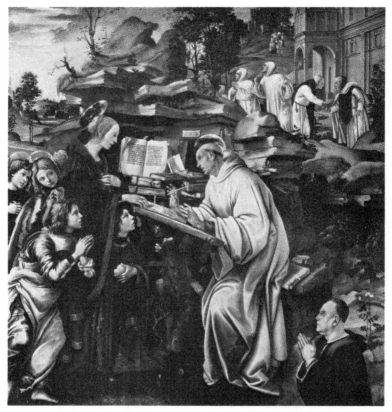

49. FILIPPINO LIPPI: *The Madonna appearing to St. Bernard*. Florence, Badia

friendly personality of Raphael. That which all those who lived with him praised most highly, the charm and amiability of his character, still shines forth from his works.

It is impossible, as has already been said, to speak of Raphael's art without first discussing Perugino. Once upon a time, the infallible recipe for gaining a reputation as a connoisseur was to praise Perugino,[1] although now the opposite would be more advisable. We know that he repeated these sentimental heads in the way of trade and we evade them even if we see them only at a distance, yet, if only one of these heads had been sincerely felt we should still be forced to ask what kind of man it was who, in the Quattrocento, had created this intense and soulful expression. Giovanni Santi knew why he placed Perugino and Leonardo side by side in his rhymed Chronicle, '*par d'etade e par d'amori*'. Perugino possessed, in addition, a lyrical quality of line which he learnt from

[1]Goldsmith's *Vicar of Wakefield*.

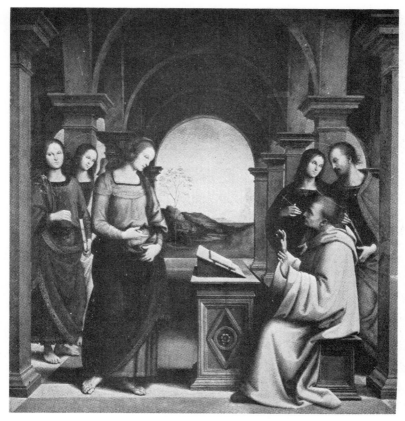

50. PERUGINO: *The Madonna appearing to St. Bernard*. Munich, Pinakothek

no one else. Not only is he much simpler than the Florentines, but he has a perception of repose and a calm, flowing rhythm which contrast strikingly with the animation of the Tuscans and the elaborate complexities of late Quattrocento style. Compare two pictures of the same subject: Filippino's *Madonna appearing to St. Bernard*, in the Badia of Florence, and Perugino's in the Pinakothek at Munich (*Figs.* 49, 50). In the former, the line is restless and the many objects in the picture are confused and chaotic, in the latter, there is complete peace, calm simple outlines, noble architecture with a wide panorama extending into the far distance, a beautiful effect of mountains fading away into the horizon beneath a clear sky, and, over all, a brooding silence so that one would expect to hear the murmur of the slender trees when the evening breeze rustles their leaves. Perugino was sensitive to landscape and to architecture, and his simple, spacious halls are constructed as part of the harmony of effect and not, as for example Ghirlandaio's are, as agreeable decorative adjuncts. No one before

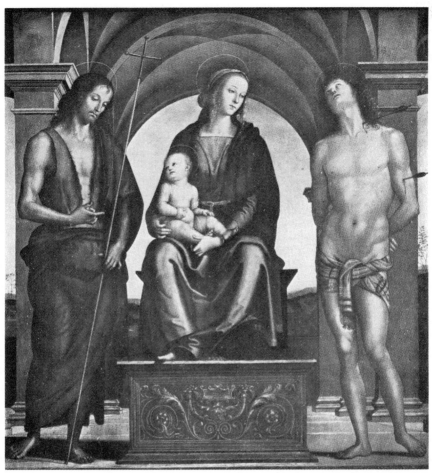

51. PERUGINO: *Madonna and Child with St. Sebastian and St. John the Baptist.* Uffizi

him had so effectively related figures to architecture (*cf.* the *Madonna* of 1493, in the Uffizi, *Fig.* 51); he had an innate feeling for architectural construction and where he had to deal with several related figures he constructed the group according to a geometrical plan. His composition of the *Pietà* of 1495 (Pitti) would have been criticised by Leonardo as empty and insipid, but in Florence at that time it had a special significance. With his principles of simplification and the imposition of pictorial laws, Perugino forms an important element in the dawn of classic art and it is clear that he greatly helped to shorten the road travelled by Raphael.

1. The *Sposalizio* and the *Entombment*

THE *Sposalizio* (Milan, Brera) bears the date 1504 (*Fig.* 52). It is the work of Raphael at the age of twenty-one, and the pupil of Perugino here shows what he had learnt from his master: we can the more easily distinguish his own contributions from that which he took over from his master, since Perugino also painted the same subject (Caen). The composition is almost the same, except that Raphael has transposed the two sides, setting the women at the left and the men at the right, otherwise the variations seem unimportant; and yet, the two pictures are separated by all the difference between a painter who works according to a set pattern and a sensitive, talented pupil who seeks, though still cramped in style, to infuse fresh life into every particle of a traditional theme. It is necessary, first of all, to understand the theme itself, for the ceremony of the betrothal is performed here in a way rather different from the one to which we are accustomed. It is not an exchange of rings, for the bridegroom alone holds out a ring to his bride who puts her finger into it, while the priest superintends the operation, holding the wrists of both. The minutiae of the ceremony present a difficult task to the artist and one has to look closely at Perugino's picture to discover exactly what is happening. This is where Raphael brings an individual contribution, for he places Mary and Joseph further apart and distinguishes between their poses: Joseph has completed his movement, bringing the ring into the middle of the picture, so that Mary is about to advance, focusing the attention of the spectator on the gesture of her right arm. This is the focal point of the whole action and it provides the reason for Raphael's reversal of the positions of men and women—he had to have the significant right arm in the foreground and uncovered by anything else. Not only this; the general flow of movement is taken up by the figure of the priest who guides Mary's hand and does not form a stiff vertical axis in the centre, as in Perugino, for his whole body accompanies the action and the swing of the upper part of his body is an injunction to put on the ring, audible at any distance. This is the work of a born painter, who senses the pictorial equivalents for the story he has to tell. The standing figures of Joseph and Mary are the stock-in-trade of the School, but Raphael takes the type-figures and endeavours always to endow them with personal qualities as well—notice the difference in the way the priest holds each of the two hands.

The accompanying figures are disposed so as to concentrate the action rather than dissipate it and the symmetry is almost audaciously upset by the youth breaking his rod on the right-hand side, a figure also employed by Perugino, who places him further back. The charming little temple in the background is placed high up, so high that its lines cannot clash with the foreground figures,

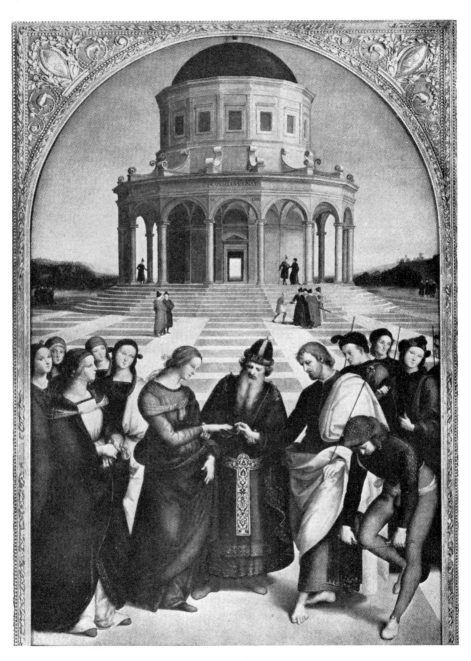

52. RAPHAEL: *The Sposalizio*. Milan, Brera

and this again is in Perugino's purest style, for he disposed his great fresco in Rome, *Christ giving the Keys to St. Peter*, in just this way, so that the figures and architecture are kept separate, like oil and water. The human figures are intended to stand out in sharp silhouette against the foil of a pavement in perspective.

How different is the story of the Marriage of the Virgin when told by a Florentine! The scene is filled with bustling figures, some clad in bright and modish dresses; the public is standing gaping, and instead of the gently resigned suitors there is a band of hefty youths who are setting about the bridegroom. Indeed, a free-for-all seems to be in progress and one wonders how Joseph can keep so calm. What does it all mean? The motive occurs as early as the fourteenth century[1] and has a juristic significance—the blows are supposed to make the marriage-vows impressive. Perhaps some will recall the similar scene in Immermann's 'Oberhof' where the significance is rationalized into meaning that the future husband ought to know how it feels to be beaten.

It was into this Florence that Raphael came to undergo a second schooling, and he was scarcely recognizable as the same man when he painted, after three or four years of this, the *Entombment*, now in the Borghese Gallery, Rome (*Fig.* 53). He had given up all he formerly possessed, soft outline, clear grouping, gentle sensibility; Florence had stirred up all his ideas, so that his main interests were now the nude figure and movement. He wanted animation, powerful effects and strong contrasts, for the impression made by Leonardo and Michelangelo was having its effect on him and he must have felt that his own Umbrian style was feeble by comparison.

The commission for the *Entombment* came from Perugia, but it is certain that what was expected was not this scene but something like a *Lamentation over the Dead Christ*, as painted by Perugino, for example, in the picture now in the Palazzo Pitti (*Fig.* 54)[2] where there is no attempt at movement but simply a ring of mourning figures standing round the dead body—a collection of faces expressing sorrow in elegant poses. In fact, Raphael's first idea was a simple *Lamentation*, and some drawings exist for this. Then he suddenly got the idea of the carrying of the corpse, and painted two men dragging the burden to the tomb on the hillside, making them different in age and character, and complicated the idea still further by making one walk backwards, feeling with his heels as he goes up some steps. Amateurs are slow to grasp the point of such purely physical motives, seeking rather spiritual expressiveness, yet everyone must

---

[1] *Cf.* Taddeo Gaddi (Sta. Croce), also Ghirlandaio (Santa Maria Novella) and Franciabigio (SS. Annunziata).

[2] At this point it may be mentioned that the youthful figure at the extreme right-hand edge corresponds, line for line, with the *Alessandro Braccesi* in the Uffizi, formerly ascribed to Lorenzo di Credi.

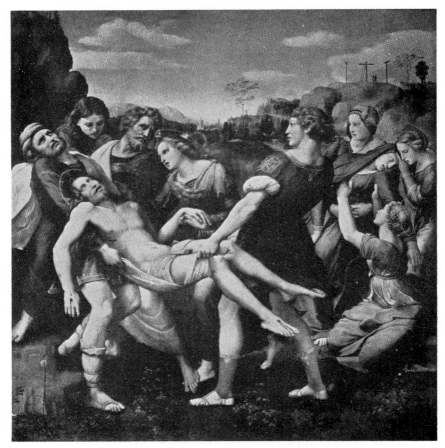

53. RAPHAEL: *The Entombment*. Rome, Borghese Gallery

agree that in all circumstances it is an advantage to introduce contrasts into a picture, so that repose is more striking by being juxtaposed with movement, and the sympathy of those concerned in the action is made patent by contrast with the indifference of those whose attention is taken up by the mechanical labour they perform. Where Perugino leaves the beholder apathetic, because all his heads have the same intensity of expression, Raphael is able to increase the dramatic tension by strong contrasts.

The chief beauty of the picture is the body of Christ, with its upthrust shoulder and drooping head—the same motive as Michelangelo's *Pietà*. The anatomy is still superficial, the heads are lacking in strong characterization, and the articulation of the joints is feeble. The younger of the two bearers does not stand firmly on his feet and the doubt about his right hand is painful, while the elder one jars on us because his head has the same inclination as that of Christ,

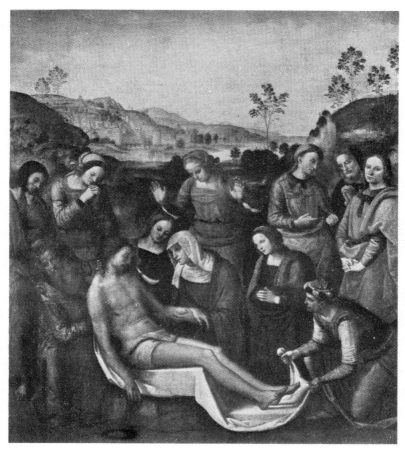

54. PERUGINO: *The Lamentation over Christ*. Pitti

a fault which was avoided in the preparatory drawings. Again, the composition as a whole is confused—the tangle of legs has always been censured—and what is the second old man, Nicodemus, doing? Here again it would seem that an idea which was originally clear has become confused in execution, for he was looking at the Magdalen as she hurries forward, but now he stares incomprehensibly into space, and the complete obscurity of the rest of his pose increases the feeling of discomfort created by the cluster of four heads stuck in the corner. The beautiful motive of the Magdalen holding Christ's hand as she accompanies the procession may be derived from an antique prototype,[1] but the gesture of her right arm remains mysterious. The group with the swooning Virgin far surpasses anything of Perugino's and the kneeling figure in front of her is

[1] Relief in the Capitoline Museum (*Hector*?): Righetti, *Campidoglio*, Vol. 1, pl. 171; H. Grimm has already noted the connection.

certainly due to Michelangelo's Madonna in the *Holy Family*; it is noteworthy that the once so sensitive Raphael now asks us to accept such harsh overlappings of forms as those in the arms. As a whole, the group is somewhat unfortunately cramped into the picture, and Raphael's original idea was much sounder—to include the Holy Women in the movement of the principal group, following it at a short distance: as it is, the picture falls apart. One other thing must be said: the square format is, in itself, a hindrance to the effect of the picture, for in order to give the impression of a procession it is necessary that the picture-surface itself should have a dominant direction. Titian's *Entombment* owes a great deal to the mere shape of the canvas.

How much of the *Entombment* is due to the second hand which completed it is still controversial. It is certain that the picture presented Raphael with problems which, for the time being, he was unable to solve completely. He had sought out Florentine problems with admirable intentions in a deliberate attempt to learn, but in the process of working them out he momentarily lost himself.

2. The Florentine *Madonnas*

THE *Madonnas* are more successful than the *Entombment* in fitting means to ends, for Raphael won lasting popularity as a painter of Madonnas and it may well seem superfluous to attempt to catch the magic of these pictures with the clumsy weapons of formal analysis. We have been familiar with them from childhood onwards, through a far greater mass of reproductions than any other artist in the world has ever had, and they appeal so strongly with their traits of motherly love and childish gaiety, solemn dignity and a strange supernatural quality, that we do not seek any further artistic meaning. Yet a glance at Raphael's drawings would show that the problem, as the artist saw it, did not lie where the public would think and that the task was not just a question of a single charming head or this or that childish attitude, but that it was the structure of a group as a whole, the harmonising of the general directions formed by the movements of different heads and limbs. This should not hinder anyone from approaching Raphael from the point of view of emotion and charm, but an essential part of the artist's intentions is revealed only to the spectator who goes beyond the pleasurable emotions aroused at first sight and is able to consider the picture from a formal point of view.

There is much to be said for arranging pictures of the same subject as a series corresponding to the stages of the artist's development, and it is irrelevant here whether the Madonna holds a book or an apple, whether she is sitting indoors or out: these material classifications are not the basis for a scheme of categories, but rather the formal classifications such as whether the Madonna is in half-length or full figure, whether she is grouped together with one or two children, whether other adult figures are introduced—these are the artistically important questions. Let us begin with the simplest case, the half-length Madonna, for which the *Madonna del Granduca* (Pitti) will serve as an example (*Fig. 55*). Perfectly simple in the vertical axis of the standing figure and the still somewhat constrained seated Child, its essential life comes from the extraordinary effect of the *one* change of direction in the tilted head.

However perfect the oval of this head, however miraculously sensitive in expression, the effect would not be obtained without this quite simple use of direction, where the diagonal of the head, tilted but still seen full-face, makes the only variation. This quiet picture still has a Peruginesque air about it, but

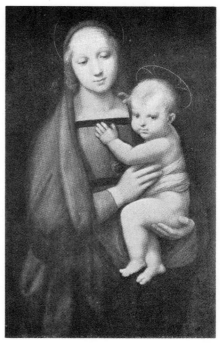

55. RAPHAEL: *Madonna del Granduca.* Pitti

in Florence the demand was for something quite different, freer and more animated. The right angles in the pose of the seated Child are already abandoned in the *Casa Tempi Madonna* in Munich, then completely superseded by a half-

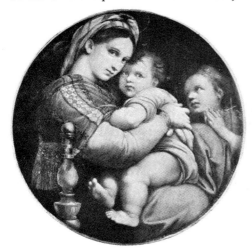

56. RAPHAEL: *Madonna della Sedia.* Pitti

lying position with the Child turned round and threshing His limbs about in an unruly fashion (*Orleans* and *Bridgewater Madonnas*): His mother is now seated instead of upright, and, according to whether she bends forward or sideways, so the picture is at once enriched with a variety of axial directions. The course of the development is unfolded in a perfectly regular fashion from the *Granduca* and *Tempi Madonnas* up to the *Madonna della Sedia* (Pitti) where the young St. John is introduced (*Fig. 56*), increasing

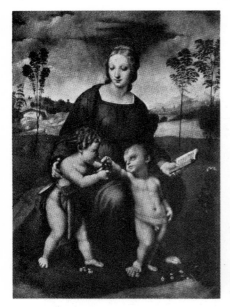

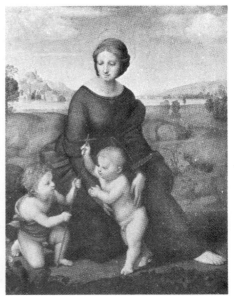

57. RAPHAEL: *Madonna del Cardellino.*
Uffizi

58. RAPHAEL: *The Madonna of the Meadow.*
Vienna, Museum

the plastic effect still further in depth and complexity, all the more effective since the group is firmly knit together and harmonised with the closely encircling frame.

The development is analogous in the treatment of a second theme, that of the full-length Madonna with Jesus and St. John. Timidly at first, Raphael constructs a sober pyramid, bounded by a carefully rhythmic outline, in the *Madonna del Cardellino* (Uffizi), with the children equally disposed on either side of the seated Virgin, and the whole composition based on an equilateral triangle (*Fig.* 57). The contours have a tender sensitiveness unknown in Florence and the masses are balanced, one against the other, as though on a jeweller's scale. Why does the Virgin's cloak slip off her shoulder? It is to prepare the way for the projection from the silhouette made by the book, so that the contour appears to glide down in an even-flowing rhythm. Then gradually there arises a need for greater movement: the children are more sharply differentiated and St. John must kneel down (*Belle Jardinière*, Louvre) or both children are placed on the same side (*Madonna of the Meadow*, Vienna; *Fig.* 58). Simultaneously, the Madonna is seated lower down, so that the group can be closed up still more and the contrasts of direction can be made more vigorous and effective, until finally there comes a picture of the concentrated richness of the *Casa Alba Madonna* (*Fig.* 59; formerly The Hermitage, now National Gallery of U.S.A.),

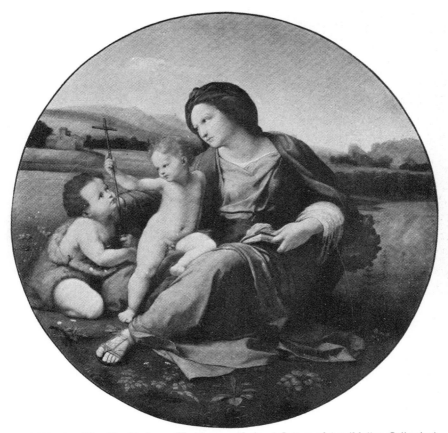

59. RAPHAEL: *The Alba Madonna*. Washington, National Gallery of Art (Mellon Collection)

which, like the *Madonna della Sedia*, is a work of the mature Roman period.[1] An echo from Leonardo's *Madonna and St. Anne* (Louvre; *Fig.* 17) cannot be denied.

Still more complex in theme are the Holy Families such as the Munich *Canigiani Madonna* (*Fig.* 60) where Mary, Joseph and the mother of St. John are united around the two children, that is to say, a group of five figures had to be planned. Here again, the original solution was a simple pyramid with the base formed by the two kneeling women holding the children between them, and the standing figure of St. Joseph as the apex. The *Canigiani Madonna* is a masterpiece of formal articulation, already far exceeding the capacities of a Perugino; Umbrian in its transparent clarity but full of the Florentine variety of movement.

---

[1] The *Madonna of the Diadem*, Louvre, enjoys a notable popularity (engraving by F. Weber), but it shows how little of this mastery passed into Raphael's closest following. The clumsy Madonna motive, the awkward seated pose and the gesticulation make it unthinkable as an original composition. (According to Dollmayr it is by G. F. Penni.)

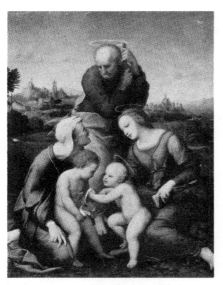

60. RAPHAEL: *The Canigiani Madonna.*
Munich, Pinakothek

The development of Raphael's ideas in Rome led on to monumental forms and strong contrasts and the Roman counterpart from his later period would have been the *Madonna del divin Amore* (Naples), which, though not autograph in execution, yet gives a complete picture of the new ideas.[1] The typical alterations are to make the earlier equilateral triangle into one with unequal sides, the earlier tall group has been lowered, and what was light becomes heavy and massive. The two women sit together on one side balanced by Joseph on the other, an isolated figure pushed far into the background. In the *Madonna of Francis I* (Louvre) with its many figures, the construction of a group is completely rejected and we have instead a picture composed in terms of a tangle of masses of light and shade which makes any comparison with the earlier compositions quite impossible.[2]

Finally, the Florentine Raphael expressed his conception of the Madonna enthroned and surrounded by saints in the large and important *Madonna of the Baldacchino*, where Peruginesque simplicity is combined with motives from the circle of Fra Bartolommeo, the powerful personality with whom Raphael was most closely connected in Florence. The simplicity of the throne is quite in Perugino's manner, but the splendid figure of St. Peter, on the other hand, with its closed contour is unthinkable without Fra Bartolommeo.

A complete estimate of the picture would, however, have to take account not only of these two factors, but also of the additions apparently made later in Rome, namely, the angels at the top, probably the whole of the architecture in the background, and certainly the addition of a considerable portion of the top.[3]

Roman taste required more space and had Raphael been free to do so, he would also have closed up the groups of saints into more compact masses, brought the

---

[1]Dollmayr (*Jahrbuch der Sammlungen des allerhöchsten Kaiserhauses* 1895) ascribes both idea and execution to G. F. Penni, 'il Fattore'.

[2]Dollmayr (*op. cit.*) does not deny a Raphaelesque origin for the group with the Virgin, at least. Penni and Giulio Romano probably had a share in the execution.

[3]The St. Augustine seems to have been added by a much weaker artist. On the other hand, the boy angels certainly belonged to the original form of the picture, in spite of contrary opinions expressed, *e.g.* in the *Cicerone*, 10th ed.

figure of the Madonna lower down in the picture and given a more massive aspect to the whole combination of figures. In the Palazzo Pitti itself one can make the clearest possible comparison with the way in which, ten years later, the question was to be settled, for one has only to compare it with Fra Bartolommeo's *Resurrected Christ with the Four Evangelists,* which is simpler and yet richer, more varied and yet more unified. In making the comparison one comes to the conclusion that the maturer Raphael would not have introduced the two naked boy angels who stand in front of the throne, charming as they are, since there are already enough verticals in the picture: what is needed here is a contrasting form, and for that reason Fra Bartolommeo's boys are seated.

3. The Camera della Segnatura

IT was fortunate for Raphael that when he first arrived in Rome he was not given commissions for subjects of a dramatic nature, but for quiet assemblies of idealized humanity, pictures of calm gatherings well suited to the exercise of inventiveness in simple gesture and sensitivity in grouping, which were precisely his talents. Now he could demonstrate on a large scale that sensitive perception of harmonious outline and balance of mass in which he had trained himself in his Madonna compositions, and in the *Disputà* and the *School of Athens* he was to develop the composition in depth and the combination of groups which served as a basis for the later dramatic works.

The modern public finds it difficult to appreciate this artistic content and looks elsewhere for the merit of the pictures, in the expressions of the faces, in the 'literary' relationship between individual figures. Above all, it demands to know what the figures mean and is uneasy if all the figures cannot have names attached to them, listening gratefully to the guide who knows the name of each person represented, convinced that such explanations make the pictures more comprehensible. For the majority of travellers this is enough, though a few conscientious people attempt to project themselves into the emotions expressed by the faces, on which their attention is concentrated. Few are able to grasp the action of the figures as wholes, apart from the facial expressions, appreciating the motives of reclining, standing or sitting as beautiful actions in themselves, and fewer still suspect that the real value of these pictures has nothing to do with details, but is to be sought in the general disposition, the articulation of the whole and the rhythm and animation of the treatment of space. They are decorations in the grand style,[1] but decorative in a rather uncommon sense, for

---

[1] Böcklin already uses the phrase. In Rudolf Schick's *Journal* (Berlin, 1900) we read (p. 171) that during his second stay in Rome the Stanze (in particular, the Stanza d'Eliodoro) had the greatest influence on him. 'It seemed clear to him that it was the decorative grandeur (*Gross-Dekorative*) of the pictures which impressed even the most insensitive and uneducated, and it was this which he sought to emulate in his own subsequent pictures.'

I mean paintings in which the chief stress is laid, not on the individual head, or on psychological relationship, but on the disposition of the figures on the plane surface and the relationship between their positions in space. Raphael had a feeling for that which is agreeable to the eye which none of his predecessors possessed.

Historical learning is not essential for the understanding of these frescoes,[1] which deal with familiar subjects, and it is quite wrong to attempt interpretations of the *School of Athens* as an esoteric treatise in historical and philosophical ideas, or of the *Disputà* as a synopsis of church history. When Raphael wanted to make his meaning unmistakable he employed inscriptions, but this happens only rarely and there are even important figures, protagonists of the compositions, for which no explanations are given, since Raphael's own contemporaries did not feel the need for them. The all-important thing was the artistic motive which expressed a physical and spiritual state, and the name of the person was a matter of indifference: no one asked what the figures *meant*, but concentrated on what they *are*. To share this point of view needs a kind of visual sensuality, rare enough nowadays, and it is especially difficult for the Northern races to appreciate fully the value which the Latin races set upon physical presence and deportment. One must not, therefore, lose patience with the Northern traveller if he experiences a disappointment at first when he had expected to find in this place a representation of the most profound spiritual forces: it is perfectly true that Rembrandt would have painted Philosophy quite differently.

Whoever persists in his desire to understand more of these pictures will find no other way to do so than by analysis of the figures one by one, learning them by heart, and then looking at the connection between them, one part presupposing another and making its position inevitable. All this advice is given in the 'Cicerone,' but I do not know how many people follow it, since there is never the time and it takes a great deal of practice before one achieves anything. Our vision has become so superficial from the mass of day-to-day illustrative painting, aiming only at making an approximate general impression, that, when we come up against such old works as these we have to begin all over again, learning the alphabet.

The *Disputà*

Around an altar with a monstrance there sit the four Doctors of the Church, the formulators of doctrine, Jerome, Gregory, Ambrose and Augustine (*Figs. 61, 62*), and, around them, the circle of the faithful; dignified theologians standing in calm contemplation, spirited youths pressing forward with praise and adoration; on the one hand reading, and on the other disputation. The assemblage

---

[1] *Cf.* the illuminating essay by Wickhoff, *Jahrbuch der preussischen Kunstsammlungen*, 1903.

contains famous personages and personified types side by side, with a place of
honour reserved for Sixtus IV, uncle of the reigning Pope. That is the earthly
scene, but, above it, the Persons of the Trinity are enthroned and surrounded by
a flat arc of saints, with a parallel row of flying angels above them. The whole is
dominated by the seated figure of Christ, showing His wounds, and attended
by the Virgin and St. John: above Him is God the Father in benediction, and
below Him is the Dove, its head marking the exact centre of the vertical axis
of the picture.

Vasari calls it the *Disputà del Santissimo Sacramento*, an inaccurate title which
has lasted to the present day. There is no dispute in this assemblage, hardly
even any speech: what is intended is the representation of supreme wisdom, the
assured presence of the profoundest mystery of the Church confirmed by the
apparition of Divinity itself.

One may attempt to reconstruct the solution to the problem which would
have been offered by the earlier men. In essence, nothing more was required
than that which has furnished the subject of so many altar-pieces: a number
of devout people in peaceful co-existence, with the Divine manifestation above
them, calm as the moon above the forest. From the beginning, Raphael saw
that it would not be enough to have a few simple motives of standing and sitting
and that the peaceful community must be compensated by a gathering of
people in movement, undertaking some animated action, and so he began by
distinguishing the four chief figures, the Doctors of the Church, as the four
successive states of reading, meditation, visionary ecstasy, and dictation. He
invented the fine group of young men pressing forward as a counterpart to the
calm of the standing figures of the Churchmen, and the same contrast is repeated
in a more subdued fashion by the expressive figure, seen from behind, on the
altar-steps; as a contrast to it, Pope Sixtus on the other side, calm and assured,
with his head held high, is looking steadily before him, a true Prince of the
Church. Behind him there is a purely secular motive: a young boy leans over the
parapet while a man points out the Pope to him,[1] and, in the corresponding
place on the other side, the same group recurs in reverse, with the younger
man pointing. The older man stands behind a balustrade, bent over a book which
others also are reading and which he seems to be expounding, but the youth
invites him towards the altar on which everything is centred. It may be said
that Raphael wanted to paint here the personification of obstinate heresy,[2]
but it certainly is not meant as a portrait of anyone in particular and it is hardly
even likely to have been part of the written programme drawn up for him,

---

[1] As has often been observed, the man pointing at the Pope is derived from Leonardo's *Adoration of
the Kings*, where he occupies the same position in the picture.
[2] *Cf.* the similar group in Filippino's *Triumph of St. Thomas Aquinas*, Santa Maria sopra Minerva,
Rome.

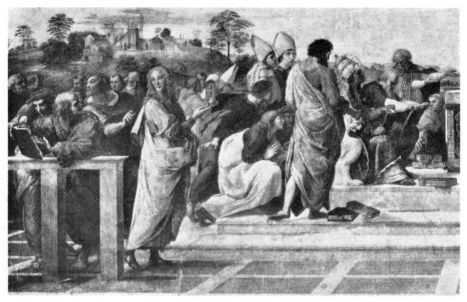

61 RAPHAEL: *The Disputà*. Detail with Sts. Gregory and Jerome. Vatican

which would have specified the four Doctors, Pope Sixtus, and one or two other people who happened to be celebrities of particular interest at that moment. Raphael complied with all this but he reserved his right to develop the groups of anonymous figures in whatever way seemed necessary for his composition. This brings us to the root of the matter, for the meaning of the picture lies not in its details but in its fugal effect, the dovetailing of all its elements, and we can only begin to appreciate it properly when we realize how every detail is pressed into the service of the general effect, and that each detail has been designed with its effect on the whole kept clearly in view. Yet no one should be disappointed because the psychological side is not the most interesting thing in the picture; Ghirlandaio would have created more convincing heads and Botticelli would have had far more sympathy for the expression of religious feeling—there is no one figure here which could be matched with the *St. Augustine* in Ognissanti, Florence. Raphael's strength lies in a different direction, for it was something unprecedented to have painted a fresco of such size with so much depth, such variety of attitudes, so lucidly developed and so rhythmically articulated. The first problem of the composition was the four Doctors of the Church who formed, by themselves, the principal figures and as such had to be given due prominence. If they were to be large in scale then they could not be placed too far back on the imaginary stage, but if they could not be set back in depth the picture would become a mere strip-like procession; in order to

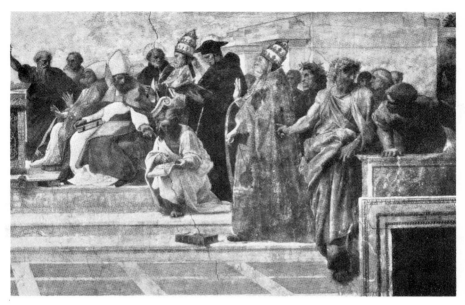

62. RAPHAEL: *The Disputà*. Detail with Sts. Ambrose and Augustine. Vatican

gain depth, after some hesitation at the beginning, Raphael decided to push
the figures of the Doctors into the background and to build a flight of steps
below them. This was the happiest solution, for the motive of the steps revealed
extraordinary possibilities, linking all the figures together and leading up to the
centre. A further result was achieved by the addition of the men gesticulating
vigorously on the far side of the altar, who are only there to emphasise the
figures of Jerome and Ambrose seated at the back; yet these men were after-
thoughts, added at the last moment.

There is a distinct flow of movement from the left towards the centre: the
pointing youth, the praying figures, the expressive figure seen from behind,
combine to form a sequence of related actions which the eye follows with pleasure,
and Raphael always took this guiding of the eye into consideration, even in his
later works. If, now, the last of the principal figures, the dictating Augustine,
turns to one side, we see the point of this movement—it is introduced as the
connecting link with the right-hand side where the action is allowed to die away
and come to a stop. Such deliberate formal considerations are complete innovations on fifteenth-century practice. Otherwise, Raphael has chosen perfectly
simple points of view for the Doctors; a lowered profile and a raised profile for
the first two, and the third but slightly varied, while the seated positions are
as simple as possible. This is Raphael's economy; indeed it is impossible to
treat distant figures in any other way if they are to have a grand effect, as is shown

by a Quattrocento picture such as Filippino's *Triumph of St. Thomas* which fails in this respect. The action becomes more complex as the figures approach the foreground, the most complicated being the bending figures and their companions in the corners, which are symmetrically disposed and linked with the central figures in the same way by means of pointing figures.[1] Symmetry is the ruling principle of the whole picture, although it is more or less concealed in the details. Even in the middle zone, where the major divergences from symmetry occur they are not very great, since Raphael is still proceeding cautiously, intent on unity and calm, not on agitation and dislocation. The contours are drawn with a delicacy of feeling that might almost be called reverent, so that no line clashes with another and a feeling of calm peace dominates the variegated effects. In the same sense, the line of the background unites the two halves of the assembly and harmonises them with the upper row of figures. With all this gentle flow of line there is preserved a still higher aspect, which is the clarity of appearance given by Raphael to every figure. Where the older painters packed their canvases, crowding head behind head, he, as a result of his education in Peruginesque simplicity, keeps the figures separate so that each can be developed in full view. This is yet another example of a new visual standard being taken into account: the treatment of crowds of figures in Botticelli or Filippino demands intensive and close-up study if one is to make anything of the individuals in the welter of figures. The art of the sixteenth century, which focuses attention on the whole, requires simplicity as a basic principle.

It is qualities such as these which determine the value of the *Disputà*, not details of draughtsmanship. It is undeniable that the fresco contains a considerable amount of essentially new motives even though much of it is still tentative and uncertain, as for example the rather vague figure of Sixtus IV, where it is not clear if he is moving or standing still, and it takes a few moments to discover that he is propping a book against his knee. The pointing youth opposite him is an unfortunate invention, derived from a Leonardesque motive known from a drawing—the so-called *Beatrice*. Where the heads are not portraits they are so empty as to be almost unpleasing: one hardly dare imagine what the picture would have looked like if Leonardo had represented the community of the faithful by types of *his* creation.

---

[1]The idea of the parapet is due to the door which cuts into the picture-plane on one side, and which Raphael sought to minimize by building the little wall over it and repeating the motive as a balustrade on the other side. Later in the Cinquecento, such incursions into the picture space could not be tolerated and so the frescoes of the Camera d'Eliodoro have their base line set at the level of the tops of the doors. It is typical of Venice that Titian, in his *Presentation of the Virgin in the Temple*, cheerfully sacrifices the legs of some of the figures to a door-opening: in Rome such a crudity would not have been endured.

Yet, as has already been said, the great attributes of the *Disputà*, and the intrinsic factors of its effect, are the generalisations: the division of the surface planes as a whole, the way in which the lower figures lead inwards, the swing of the upper curve of saints, the contrast between figures in movement and those solemnly enthroned, the combination of variety and repose, all result in a picture which has often been lauded as a supreme example of the monumental style of religious painting. Its special character derives from the charming balance it strikes between the limitations of youthful and delicate perceptiveness and budding powers.

The *School of Athens*

ON the wall opposite Theology we find a representation of Philosophy, secular knowledge, in the picture which is called *The School of Athens* (*Fig.* 1), although the name is almost as arbitrary as that of the *Disputà*. One could, if one wished, rather speak of this as the Disputà since the principal motive is the two leaders of philosophy, Plato and Aristotle, engaged in argument and surrounded by their audience. Nearby is Socrates with his own circle, plying his questions and counting off on his fingers each point as it is made. In the dress of a man above the needs of this world, Diogenes lies on the steps. An elderly man, who may be Pythagoras, writes something down, while a tablet inscribed with the harmonic scale is held out in front of him. The historical content of the picture is completed by the addition of the astronomers Ptolemy and Zoroaster and Euclid the geometer.

The composition presented greater difficulties here than was the case in the *Disputà* because the circle of Christ and the Saints was lacking. Raphael had no other way out of the difficulty than to invoke the aid of architecture, so he constructed an imposing, vaulted hall with four very high steps in front of it, extending across the entire breadth of the picture: in this way, he obtained a double stage—the space below the steps and the platform above them. In contrast to the *Disputà*, where all the parts tend towards the centre, here the whole is broken up into a sum of individual groups, even individual figures—the natural expression of the ramifications of philosophical inquiry. A search for specific historical allusion is as pointless here as in the *Disputà*. The idea that the physical sciences are grouped together in the lower part, leaving the upper space free for the speculative thinkers is illuminating as an idea: yet, even so, it may well be that this interpretation is beside the mark.

The motives expressing mental states by physical actions are much more varied here than in the *Disputà*; in itself, the subject demanded greater variety of treatment but it is clear that Raphael himself had developed and become more inventive, for the situations are more sharply characterized, the gestures more telling, and the figures more easily remembered. Raphael's handling of the group of Plato and Aristotle is of primary importance. The theme was an old one and a comparison can well be made with Luca della Robbia's *Philosophers* relief on the Campanile in Florence—two Italians argue with typical Southern vehemence, one insisting on the literal truth of his text, while the other gesticulates with both hands and all ten fingers, insisting that it is nonsense. The bronze doors by Donatello in S. Lorenzo have other examples of disputing figures, yet Raphael had to reject all these prototypes since sixteenth-century taste was in favour of reticence of gesture. The two Princes of Philosophy stand side by side in noble calm; the one with arm outstretched, whose hand, palm down, makes a sweeping gesture over the earth, is Aristotle, the 'constructive' man; the other, Plato, with uplifted finger points heavenwards. We do not know what inspired Raphael to characterise the opposite qualities of the two personalities in this way, which makes them plausible as images of the two philosophers.

Standing at the right-hand edge of the picture is another group of impressive figures. The isolated figure of a man with a white beard, closely wrapped in his mantle and absolutely simple in silhouette, is a noble and tranquil presence. Next to him is another man leaning forward on the base of a pilaster and watching a boy, who is seen from the front, bending forward with his legs crossed as he sits writing: it is by figures like these that we must measure Raphael's progress. The lying motive in the figure of Diogenes is absolutely new—it is the beggar who makes himself comfortable on the steps of a church. The variety and inventiveness go on increasing: the scene of the geometrical demonstration is not only admirably acute in psychological observation, showing the different degrees of understanding in the various students, but the actual physical movements of kneeling and bending are realized in each figure in a way which deserves the closest study and might even be learned by heart.

The group around Pythagoras is still more interesting *(Fig. 63)*. A man in profile sits writing on a low seat, with one foot on a stool; and behind him are other figures pressing forward and leaning over him—a whole garland of curves. A second man also sits writing, but he is seen from the front and his limbs are disposed in a more complex pattern; between these two there is a standing figure supporting an open book against his thigh, apparently citing a passage in it. There is no need to puzzle one's head over the meaning of this figure, for in the intellectual sense of this group he has none, and he exists solely as a physical motive, for formal reasons. The raised foot, the outstretched arm, the twist of the upper part of the body and the contrasting tilt of the head give it a plastic significance of its own, and if the Northern spectator is inclined to think this an artificial reason for so emphatic and elaborate a motive he must

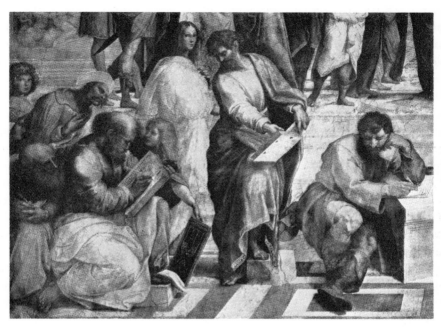

63. RAPHAEL: *The School of Athens*. Detail with Pythagoras. Vatican

be warned not to make over-hasty judgements, for the Italian is so much more given to gesticulation than we are, that for him the limits of the natural are quite different. Here, Raphael is obviously following in Michelangelo's footsteps and under the influence of the more powerful personality he has, for the moment, lost his natural sensibility.[1]

Analysis of the fresco should not stop short at single figures, for Raphael's rendering of movement in individual figures is a lesser achievement than the skill with which he builds up his groups and there is nothing in earlier art which can in any way be compared with this polyphony. The group of the geometers is a solution to a formal problem which few have ever attempted— five figures directed towards a single point, clearly developed in space, pure in outline, and with the greatest variety in attitude. The same may be said of the still more nobly planned group on the opposite side, where the highest art is manifested in the way in which the most varied poses complement one another and the many figures are brought into an inevitable cohesion, uniting like the

---

[1] The prototype for this very figure is, however, to be found in Leonardo and not Michelangelo: it is developed from the motive of the *Leda* (*Fig.* 18) and a drawing by Raphael after the *Leda* is preserved. The borrowings from Donatello's Paduan reliefs (*cf.* Vöge, *Raffael und Donatello*, 1896) are confined to such subordinate figures that one may well believe them to have been incorporated into the composition almost as a jest. In any case, one must not consider these borrowings as evidence of poverty of imagination.

voices in a chorus, so that the whole appears self-explanatory and logical. If one looks at this group as a whole, one sees the point of the young man who stands right at the back: he has been thought to be the portrait of some prince, which may or may not be the case, but what is certainly true is that he has the formal function of supplying the necessary vertical in the tangle of curves.

As in the *Disputà*, here, too, the greatest variety is displayed in the foreground: at the back, on the platform, there is a forest of verticals; at the front, where the figures are large, the lines are curved and interlace in a complex way. Around the central figures symmetry reigns, but this is relaxed on one side to allow the upper mass to stream unsymmetrically down the steps and destroy the equilibrium, which is again restored by the asymmetry of the foreground groups.

What is certainly extraordinary is that the figures of Plato and Aristotle, standing so far back in the crowd, can still dominate the composition; and it is the more incomprehensible when one takes the scale of proportions into account, for, according to strict reckoning, there is too rapid a diminution towards the background—Diogenes on the steps has, abruptly, quite different proportions from those of the neighbouring figures in the foreground. The miracle explains itself by the method of disposing the architecture: the disputing philosophers stand exactly in the opening of the last arch, and they would be lost without this halo which is echoed, and powerfully reinforced, by the concentric lines of the nearer arches. I call to mind the use of a similar motive in Leonardo's *Last Supper*—take away the architecture and the whole composition falls to pieces.

Yet here the relationship between the figures and the space they occupy is thought of in an entirely new way—high above the heads of the figures the great vaults recede into the distance and the spectator shares the calm and serene atmosphere of this basilica. Bramante's new St. Peter's was conceived in such a spirit, and, according to Vasari, Bramante should be accounted the author of the architecture in this fresco.

*   *   *   *   *

THE *Disputà* and the *School of Athens* are best known in Germany from engravings and the powerful spatial impression of the frescoes is reproduced better, even in a superficial engraving, than in any photograph. In the eighteenth century Volpato made a series of seven engravings of the Stanze, which for generations were the souvenirs brought home by visitors to Rome, and even now these plates are not to be despised, though Keller and Jacoby have taken up the task with other eyes and other means. Jos. Keller's *Disputà* of 1841–56 superseded all earlier versions by the size of the plates, and while Volpato sought only to reproduce the general configuration, and in so doing arbitrarily increased the painterly appearance, the German sought a more literal rendering and tried to reproduce with his graver all the characteristics of Raphael. Clear, firm, strong in chiaroscuro, but without any feeling for painterly effects, he set his figures on the surface and sought, above all, to be precise in the form, disregarding the colour harmony and, more particularly, the light tonality of the fresco. Jacoby began at this point. His *School of Athens* was the result of ten years work (1872–82) and the layman can have no conception of the critical judgement required to find a corresponding tone on the copper-plate for every colour value of the original, to reproduce the softness of the painting, and to retain spatial clarity within the bright tonal scale of fresco. The engraving appeared as an unequalled achievement. Perhaps, however, his intentions overstepped the limits which in these cases are set upon the graphic arts, and there are still art lovers who, since the reduction of scale is so great, prefer the more summary handling of Volpato, with his relatively simpler linear means, just because it is thus easier to preserve something of the monumentality of the general impression.

Parnassus

IT may well be thought that Raphael was glad not to have a similar wall-space for his third task, the fresco of the poets (*Fig.* 64). The narrower surface, with the window in the middle, of itself suggested new ideas, and Raphael constructed the actual hill of Parnassus around it, obtaining in this way two small foreground spaces below and beside the window-opening, with a broad podium above it, the place where Apollo and the Muses sit. Homer, too, is admitted to this place, and in the background, Dante and Virgil[1] are recognizable. The rest of the poets crowd around the slopes of the hill, wandering by themselves, or standing in groups and conversing idly, or listening fixedly to some animated recitation. It was difficult to make a group portrait of poets with any psychological penetration, since poetry is not made in company, and Raphael confined the expression of inspiration to two cases, the god himself who plays the violin and looks upward, ravished; and Homer, who looks up, but with his blind eyes, as he pours out his inspired words. Artistic economy dictated less emotion for the other groups, and the divine madness is proper only in the vicinity of the god: lower down, we are in the company of fellow-mortals. Here again, it is not necessary to know the names, although Sappho is identified by an inscription, since, otherwise, no one would have known what a woman was doing there; yet it is clear that Raphael really included her in order to have a female figure as a contrast. Dante is quite small and almost incidental. The really striking figures are nameless ideal ones,

---

[1]Virgil is no longer fantastically dressed, with a pointed crown, as Botticelli had still made him, but is now antique, the Roman poet, as he was first represented by Signorelli at Orvieto. *Cf.* Volkmann, *Iconografia Dantesca*, p. 72.

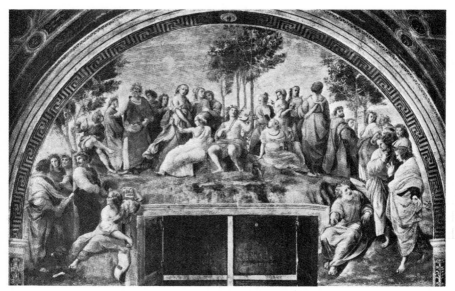

64. RAPHAEL: *Parnassus*. Vatican

and only two portraits leap to the eye from among the throng: one, on the right at the extreme edge, is apparently Sannazaro; the other, who takes the pose used in Raphael's self-portrait, has the air of a portrait but has not yet been satisfactorily identified.

Apollo and two of the Muses at his side are seated; he is in full face and they in profile, forming a broad triangle which is the centre of the composition, with the other Muses disposed around it. The chain of movement ends at the right with a majestic figure seen from behind, and, on the left, with the corresponding figure of Homer seen from the front, the two figures together forming the angle-pillars of the Parnassian assembly. The grand construction of the whole group is resolved by the figure of the boy who sits near Homer's feet and takes down his words with a stylus, but the composition develops in depth in an unexpected way on the other side, for the man next to the female figure seen from behind is only three parts visible as he strides into the picture from the far side of the hill. The effect of this movement is heightened by the laurel bushes coming forward from the background, and if one concentrates on the trees in the picture it will be seen how much calculation went into their composition, for they add a diagonal movement which breaks up the rigid symmetry, and Apollo would be lost among the Muses were it not for the central tree-trunks.

The groups in the foreground are contrasted among themselves in so far as the left-hand group, with the tree as its focus, appears as quite isolated, while the right-hand one maintains a connection with the figures above it. This is the same chain of movement as in the *School of Athens*.

The *Parnassus* is less beautiful in its spatial treatment than the other pictures, for there is a feeling of crowding on the too-narrow hill and few of the figure motives are really convincing, too many of them being marked by a kind of pettiness; the Muses are, perhaps, the most unfortunate of all, being mere empty effigies, none the better for their conscious 'antique' flourishes. One of the two seated Muses imitates the drapery of *Ariadne*, and the other may have a proto-type for her action in some such figure as the so-called *Suppliant Woman*; the bared shoulders, rather obtrusively repeated, is another motive taken from the antique. If only Raphael had shown more living shoulders! In spite of all the roundness of his forms, one thinks nostalgically of Botticelli's angular Graces, but there is one striking touch of nature in the neck of the standing woman with her back turned towards us—it is the true neck of a Roman woman. The best figures are the straightforward ones: the twisted figure of Sappho shows to what extraordinary lengths the search for interesting movement could lead, for Raphael temporarily lost his way and allowed himself to compete with Michelangelo, without really understanding him. It is enough to compare this unhappy poetess with any of the Sistine Sibyls to appreciate the very real difference. The sharp foreshortening of the arm of the man pointing outwards is another piece of virtuosity which we need not censure, since this kind of problem was then obligatory, and Michelangelo's own view of the matter is contained in the figure of God the Father in the *Creation of the Sun*.

One peculiarity in the spatial handling has still to be mentioned and that is the striking way in which Sappho and her counterpart appear to cut across the window-frame, which is so unpleasant because the figures seem to break out of the wall-plane. One wonders how Raphael could have committed such a crudity, but the fact is that he calculated on the opposite effect, thinking that the arch painted in perspective, with which he enframed the entire picture, would so push back the window that the spectator would be led to believe that the window itself was set back some distance into the picture-plane. It turned out to be a false calculation and Raphael never again tried anything of the kind, but later engravers have disseminated the error by omitting to include the painted frame which alone gives the clue to the spatial intentions.[1]

---

[1] I cannot accept the grisailles below the *Parnassus* as contemporary with the rest of the room. The older interpretation of them, as *Augustus preventing the burning of the Aeneid* and *Alexander hiding Homer's poems in a coffin*, seems to have much in its favour as against Wickhoff's proposed interpretation (*Jahrbuch der preussischen Kunstsammlungen*, 1893), which scarcely explains the gestures—it is not a representation of the burning of books, but the prevention of it, and it is not the removal of writings from a sarcophagus, but the putting of them into it. I believe that all unprejudiced observers will come to this conclusion.

Jurisprudence

RAPHAEL was spared the task of painting a concourse of jurists since the fourth wall needed only two fairly small ceremonial scenes from legal history on either side of the window and the arch above it is filled with figures of Fortitude, Prudence and Temperance, the virtues necessary for the administration of the law. Nobody is likely to be enchanted by these figures as expressions of the virtues they are supposed to personify, for they are uninteresting female figures, the outer pair in animated movement, the centre one rather calmer, and all three sitting low down in order to get greater contrast of movement. Temperance raises high her bridle with a ceremoniousness not altogether comprehensible, her general action closely related to the Sappho of the *Parnassus*; the twist of the torso, the arm stretched across her body, and the position of the legs all being similar, although the figure as a whole is superior, conceived on a grander scale and not so broken-up, clearly showing the stylistic development of the artist. Prudence, pleasing in herself because of her repose, has a very lovely outline and the drawing, by comparison with the *Parnassus*, shows a greater grasp of the idea of clarity, as may be seen by comparing the arm on which she leans with the same motive in the Muse at Apollo's left, where the essence of the action is not clearly brought out. From here, the course of his development leads on to the *Sibyls* in Santa Maria della Pace, marking an immense advance in variety of movement and a similar progress in clarification of motive: in particular, the third of the *Sibyls* must be mentioned here for the convincing way in which the structure of head, neck and elbow is mastered and expressed. The *Sibyls* are placed in front of a dark tapestry background, while the *Virtues* are silhouetted against a bright blue sky, and this is itself an essential characteristic of the difference in style.

The two scenes from legal history, the giving of the civil and ecclesiastical codes of law, are primarily interesting as formulations of ceremonial procedure in the taste of the early sixteenth century; but, at the point at which this fresco joins on to the *Disputà*, there is clear evidence that Raphael, towards the end of his work in the Camera della Segnatura, began to achieve breadth and calm repose, and that he had already begun to work with figures on a larger scale than his earlier ones.

It is a pity that the room no longer contains its original wooden panelling, which would have had a more harmonious effect than the present white standing figures painted on the dado, for there is always something rather hazardous in putting figures under figures. The same scheme is followed in the succeeding Stanze, but it is far less disturbing there—where it is a contemporary scheme— because the caryatides with their plastic effect form a decisive contrast with the entirely painterly style of the frescoes, and they could almost be said to give the pictures a truly pictorial effect by emphasising the effect of recession. This relationship does not exist in the first Stanza, with its comparatively unpainterly style.

4. The Camera d'Eliodoro

AFTER the allegories of the Camera della Segnatura we find the second room contains histories, and, more than this, it is the room of the new, grandiose, painterly style, with large-size figures and far greater plasticity of effect. It seems as if a hole has been cut in the wall, and the figures loom up from the dark depths; even the framing arch-mouldings have shadows cast in an illusion of reality. If one looks back at the *Disputà* it looks like a tapestry, two-dimensional and light: here the pictures contain less, but what there is is more powerful in effect. There are no subtle and highly wrought figure groupings, only powerful masses set one against the other in the sharpest contrasts; no more decorative half-truths or theatrically disposed philosophers and poets, but, in their place, vehement emotions and expressive action. The first of the Stanze may rank higher as decoration, but the Stanza of Heliodorus furnished the pattern of monumental narrative for all time.

The *Expulsion of Heliodorus*

THE Second Book of Maccabees tells how the Syrian general Heliodorus was sent by his king to Jerusalem to rob the Temple of the money belonging to the widows and orphans, who ran lamenting through the streets, foreseeing their loss, while the High Priest, pallid with terror, prayed at the altar. Neither remonstrances nor entreaties could deter Heliodorus, who broke into the treasury and emptied the coffers: then suddenly there appeared a Heavenly rider in golden armour who cast down the robber and trampled him beneath his horse's hooves, while two youths scourged him. That is the text. Raphael took the successive incidents and combined them into one picture, not as the old painters had done, calmly setting different scenes side by side or one above the other, but with due regard to unity of time and place (*Fig.* 65). He does not show the scene in the treasury, but represents Heliodorus as about to leave the Temple with his loot; the widows and orphans who, according to the story, should be running screaming through the streets, he brings into the same place, as witnesses of the Divine intervention, and the High Priest praying to God for help has thus his natural place in the picture.

For the public of that time, the greatest surprise must have been the way in which Raphael disposed his scenes, since no one was accustomed to any other arrangement than that of setting the principal action in the centre of the picture,

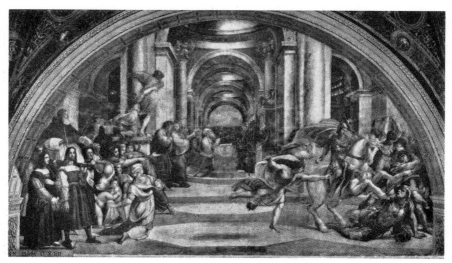

65. RAPHAEL: *The Expulsion of Heliodorus*. Vatican

yet here there is a great void in the middle, with the decisive action taking place at the extreme edge. We can now hardly appreciate to the full the impression made by such a composition, for we have been brought up with a quite different approach to formal problems; but people at that date must really have felt that they were actually watching the sudden miracle taking place. Further, the scene of retribution is worked out according to new dramatic rules. It is clear enough how the Quattrocento would have told the story—Heliodorus would be bleeding under the horse's hooves while the two men would be scourging him from either side. Raphael depicts the moment of suspense when the evil-doer has been cast down, the rider is wheeling his horse to trample him underfoot, and the two youths are just rushing forward with their scourges. This was the way in which Giulio Romano later composed his *Stoning of St. Stephen* (in Genoa): the stones are upraised, but the Saint is still unharmed.[1] In the fresco, the movement of the youths has the additional advantage that their impetuous rush is reflected in the horse so that it appears to be part of the same lightning movement. The rush of movement is admirably rendered so that their feet seem hardly to touch the ground. The horse is less good, for Raphael was no animal painter.

The fallen Heliodorus, with vengeance breaking over him, would have been represented in the Quattrocento as a vulgar scoundrel, without a single redeeming feature, as children would have him, but the sixteenth century saw things differently and Raphael did not make him ignoble, for even in humiliation he

[1]The same idea had already been used for the *Stoning of St. Stephen* in the Sistine Tapestries.

remains calm and dignified although his companions are in utter confusion. His head is, in itself, a model of Cinquecento force of expression: the painful upraising of the head, giving the essentials in a few forms, has no equal in earlier work and the motive of the body is also new and of great consequence for the future.[1]

Opposite this group are the women and children, huddled together in arrested movement, and sharply and closely outlined. The appearance of a crowd is given by the simplest means—if one counts the number of figures it is astonishing how few there are; yet all the action, the questioning glance and the answering gesture, the pressing back and attempts at concealment, are set out in clear, expressive lines and strong contrasts.

Pope Julius II is calmly seated in his litter, above the crowd, looking into the picture, although his attendants, all portraits, take no part whatever in the action. It is difficult to understand how Raphael could have allowed the spiritual unity of the picture to be thus disturbed; probably the Pope wished to be shown as present at the event, as had been the custom in fifteenth-century pictures, and it was a concession to his taste. The theoretical treatises might insist that all the persons in a picture should be represented as actually taking part in the action, but there were frequent lapses in practice, and in this case Raphael turned the Pope's whim to good use since it gave him the opportunity to make a calm contrast to all the excitement in the rest of the picture.

There are two boys climbing up on one of the columns in the background: what do they signify? It is likely that so striking a motive is no mere incident which could just as well have been omitted and indeed they are essential to the balance of the composition, as a counterpart to the prostrate Heliodorus: the scales are tipped down on the one side and rise on the other, and the contrast gives real meaning to the prostration of Heliodorus.[2]

The clambering pair have a further function in that they lead the eye into the picture, towards the centre, where we discover the praying High Priest, kneeling at the altar, unaware that his prayer is already answered. The basic theme of imploring helplessness is central in the composition.

The *Deliverance of St. Peter*

RAPHAEL tells how St. Peter lay in prison and was roused by an angel in the night; how, still dreaming, he walked out with the angel to freedom; and how the guard was aroused when his flight was discovered—all this is told in three frescoes which seem to have arranged themselves on the barely sufficient surface of a wall which is broken into by a window (*Fig.* 66). In the centre there is the

---

[1] I cannot support the view, advanced from time to time, that it is derived from an antique river-god.
[2] The occurrence of a similar motive in Donatello's relief of the *Miracle of the Ass* is not to be held against Raphael; who could talk of borrowings here?

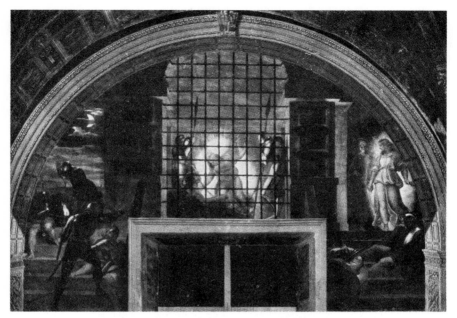

66. RAPHAEL: *The Deliverance of St. Peter*. Vatican

dungeon, the front wall of which is formed by a grating so that the interior is visible; to left and right there are steps leading up from the foreground and materially aiding the impression of depth, avoiding the feeling that the hollow space of the wall lay immediately above the void of the window-niche.

St. Peter sits sleeping on the ground, his hands on his knees as if in prayer and his head a little bowed. The angel, in a glory of light, bends down to him and touches him on the shoulder with one hand while he points the way with the other. Two guards in armour stand against the wall at either side, heavy with sleep. Could the scene be simpler? And yet it took a Raphael to see it thus, and even afterwards it was never again told so concisely and impressively. There is a picture of *Peter's Deliverance* by Domenichino, universally known because it hangs in the church in which the Saint's chains are preserved, S. Pietro in Vincoli (*Fig.* 67): in it the angel bends down and takes St. Peter by the shoulder; the old man awakes and recoils in terror at the apparition. Why did Raphael show him as sleeping? Because only thus could he represent the pious resignation of the prisoner, since terror is an emotion which does not allow of a distinction being made between a good and a bad man. Domenichino attempts fore-shortening and achieves a restless effect: Raphael gives the simplest full-length view and gains an effect of peace and calm. Again, in the Domenichino, the two guards are in the cell, one lying on the floor and the other leaning against the

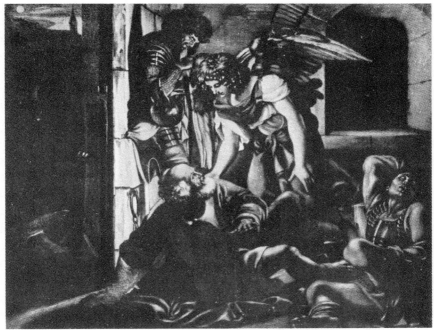

67. DOMENICHINO: *The Deliverance of St. Peter*. Rome, S. Pietro in Vincoli

wall, but their obtrusive poses and highly finished heads claim the spectator's attention as much as the principal figures do. Raphael makes a subtle distinction: his guards stand against the wall as if they were part of it, living masonry, and a glance at their rather vulgar features shows that they have nothing to detain our interest. It goes without saying that Raphael did not attempt a detailed rendering of the prison walls.

In the scene of the actual deliverance from the dungeon, which earlier artists regarded as the kernel of the story, Peter was always shown speaking, in conversation with the angel: Raphael paid heed to the text of the Scriptures—he went out as if in a dream. The angel leads him by the hand, but he sees neither the angel nor the path, his wide-open eyes stare into space and he moves like a sleepwalker, an impression heightened by the way in which he looms out of the darkness, partly hidden by the blaze of light coming from the angel: here speaks the painter in Raphael, who had already created something quite new in the half-light of the prison cell. As for the angel himself, it is the unforgettable rendering of the light-footed guide and leader.

The steps above and below are occupied by sleeping soldiers. The Bible mentions the alarm being given and it is supposed to have taken place in the morning, so Raphael preserves the unity of time, and, in order to give the halo of light at the right a counterpoise, he places a crescent moon in the sky while the dawn begins to break in the East. To this he adds one piece of pictorial virtuosity—the flickering light of a torch and its reddish reflections on the stones and the shining armour. The *Deliverance of St. Peter* is perhaps better fitted than any other of Raphael's works to lead the hesitant to a full appreciation of him.

The *Mass of Bolsena*

THE *Mass of Bolsena* is the story of an unbelieving priest, in whose hands the Host began to bleed while he celebrated Mass. This might be thought to afford a highly dramatic picture—the priest starting back in terror, the spectators overcome by the miracle—and the scene has been so painted, but Raphael took a different course (*Fig. 68*). The priest, kneeling in profile before the altar, does not spring up, but, unable to move, holds the red-stained Host before him, engaged in an inward struggle which is psychologically more penetrating than if he had suddenly become ecstatic. Because the principal figure is motionless, Raphael is able to use it as a starting-point for a whole crescendo of emotion as the miracle works on the crowd of the faithful: the choir-boys, who are nearest, whisper among themselves, their candles swaying, and the nearest boy involuntarily bows in adoration; on the steps the congregation presses and jostles until the wave of movement reaches its climax in the woman in the foreground who has jumped up and strains forward to see. Her glance, her gestures, and indeed her whole body, could be taken as an embodiment of faith. Earlier artists had imagined Fides as a figure like this, and there is a relief by Civitale, in the Museo Nazionale, Florence, which has the closest similarities in the head thrown back in half profile. The chain of movement ends in the women squatting at the base of the steps, the indifferent multitude which, as yet, has no knowledge of the event.

In this fresco, too, the Pope again wanted to be shown with his retinue and Raphael set aside half the picture for this purpose, bringing the Pope—after some hesitation at the beginning—on to the same level as the principal figure, so that the two kneel facing each other, profile to profile, the awestruck young priest and the old Pope in his ritual attitude of prayer, as unmoved as the rock of the Church. Considerably further back there is a group of Cardinals, fine portraits, but none of them comparable with their master. In the foreground, there are the Swiss Guards with the Papal litter; they are kneeling, their physical existence closely represented without any spiritual exaltation—the miracle causes only a profane eagerness among them to find out what is going on.

The composition is thus based on a great contrast of motives, suggested by the peculiarity of the wall-surface, for there was again a window cutting into the

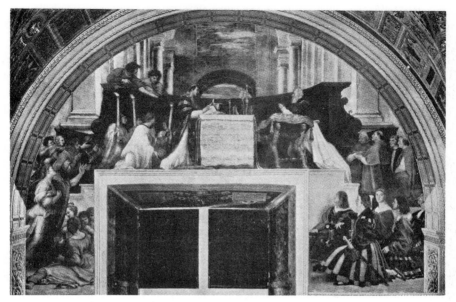

68. RAPHAEL: *The Mass of Bolsena*. Vatican

wall, which had to be taken into account, and which made the representation of a church interior unthinkable. So Raphael constructed a terrace with steps leading down at the sides, and placed the altar so that it came in the centre of the picture. He surrounded the terrace with a flat, rounded parapet and allowed a hint of ecclesiastical architecture only in the background. Since the window is not in the centre of the wall, the two halves of the picture are unequal, and this is equalized to some extent by pushing the narrower left side somewhat higher, justifying the presence of the people leaning over the parapet behind the priest, and who would have been superfluous if their only function was to point out the miracle.[1]

The last of the pictures in this room, the *Meeting of Leo I and Attila*, is a disappointment. It is clear enough that what was intended was to show the Pope and his retinue dominating the excited hordes of the King of the Huns by their calm dignity, although they occupy the less important part of the picture space; yet the effect does not come off, and the apparition of the Heavenly helpers, Sts. Peter and Paul, bearing down menacingly on Attila from above, cannot be blamed for destroying the effect. It is simply that the contrast itself is not developed properly—it is difficult to find Attila at all. Subordinate figures thrust themselves forward, misleading the spectator; there are discords in the

[1]Raphael assumes that the spectator stands exactly opposite the central axis of the picture, so that the left side of the window-frame overlaps part of the picture space.

linear rhythms and obscurities of the most destructive effect, so that Raphael's authorship of this fresco is only very partial, especially as its general tone is different from the others. From our point of view it is not relevant.[1]

For the same reason, we cannot follow the activities of the Raphael School in the third room, that of the *Fire in the Borgo*. The chief picture after which the room is named has several very fine motives in detail, but the good is mixed with the less good and the fresco as a whole lacks the closed quality of an original composition. The woman carrying water (*Fig.* 167), the men putting out the fire and the group of refugees are easily recognizable as Raphael's, and they are very informative as examples of fine detail in individual figures, created during his last years; but for the course of his development in large-scale narrative we have to go to the cartoons for the Sistine Chapel Tapestries.

5. The Tapestry Cartoons

THE seven cartoons in the Victoria and Albert Museum, all that remain of the original series of ten, have been called 'the Parthenon sculptures of modern art' and certainly they surpass the great Vatican frescoes in fame and in the extent of their influence (*Figs.* 69–75). They can be used as models for compositions with a limited number of figures and they have been widely diffused in woodcut and engraved reproductions. They were a thesaurus of forms expressing all human emotions and Raphael's fame as a draughtsman is mainly based on these achievements: Western art has sometimes seemed incapable of inventing new gestures to express astonishment, fear, the distorted grimaces of grief or the image of nobility and dignity. It is striking how many expressive heads occur in these compositions, how many figures are impelled to say something, and this leads to the *fortissimo*, almost harsh, effect of some of the pictures. They are not all of equal merit, and not one of them has any of Raphael's own work in it,[2] but some are of such a perfection that we recognize the immediate proximity of Raphael's genius.

The Miraculous Draught of Fishes. Jesus had gone out on the lake with Peter and his brother, and, at His word, the nets were cast out once again although the fishermen had toiled all night in vain; then they made such a huge haul that a second boat had to be called over to help with the catch. Peter is seized with

---

[1] I note some examples of the lack of clarity in draughtsmanship which are not consonant with Raphael's mature style. (*a*) Attila's horse. The hind legs are indicated as far as the hoofs in a ridiculously fragmentary way. (*b*) The man pointing, between the black and white horses. His second leg is also fragmentary. (*c*) One of the two lancers in the foreground is extremely ill-drawn. The ground and the landscape behind it are also unRaphaelesque. An unknown hand collaborated here, talented but still rough and crude. The best parts are on the left.

[2] *Cf.* H. Dollmayr, *Raffaels Werkstätte* in *Jahrbuch der kunsthistorischen Sammlungen des allerhöchsten Kaiserhauses*, 1895. 'In the main, only one hand worked on the cartoons, and that was Penni's' (p. 253).

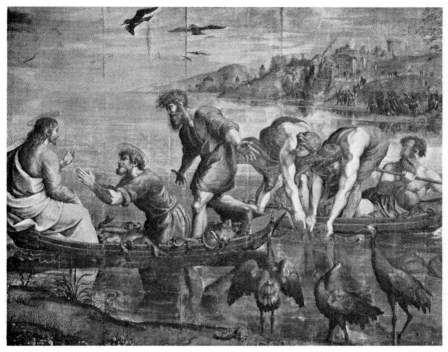

69. RAPHAEL: *The Miraculous Draught of Fishes.* Cartoon. Victoria and Albert Museum

wonder at the evident miracle—'*stupefactus est*', says the Vulgate—and throws himself at the feet of the Lord: 'Depart from me for I am a sinful man, O Lord', and Christ gently calms the excited man: 'Fear not'.

So much for the story. There are two boats on the open water, the net has been hauled in and there are fish everywhere, and, in this confusion, the scene between Christ and Peter takes place. The first great difficulty was to emphasise the principal figures among so many men and so much incidental material, especially as Christ could hardly be otherwise than seated. Raphael made the boats small, unnaturally small, in order to ensure the domination of the figures, just as Leonardo treated the table in the *Last Supper*: the classic style sacrifices actuality to the essential. The flat boats are close together, both seem almost entirely unforeshortened, with the first overlapping the second only a little, and the representation of all the toil is relegated to the second boat, further away, where two young men are drawing in the net—Raphael was the first to show the draught completed—and the oarsman is seated, balancing the boat with difficulty. However, these figures have no independent existence in the composition, serving only as a preparation or introduction to the group in the nearer boat where Peter kneels before Christ. With astonishing skill Raphael brought all the occupants of the boats into one major line, beginning with the oarsman, rising over the two men bending forward, coming to a climax in the standing figure and then turning abruptly downwards, rising again to its conclusion in the figure of Christ: everything leads up to Him, He is the goal of all the action, and, although quite small as a mass and placed at the very edge of the picture, He dominates everything. No one had composed like this before.

The pose of the central standing figure is decisive in the total impression and it is noteworthy that it was determined only at the last moment: it had been decided quite early that an upright figure was necessary at this point in the picture, but the original plan was for an oarsman who played no greater part in the action than that of being needed in the boat. Then Raphael decided the emotional tension needed heightening and he included the man (he must be identified with Andrew) in Peter's action, thus adding unusual impressiveness to the act of adoration. The kneeling movement is, as it were, shown in two phases of development, and by using two simultaneous images in this way it is possible for the visual arts to achieve the impossible—the effect of successive movements. Raphael frequently used this method, as witness the horseman and his attendants in the *Heliodorus*. The group is worked out with perfect rhythmic freedom, yet it has the inevitability of an architectural composition and every part, down to the last detail, is related to the whole; each line is calculated to fit in with its counterparts elsewhere, and every detail of the picture-surface seems to exist solely for the subject which is contained in it. For this reason the composition as a whole seems full of repose. The shapes of the landscape are also created with a definite pictorial purpose: the line of the river bank exactly follows the ascending contour of the figure group, then there is a gap on the horizon, and only above Christ does a hilly bank recur, so that the landscape gives emphasis to the important cæsura in the figure composition. Earlier works had trees, hills and valleys on the principle of the more the better, but now landscape is used in the same way as architecture, to help the figures. Even the birds, which formerly flew aimlessly about, are here brought in to aid the principal action; flying towards us from the background the nearest one drops downwards exactly where the cæsura occurs, so that even the wind is pressed into the service of the general movements.

The apparent strangeness of the high horizon is probably to be explained by Raphael's desire to give his figures the uniform, quiet background of a sheet of water, and, in doing so, he repeated the lesson he had learned from Perugino's *Christ giving the Keys to St. Peter*, which shows precisely the same intentions in placing the buildings far into the background. In contrast to the uniform, mirror-surface of the water, the foreground is animated and broken up, and a piece of the bank is visible although the scene should take place on the open

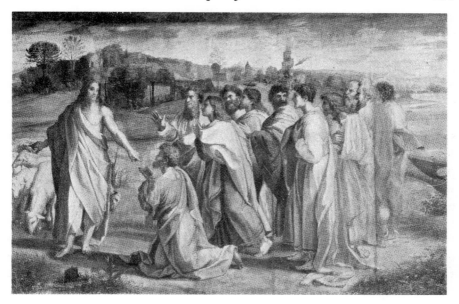

70. RAPHAEL: *'Feed my sheep'*. Cartoon. Victoria and Albert Museum

water.[1] Some herons stand on the bank, superb birds but perhaps too conspicuous if the picture is known only from black and white reproductions; in
the tapestry itself their brownish tones are quite close to the tone of the water
and, by comparison with the luminous tones of the figures, they attract little
notice. Raphael's *Miraculous Draught*, along with Leonardo's *Last Supper*, is one
of those representations of a theme which cannot henceforth be conceived
otherwise. How much even Rubens is inferior to Raphael! By the one motive,
that of making Christ spring up, his representation of the scene loses its nobility.

'*Feed my Sheep*'. Raphael's theme here is similar to one already painted by
Perugino in the Sistine Chapel, the place for which the tapestries were designed.
Perugino's was the *Delivery of the Keys* (Matthew XVI. 19); here it is the words
of the Lord, 'Feed my sheep' (John XXI. 15–17). The motive is basically the
same and it is immaterial whether Peter already holds the keys or not:[2] in order
to make the sense clear it was necessary to include an actual flock of sheep in the
picture and Christ gives expression to the command by an energetic gesture of
both arms, so that what in Perugino is only an emotional pose is here an effective
action, and the moment is perpetuated with historical seriousness. This seriousness is to be found also in the kneeling figure of St. Peter, gazing intensely

---

[1]Was it from a sense of style that Raphael wanted to have something solid in the foreground?
Botticelli, too, in his *Birth of Venus* did not bring the water right up to the edge; and although the
Galatea is a contrary example, a mural painting is not bound by the same considerations.
[2]Raphael's original intention was to show Peter without the keys.

upwards, and filled with a sense of the urgency of the moment. And the others? Perugino has a row of beautiful standing poses and tilted heads: what else could he do? The Disciples have nothing to do, and it was awkward that there were so many of them since it makes the scene somewhat monotonous. Raphael adds something new and unexpected, for they stand bunched closely together with Peter scarcely separated from the mass, but in this crowd there is the greatest variety of expressions—the nearest, attracted to the radiant form of Christ, devour Him with their eyes and are ready to fall on their knees like Peter; then there is a pause, a feeling of doubt, a questioning interplay of glances, and finally a distinct holding back in distrust. Such a treatment of the theme requires great power of psychological expression, quite outside the range of the earlier generation.[1]

In Perugino's fresco, Christ and St. Peter occupy the centre of the picture and the spectators are grouped symmetrically on either side; here Christ stands alone and apart from all the others, not turned towards them, but walking past them so that the Disciples see Him only from the side—in a moment from now He will have vanished. He is the only figure on whom the light falls fully, while all the others have the light behind them.

The Healing of the Lame Man. The first question which is always asked in front of this picture is: what do these great twisted columns mean? The spectator has the buildings of the Quattrocento in his head, open and lucid constructions, and it is difficult to grasp how Raphael arrived at the elephantine forms which take up so much of the picture. It can be shown that the source of the idea of twisted columns is in St. Peter's, where such a column is preserved which, according to tradition, came from the Temple of Jerusalem; and the Beautiful Gate of that Temple was the scene of the healing of the lame man. Yet the really striking thing is not so much this peculiarity of form as the linking of the figures with the architecture: Raphael does not use the columns as coulisses or as a background, but to form a hall to enclose the spectators, a whole throng of them, and in this way he gets his effect with comparatively simple means, since the columns themselves occupy a good part of the picture space. It is now easy to see how desirable the columns were as divisions and as a means of enframing the main subject, since the neat rows of bystanders of the Quattrocento painters were no longer good enough, and yet, if a real press of people were to be painted it meant running the risk of losing the principal figures in the crowd. This risk has been avoided here, but the spectator notices the happy effect of this disposition long before he sees how it was done.

---

[1]Another interpretation of the picture is possible—that it shows some doubt among the Apostles as to whether the Resurrected Christ who appears to them is indeed He or an illusion. This interpretation would be kinder to the Apostles, but it is not the accepted ecclesiastical one.

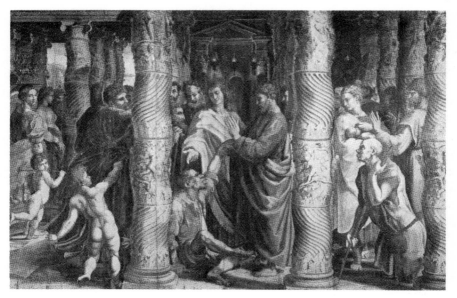

71. RAPHAEL: *Peter and John at the Beautiful Gate*. Cartoon. Victoria and Albert Museum

The scene of the actual healing is a good example of the virile style which Raphael had by now evolved for such subjects. The healer does not strike an attitude, for he is no conjuror pronouncing magic formulas, but the man of power, the physician, who quite simply takes the cripple by the hand and blesses him with his own right hand. The whole thing takes place with the minimum of fuss and the Apostle remains quite upright, only bending his powerful neck a little, where earlier artists made him bend right down to the sufferer; yet Raphael's way makes the raising up seem miraculous. St. Peter gazes steadfastly at the cripple, who looks at him eagerly and expectantly: they are profile to profile and the nervous energy passing between them is almost tangible. There is no other representation of the scene of such psychic insight.

St. Peter is accompanied by St. John, standing by with slightly bowed head and a gesture of friendly encouragement, while the cripple has his antithesis in a fellow-cripple who looks on stupidly and spitefully. A variety of different expressions is presented by the crowd pressing forward in curiosity or doubt, and some completely indifferent passers-by serve as a neutral foil for the others, while a different kind of contrast is afforded in this picture of human misery by the introduction of two naked children, idealized in form, whose luminous flesh shines out of the picture.

The Death of Ananias is a thankless task for a painter, since it is impossible to represent his death as the consequence of disobedience: it is possible to paint the

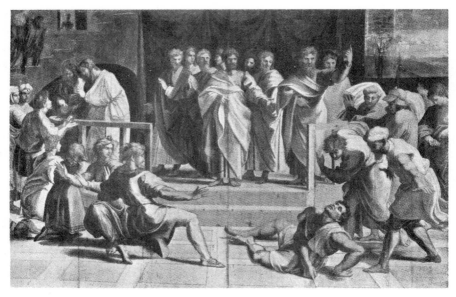

72. RAPHAEL: *The Death of Ananias*. Cartoon. Victoria and Albert Museum

collapse of Ananias, the surprise and terror of the bystanders, but how is it possible to point the moral that this is the death of a transgressor? Raphael has done everything possible to express at least the outward story in a rigidly composed picture, with the body of Apostles raised like a chorus upon a central podium, a closed and most impressive group before a dark background. To the left, the goods of the community are brought in, to be divided at the right, an arrangement which is both simple and clear: then in the foreground comes the dramatic event, with Ananias convulsed upon the ground. The people nearest him recoil in horror, and the circle of these foreground figures is so constructed that Ananias, in collapsing backwards, tears a hole in the composition which is visible even at a distance, and this shows why everything else in the picture is so rigidly ordered: for this one asymmetry is the more powerfully reinforced by it. Like a thunderbolt, the judgement has torn the ranks apart and struck down its victim. The relationship of this to the upper group of the Apostles is now perfectly clear, for they represent Destiny. The eye is led directly to the centre, where St. Peter stands, a minatory arm outstretched, yet it is not an excited gesture and Peter does not fulminate: he merely pronounces the judgement of God. The Apostles themselves remain calm and unaffected by the occurrence and only the crowd, ignorant of the sequence of events, breaks up in violent agitation. They are few in number but Raphael makes each one a type of intense and amazed horror and each has been repeated, times without number, in the art of the following centuries, for they became academic exercises in expression, causing endless mischief by transplanting these Italian gesticulations on to Northern soil. Yet even the Italians themselves lost, from time to time, the feeling for the natural in such a language of gesture and lapsed into conventional gesticulation; and we, as foreigners, are in no position to judge how far the gestures in this picture are still natural, but it can safely be said that here we can very clearly observe the transformation of the 'character head' into the 'expressive head'—the interest in the expression of passion and emotion had become so strong in itself that individuality of feature in the painting of a head was renounced in favour of this expressiveness.

The Blinding of Elymas. Elymas the sorcerer was struck with sudden blindness when he tried to prevent the Apostle Paul from converting the proconsul of Cyprus: it is the old story of the Christian Saint triumphing over his adversary in the presence of a pagan ruler, and the idea of the composition which Raphael used is thus the same as that which was already known to Giotto when he painted the fresco in Santa Croce of St. Francis and the priests of Mahomet before the Sultan. The proconsul is in the middle with the opposing parties on either side of him, just as Giotto arranged it, but here the story is told with greater dramatic concentration; Elymas has pressed forward towards the centre of the stage when

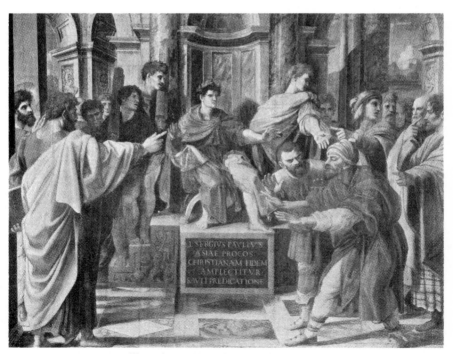

73. RAPHAEL: *Elymas struck blind.* Cartoon. Victoria and Albert Museum

the darkness falls upon him and he recoils, throwing out both hands and twisting his head upwards, the unsurpassed image of blindness. Paul stands quite calmly, right at the edge of the picture and turned three-quarters into it; his face is in shadow and in *profil perdu*, while the light falls full on Elymas. His arm stretched out towards Elymas is eloquent, not impassioned, but most impressive because of the simple conjunction of the horizontal with the powerful vertical of his calm and erect figure: he is the rock from which evil must recoil. Compared with these protagonists the other figures would be of little interest, even if they were less indifferently executed. Sergius, the proconsul, who is only a spectator, throws back his arms in the characteristic Cinquecento gesture, which may have been part of the original design, but the remaining spectators are more or less super-fluous and distracting extras who give a rather restless effect to the picture when combined with the florid architecture and certain rather petty, picturesque details. Raphael does not seem to have supervised the completion of the work.

This impression is still more strongly conveyed by the *Sacrifice at Lystra*. This very famous picture is a complete enigma, for no one could guess that a sick man had been healed and that the people wish to sacrifice, as to a god, to the man who worked the miracle, and that he, the Apostle Paul, is so enraged by this that he rends his garments. The principal emphasis is laid on the reproduction of an antique scene of sacrifice, imitated from an antique sarcophagus relief, and the interests of archæology take precedence over all else. The full use made of the prototype is, in itself, enough to make one rather dubious about Raphael's

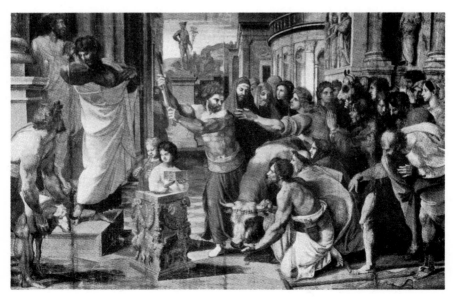

74. RAPHAEL: *Paul and Barnabas at Lystra*. Cartoon. Victoria and Albert Museum

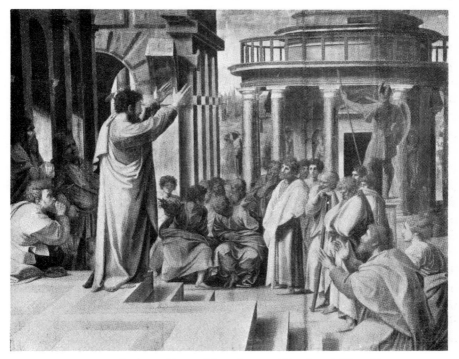

75. RAPHAEL: *Paul preaching at Athens*. Cartoon. Victoria and Albert Museum

authorship, and, in addition, every deviation from the model is for the worse, for the composition is awkward in its spatial relationships and confused in the main lines of direction.

On the other hand, the picture of *Paul preaching at Athens* is a great original invention. The preacher, both arms upraised, is a figure of great seriousness, without any attitudinizing or the rhetorical effect of agitated draperies. He is seen only from the side, almost from the rear, raised above his audience and preaching into the picture, standing almost on the very edge of the steps, and this advance gives him an urgent air in spite of the general calm. His face is in shadow and all the expression is concentrated into the noble simplicity of outline of the figure which resounds triumphantly through the picture—all the preaching saints of the fifteenth century are but tinkling cymbals beside this orator.

The figures of the audience below are much smaller, as a deliberate calculation, and the effect of the sermon, as shown in so many faces, was a task much to the taste of Raphael in those years. Some individual figures are worthy of him, others give an irresistible feeling of another hand at work, particularly in the clumsy heads at the front. The architecture is a trifle obtrusive: the background of St. Paul is well adapted to its position, but the circular temple (Bramante's) would have been better replaced by something different. The statue of Mars, strengthening the diagonal movement, effectively corresponds to the Christian preacher.

Those compositions which are extant only in the tapestries and of which the cartoons are lost, may be omitted save for the important proviso of a note on the relation between the cartoon and the executed tapestry. As is well known, the working of a tapestry involves reversing the cartoon, as in a mirror, and one would expect to find the cartoons allowing for this. Strangely enough, not all of them do so. The *Miraculous Draught*, the *Charge to Peter*, the *Healing of the Lame Man*, and the *Death of Ananias* are so drawn that their full effect appears only in the tapestry, while the *Sacrifice at Lystra* and the *Blinding of Elymas* lose by reversal, and the *Sermon at Athens* is not affected either way.[1] It is not merely a question of the left hand becoming the right when reversed so that, for example, a benediction made with the left hand spoils the effect; it is that a composition by Raphael in this style cannot be reversed at will without losing some part of its beauty. As a result of a disposition reinforced by upbringing, Raphael leads the eye from left to right, and the flow of the composition goes in this direction even in works like the *Disputà* which have no active movement, while the same is true of the great dramatic pictures—Heliodorus has to be expelled towards the right-hand corner, since the movement appears so much more convincing that way. When, in the *Miraculous Draught*, Raphael wishes to lead us along the curve of the fishermen up to the figure of Christ, it is again natural for him to go from left to right; but when he wants to make the violent staggering backwards of Ananias even more emphatic, he makes him collapse in a direction contradicting the general tendency.

6. The Roman Portraits

In passing from the history pictures to the portraits it may well be said that the portrait was now destined to become a history picture. Quattrocento portraits have a somewhat naive air, as of studies from models, giving the form of the person without searching for characteristic expression, and the sitters gaze out from the pictures with equanimity and in a pose taken for granted. The aim was a striking likeness, not the portrayal of a characteristic mood. There are exceptions, but the general rule was to be content with grasping and recording the permanent forms of the sitter's head, and it did not seem to impair the impression of living actuality if conventional attitudes were retained.

---

[1] Yet it seems to require reversal, since it is only thus that the figure of Mars can be made to hold his shield and spear correctly.

The new art demanded the specifically personal approach, the effect of a given moment in an individual life, as lived by that person. The form of the head is no longer sufficient in itself but expression must be reinforced by movement and gesture: a dramatic style is evolved from a descriptive one. The heads themselves possess a new expressive vigour, and it is quickly seen that this art possesses greater resources of characterization, utilising chiaroscuro, outline and the distribution of masses in depth, all in order to obtain a specific and characteristic expression. For the same reason, to allow the essential personality to make the strongest possible impression, certain forms are emphasised above others, where the Quattrocento had treated every part with almost equal thoroughness.

This style is not to be found in Raphael's Florentine portraits, for it was in Rome that he first became a painter of human beings. Like a butterfly, the youthful artist fluttered around the visual appearance, for, as yet, he completely lacked a firm grasp of form, and the power of extracting its significance for character. The *Maddalena Doni* is a superficial portrait and, to me, it seems impossible to ascribe the excellent portrait of a woman (the so-called *Doni's Sister*) in the Tribuna to the same painter—at that time, Raphael obviously did not have an eye which could absorb so much.[1] His development presents a curious spectacle in that the grandeur of the style is accompanied by increasing grasp of characterization.

The first of the great works was undoubtedly the portrait of Julius II (in the Uffizi),[2] which really merits the name of a history picture, for the Pope is seated with his head bent, his mouth firmly closed in a moment of reflection, so that it is not a picture of a posed model but a fragment of history—the Pope in a typical attitude. The eyes no longer look at the spectator; the eye-sockets are in shadow so that the rock-like forehead and the strong nose are emphasised and form the principal elements of expression with a uniform high light over them; these are the accentuations needed by the new style and later they would have been still more strongly emphasised—how one wishes that Sebastiano del Piombo had also painted this head!

The *Leo X* in the Pitti (*Fig.* 76) presented a different problem, for the Pope had a thick fleshy face with fat concealing the form and it was necessary to divert attention from the sallow expanse of flesh by the charm of the play of light and by allowing the spirituality of the head to shine through in such things as the refinement of the nostrils and the wit of the sensuous and eloquent mouth. The dim, short-sighted eye has acquired a notable power without altering its

---

[1]Davidson's arguments in *Repertorium*, 1900, XXIII, p. 211, would lead one to drop the identification with Maddalena Doni, even if the authorship of Raphael is not abandoned. I believe the Tribuna female portrait to be by Perugino, for its close relationship with the 'Timete Deum' portrait in the Uffizi (Francesco dell' Opera, *Fig.* 78) seems to make this conclusion inescapable.
[2]The Pitti version is certainly later and it is a question whether it is by Raphael himself.

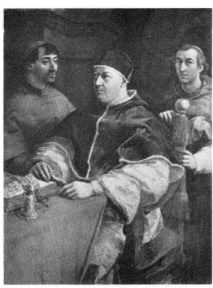

76. RAPHAEL: *Pope Leo X*. Pitti

character. The Pope is represented in the act of glancing up from an illuminated manuscript which he has been studying, and there is something in the glance which characterizes the ruler better than if he had been portrayed enthroned and wearing the Tiara. The hands are perhaps even more individual and characteristic than those of Julius. The accompanying figures, very important in themselves, are yet only foils and, as such, subordinate to the chief motive.[1] Not one of the three heads is inclined and Raphael thus obtains a threefold vertical which gives a kind of hieratic stillness to the whole picture. Where the *Julius* has a uniform green background, here there is a wall with pilasters seen in perspective, which possesses the double advantage of heightening the illusion of plasticity and of offering both lighter and darker foils to the principal tones. But there has been a great toning down of the actual colour towards neutral tints, for the old-fashioned bright background has been abandoned, so that the foreground colours alone make a powerful impression, as in this case, where the Papal purple has the richest possible appearance in contrast to the greenish grey behind it.

A different kind of momentary animation was given by Raphael to the squinting scholar Inghirami (the original formerly in Volterra, now in Boston: old copy in the Pitti). Without underlining the natural defect and without concealing it, he was able to disregard the unfortunate effect because of the serious and spiritual expression he gave to the head. Here, an indifferent look would be unendurable, but the spiritual exaltation depicted in the upturned head of this scholar soon makes the spectator's attention take another turn. This portrait is one of the first he painted in Rome, and, if I mistake not, Raphael later would have avoided so strong an emphasis on momentary action and would have chosen a motive of greater repose for a portrait which was intended to bear close and repeated inspection. His art, in its perfection, could render the charm of the momentary even in apparent repose, as may be seen in the Louvre *Castiglione* (*Fig.* 77), extremely simple in pose, yet the slight tilt of

---

[1] Is it artistic licence that makes them appear so low down, or are we to assume that the Pope is seated on a dais ?

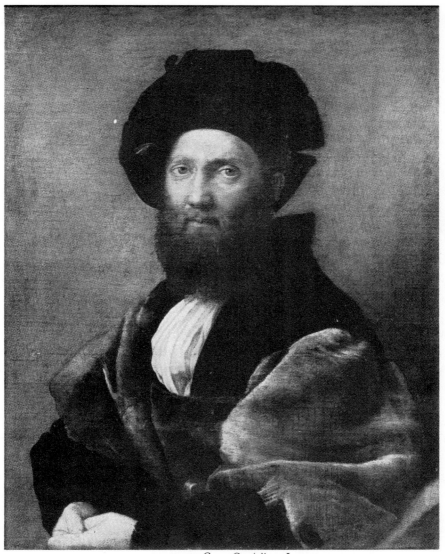

77. RAPHAEL: *Count Castiglione*. Louvre

the head and the folding of the hands have an infinitely personal and transitory quality. The man gazes calmly out of the picture, his soul in his eyes, yet without obtrusive sentiment, for Raphael was painting the aristocratic courtier, the embodiment of the complete gentleman, as described by Castiglione himself in his little book, 'Il Cortigiano', with modesty as the basic trait of his character. The nobility of the man is shown, not by any hauteur of bearing, but by his unpretentious and restrained calm, and the richness of the picture is due to

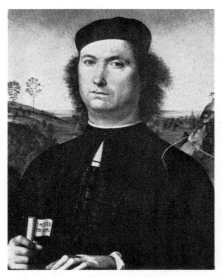

78. PERUGINO: *Francesco dell'Opera*. Uffizi

the twist of the figure—similar to that of the *Mona Lisa*—and the splendid distribution of the large masses in the costume. The silhouette has a grandiose effect best seen by comparison with an older picture, such as Perugino's male portrait in the Uffizi (*Fig.* 78), when it becomes clear at once that the figure has a totally new relationship to the space around it, so that the sitter's imposing appearance is greatly helped by the wide space around it and the large and simple plane of the background. Already the hands are beginning to disappear, for it seems that, in this size of portrait, there was a fear that the hands might distract attention from the head; and where the hands were intended to play an important part in the whole, the three-quarter-length type of portrait was evolved. Here the background is a neutral grey, with some cast shadows, and the costume is also grey (and black), so that the flesh parts alone are warm in tone, while the white of the shirt was employed in this kind of scheme also by other colourists such as Andrea del Sarto and Titian.

The clarification of outline perhaps reached its highest point in the Madrid *Portrait of a Cardinal* (*Fig.* 79), where the drawing is simple in the extreme, giving a total effect as large and reposeful as architecture: it is the very type of the great Italian prelate and one may well picture him in imagination walking noiselessly down vaulted corridors.[1]

---

[1]According to H. Hymans, the Madrid *Cardinal* represents the young Scaramuccia Trivulzio, Bishop of Como, and, from 1517, Cardinal (*Burlington Magazine*, 1911, XX, p. 89). R. Durrer thinks it is the Swiss, Matthäus Schinner, Bishop of Sitten (*Monatshefte für Kunstgeschichte*, 1913, p. 1), in which case the picture must have been painted in 1513. It is a fact that an identical, or at any rate very similar, head once passed for Schinner, although the medals which were made for Schinner himself show quite a different type.

By way of commentary on the illustration, here is the considered opinion of a modern painter. Israels (*Spanien*, Berlin, 1900) says of this 'modern masterpiece': 'There is no splendour of colour, no virtuosity; it is rather the thought, the soul, the character of the man which grip, enchain and seduce us. There is a rare economy of light and colour, for it is the triumph of the nobility of form. It is a tall figure, with the face eloquent of continence and peace, the eyes deep and penetrating, and the pallor of the thin and sallow cheeks distinguishing the man of the church and the convent. The finely curved nose betrays a patrician Italian origin and the lightly closed lips the man of reflection and gentleness. This one portrait has more poetry in it than many a picture of saints and angels hanging there (in the Prado).'

The question of identity is still debatable and Müntz's essay (in *Archivio storico dell'Arte*, 1890) does not seem to me to throw any further light on it, but the *Cicerone* (presumably relying on Passavant's opinion) is definitely wrong in saying that the *Cardinal Bibbiena* of the Pitti is an 'inferior copy' of the Madrid *Cardinal*. There is no connection whatever between the two pictures.

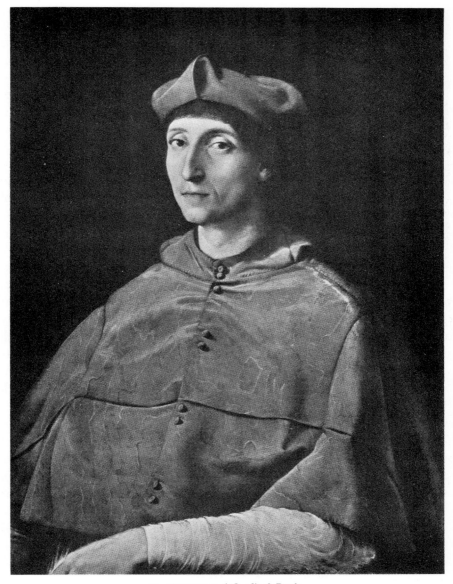

79. RAPHAEL: *A Cardinal*. Prado

The portraits of the two Venetian *literati*, Navagero and Beazzano, in the Doria Gallery, are not absolutely certainly by Raphael himself, but they are splendid examples of the new style and saturated with character and life: Navagero's pose is a stressed vertical, the head twisted sharply to look back over the shoulder and a diffused light falling on his bull-neck, with the emphasis

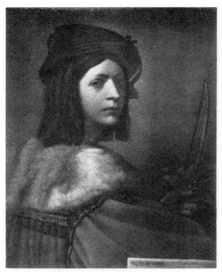

80. SEBASTIANO DEL PIOMBO: *The Violinist.*
Rothschild Collection

everywhere on the bone structure so that the total effect is one of an active man, where the antithesis is Beazzano, the passive Epicurean, his head gently inclined and softly illuminated.

The *Violinist* (formerly Sciarra, Rome; now Alphonse Rothschild, Paris) has also been given to Raphael, but is now generally regarded as by Sebastiano del Piombo (*Fig.* 80). This most attractive head, with its questioning glance and determined mouth which is eloquent of his calling, is remarkable as a Cinquecento conception of the portrait of an artist even when compared with Raphael's youthful *Self-portrait*, for it is not merely a difference of model, but a difference in approach, with its new restraint of expression and its incredible power and certainty of effect. Raphael had already tried pushing the head to one side of the picture, but Sebastiano goes still further and he also gives a slight, almost imperceptible, tilt to the head. He uses a simple kind of lighting with one side entirely in shadow and the forms very sharply accentuated, and then there is the great contrast in direction with the head looking over the shoulder, and enough of the nearer arm is shown to make a decisive contrast of direction with the vertical of the head.

Raphael painted few female portraits and he left unsatisfied the curiosity of posterity as to the appearance of his 'Fornarina'. Here again, at one time, Sebastiano's pictures were borrowed, rechristened Raphael, and any beautiful woman was regarded as his *inamorata*, as for example, the *Venetian Girl* of the Tribuna, or the so-called *Dorothea* (formerly Blenheim, now Berlin): nowadays, we try to make up for it by taking the *Donna Velata* (Pitti), which is an accepted Raphael, to be not only the model for the *Sistine Madonna*, but also an idealized portrait of the sought-for Fornarina. The first relationship is obvious; the second has, at any rate, an old tradition behind it.

The '*Fornarina*' of 1512 in the Tribuna is a somewhat mediocre piece of Venetian prettiness and is, in any case, far surpassed by the Berlin *Dorothea* (*Fig.* 81), a later work, which already possesses the aristocratic composure, the grand rhythms and the amplitude of movement of the High Renaissance, so that one is involuntarily reminded of Andrea del Sarto's beautiful wife in his *Birth of the Virgin* of 1514. In contrast to Sebastiano's voluptuous creatures,

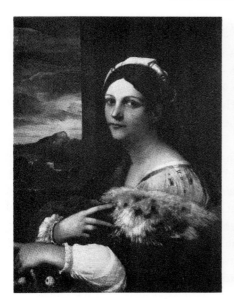
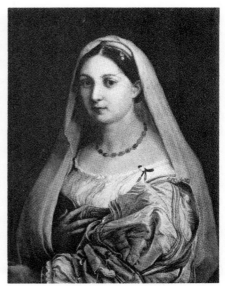

81. SEBASTIANO DEL PIOMBO: *Dorothea.*
Berlin, Museum

82. RAPHAEL: *Donna Velata.* Pitti

Raphael shows us exalted womanhood in his *Donna Velata* (*Fig.* 82): her bearing is majestically upright, her costume rich but subdued by the solemn sweep of the unifying, simple head-cloth, and her glance is not searching, so much as steady and unwavering. The flesh gains in warmth against the neutral background and even holds its own against the white satin. Comparison with an earlier female portrait, such as the *Maddalena Doni*, at once shows the grand grasp of form of this style and the certainty with which effects are combined into a whole, but the basis of it all is a conception of human dignity which the young Raphael did not yet possess.

The *Donna Velata* shows so striking a similarity to the *Dorothea* in its general lay-out, that the idea that both may have been painted in some sort of rivalry constantly recurs. A third picture might be added if one considers at the same time *La Bella* (formerly Sciarra Collection, now Alphonse Rothschild, Paris), which is certainly an early Titian,[1] and, in any case, must date from this period. It would be an instructive sight if we could see, hanging side by side, these three examples of the new ideal of beauty developed by the Cinquecento.

From this prototype of the *Sistine Madonna* we must hasten on to the picture itself, but the road has several stages, and of the Roman altar-pieces, the *St. Cecilia* has the right to be taken first.

---

[1] It is now generally ascribed to Palma, but its similarity to the so-called *Maîtresse de Titien* in the Salon Carré of the Louvre is so evident that it would seem advisable to return to the old attribution.

7. Roman Altar-Pieces

THE *St. Cecilia* of the Pinacoteca at Bologna (*Fig.* 83) is a group of standing saints, the name-saint and four others—Paul and the Magdalen, a Bishop (Augustine) and John the Evangelist, with St. Cecilia, in no way specially distinguished but like a sister of the others. She has let her organ fall to the ground and is listening to the song of the angels above their heads. This tender figure bears the unmistakable stamp of Umbria, and yet, when one makes the comparison with Perugino it is astonishing to see how restrained Raphael is: the placing of the foot which bears no weight and the backward tilt of the head are different from Perugino, and simpler than he would have made them. There is no longer the yearning type of face with open mouth, the sentimentality in which Raphael himself still revelled when he painted the London *St. Catherine*, for the now mature artist gives less, but he makes that less the more effective by contrasts and he calculates on pictorial effects which have a permanent quality, for a single head with an overdone expression of rapture soon palls, where a picture retains its freshness if the expressive parts are restrained and suggestive of yet greater depths, and if contrasts are developed between the different figures. St. Paul and the Magdalen are to be understood thus: Paul, as virile, collected, gazing straight before him, the Magdalen quite indifferent in expression and serving simply as a foil, while the other two stand apart and whisper together. It does harm to the artist's intention to take the principal figure and isolate it, as some modern engravers have done, for the feeling of the whole picture requires completing, just as much as the pose of the head needs a counterpart. The upward direction of St. Cecilia's glance needs the counter-acting downcast eyes of St. Paul, and the Magdalen, who plays no active part, adds a pure vertical, a plumb-line by which all the slight variations from the perpendicular can be measured.

This is not the place to pursue an analysis of the compositional contrasts in the placing and aspect of the figures, but it may be remarked that Raphael is still very moderate, for none of his successors would have grouped together five standing figures without introducing some much stronger contrast or movement.

The related engraving by Marcantonio (B. 116) is an interesting variant of the composition, for if one is to accept Raphael as the designer—and indeed one must accept this—it must have been an earlier project, since it lacks the concentration of the picture, and just those features which give interest to the painting are absent from the engraving. In it, the Magdalen also looks emotionally upwards and so enters into competition with the principal figure, while the two saints at the back press obtrusively forward: in the painting, which is the revised

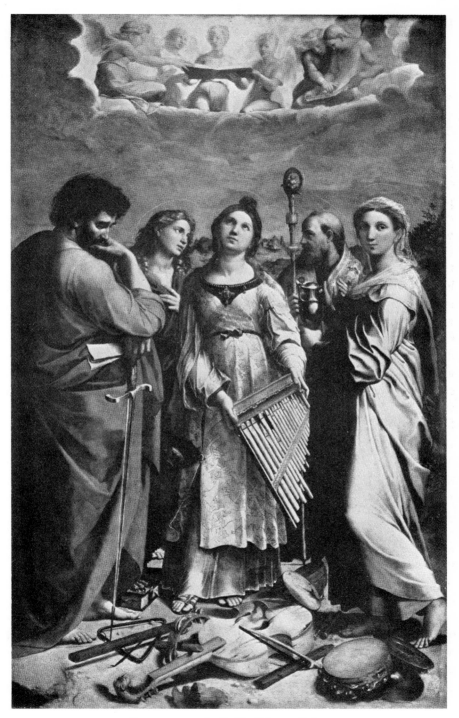

83. RAPHAEL: *St. Cecilia*. Bologna, Gallery

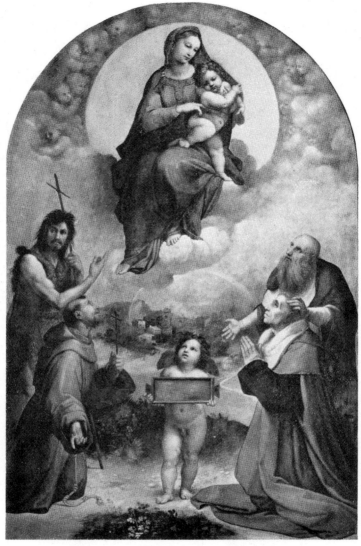

84. RAPHAEL: *The Madonna of Foligno*. Vatican

edition, the step which is the mark of all progress is first taken, namely, sub-ordination instead of co-ordination, selection of motives, so that each occurs only once, but in its own place each makes an integral and stable part of the composition.

The *Madonna of Foligno*, in the Vatican (*Fig.* 84), must date from about the same time as the *St. Cecilia*, somewhere about 1512. The theme is that of the Madonna in Glory, an old motive, but to some extent novel since it was not

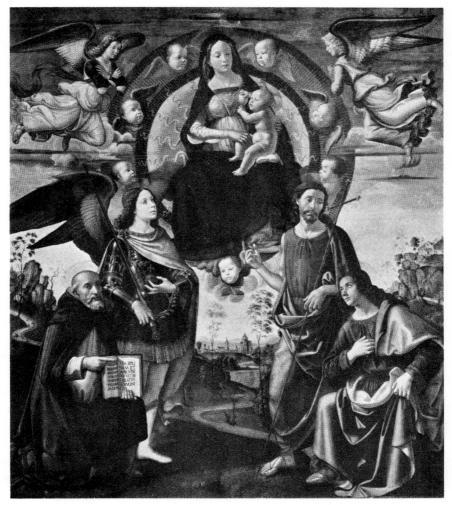

85. GHIRLANDAIO: *The Madonna in Glory*. Munich, Pinakothek

often treated in the Quattrocento. That century, unembarrassed by ecclesiastical conceptions, preferred the Madonna to be seated on a solid throne rather than floating in the air, but the changed emotional climate of the sixteenth and seventeenth centuries, which tended towards a sharper separation between earthly and heavenly things, preferred this idealized scheme for altar-pieces. For comparison, there is a picture painted right at the end of the Quattrocento— Ghirlandaio's *Madonna in Glory*, formerly on the high altar of Santa Maria Novella and now in Munich (*Fig.* 85). As in the *Madonna of Foligno*, there are four men standing on the earth below, and even then Ghirlandaio felt the need of contrasts in the action, for, as in Raphael, two of them kneel, although the latter surpasses his predecessor both by the variety and intensity of the physical and spiritual contrasts beyond all comparison with Ghirlandaio, and, at the same time, Raphael's contrasts are linked with one another. The figures have to be treated in such a way that the spiritual and emotional unity is maintained as well as the physical one, whereas in the older altar-piece no exception could have been taken to the way in which the saints stand about without any inner relationship to the subject.

One of the kneeling figures in the *Foligno Madonna* is the donor, an unusually ugly man, but the grave and important treatment of the head makes one forget his ugliness as he kneels in prayer, with his patron, St. Jerome, laying one hand on his head and presenting him to the Madonna and Child. His somewhat conventional attitude of prayer is felicitously contrasted with the figure of St. Francis gazing fervidly upwards, as if to show how the saints pray, while with one hand he gestures outwards to include the whole congregation of the faithful in his intercession. The whole upward movement of St. Francis is echoed, and the effect increased, by the upraised arm of the Baptist behind him.

The halo around the Madonna is softened and dissolved in a painterly way, but not completely so, for the old-fashioned, rigidly designed disc is retained as part of the background, but the clouds are made to flow around it while the accompanying putti, to whom the Quattrocento conceded at most a little scrap of cloud on which to rest one foot, can now tumble about in their element like fish in water.

The seated pose of the Madonna is a particularly fine motive, but, as has been said already, it is not one of his invention: the different levels of the feet, the twist of the body, the tilt of the head, go back to Leonardo's Madonna in the *Adoration of the Kings (Fig.* 10).

The Christ Child is affected in His attitude, but it was a charming thought to have made Him look down, not to the praying donor as His mother does, but to the putto who stands below, between the men, and looks upward himself. What is the meaning of this naked boy with his tablet? It could be said that it was desirable in any case to have some childish innocence among all the grave and serious men, but the boy is also indispensable as a formal link, for there is a hole in the picture at this point. Ghirlandaio did not bother about this, but the Cinquecento concept of style demanded that the masses in the picture should be kept in touch, and, above all, a horizontal was necessary at this point. Raphael met the need with a boy-angel holding a blank tablet: that is the idealism of great art.

Raphael's effects are broader and yet more massive than those of Ghirlandaio. The Madonna is so low down in the picture that her foot is level with the shoulders of the standing figures, while the lower figures are brought right up to the edge of the frame so that the eye cannot see behind them into the remainder of the landscape as was the case with earlier pictures, which, as a result, have a rather loose and thin effect.[1]

The *Madonna with the Fish* (Madrid, Prado). This *Madonna del Pesce* (*Fig.* 86) is Raphael's Roman version of the Virgin enthroned—'Maria in Trono'. A Madonna was required with two accompanying figures, St. Jerome and the Archangel Gabriel, who was usually accompanied by the boy Tobias with his fish as a distinguishing attribute of the Archangel, but where the boy used formerly to stand lost at one side, notable only for being a disturbing feature, he is now changed into the central figure of an episode so that the old-fashioned typical votive picture is itself transformed into a history picture, the presentation of Tobias to the Madonna by his guardian angel. There may be no special allusion in this: it is simply a consequence of Raphael's art, which sought organic relationships for everything in a picture. St. Jerome kneels on the other side of the throne, glancing up for a moment from his book to look at the group with the angel, while the Christ Child, who seems to have been turned towards him, has now twisted round to face the new-comers, pointing with childish interest but leaving His other hand still in the old man's book. The Virgin, very aloof and aristocratic, glances down at Tobias without moving her head: she represents the pure vertical in the composition. The timid boy approaching her and the enchanting angel, of truly Leonardesque softness and delicacy, together form a group which is unique in the world. The upward glance of the interceding angel is reinforced by the diagonal line of the green curtain, which exactly echoes the direction of his glance, and with its sharp contrast to the bright sky, this curtain forms the only decorative adjunct in a highly simplified composition. The throne is of a Peruginesque simplicity and the richness of the picture is due solely to the interlocking of all movement and the close grouping of the figures. As Frizzoni has recently shown, the execution of the picture is not original but the perfect coherence of the composition leaves no room for doubt that Raphael watched over the work to the very end.

The *Sistine Madonna* (Dresden). No longer seated on clouds, as in the *Madonna of Foligno*, but standing erect and gliding over the clouds like a momentary apparition, the Madonna which Raphael painted in this picture for the Carthusians of Piacenza is accompanied by St. Barbara and Pope Sixtus II, from whom the picture takes its name. As the merits of this picture have been discussed from so many angles already it is not necessary to mention more than a few points here (*Fig.* 87).

---

[1]The landscape was recognized as Ferrarese in type by Crowe and Cavalcaselle (Dosso Dossi), and perhaps the celebrated 'meteor' in the background is one of the well-known Ferrarese displays of fireworks and should not have any further significance attached to it. It goes without saying that the meticulously executed tufts of grass in the foreground are by this other hand.

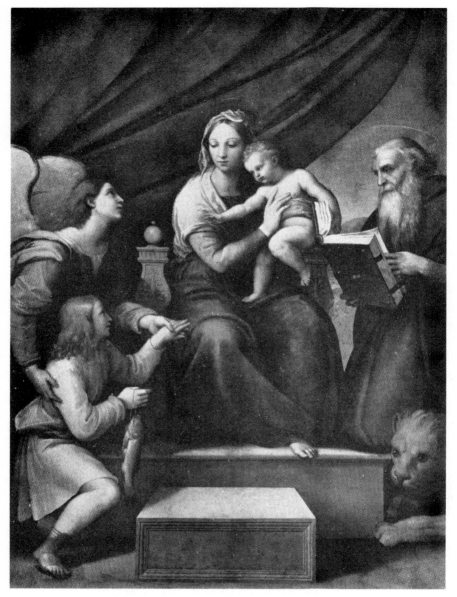

86. RAPHAEL: *The Madonna with the Fish*. Prado

The idea of a figure emerging directly out of the picture and bearing down on the spectator is inevitably connected with a certain unpleasantness of effect, although there are indeed certain modern works which aim at just this crudity, but Raphael has used every means to arrest the movement and

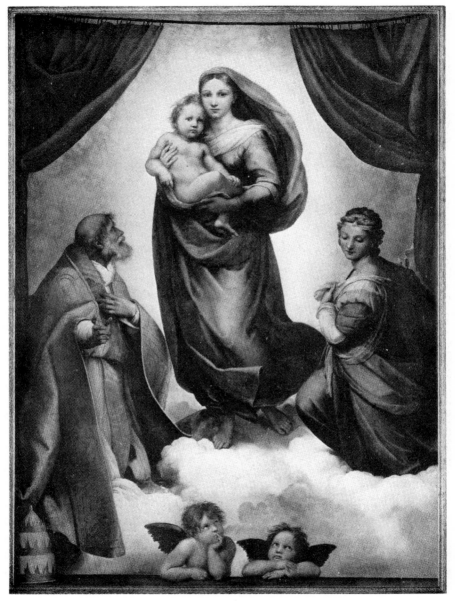

87. RAPHAEL: *The Sistine Madonna*. Dresden, Gallery

keep it within strict limits; nor is it difficult to discover what these means were.

The movement itself is a wonderfully light, floating progression and the miracle is only partially explained by an analysis of the special way in which the

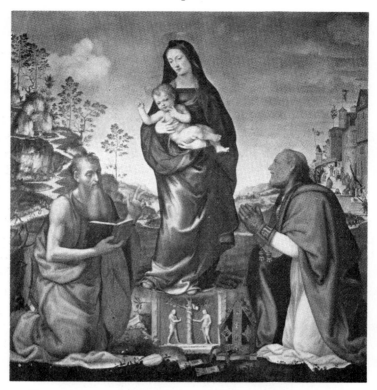

88. ALBERTINELLI: *The Madonna and Child with two Saints.* Louvre

weight of the body is distributed to maintain equilibrium, or of the use of line in the billowing mantle and the ends of the drapery which seem to be blown gently backwards. It is also significant that the saints on either side are not kneeling on the clouds but sinking into them, and that the feet of the Virgin herself are in shadow while the light irradiates only the crests of the waves in the sea of clouds, an effect which greatly heightens the feeling that she is borne along on them. The whole picture is so planned that the central figure has no counterpart but only favourable contrasts: she alone is standing and the others kneel—and kneel at a lower level[1]—she alone appears in a fully frontal pose, a pure vertical, a simple mass completely silhouetted against the bright background, while the others are tied to the edge of the frame, their costumes broken up into several parts and fragmentary as masses, not ends in themselves but existing only in relation to the figure in the centre of the picture, to which the utmost clarity and power is reserved. She is the norm, the others are variations from it which yet seem ordered by some hidden law: the main directions of

[1]Compare the arrangement of Albertinelli's picture of 1506 in the Louvre (*Fig.* 88) which is in every respect a most instructive parallel to the *Sistine Madonna.*

movement are clearly counterpoised—the upwards glance of the Pope must be balanced by the downward-looking St. Barbara, the outward pointing gesture of the one by the inward-reaching of the other[1]. Nothing is left to chance. The Pope looks up at the Madonna and St. Barbara looks down at the children on the edge of the frame, ensuring that the spectator's eye is at once led along determined lines.

It need hardly be stressed that the figure of the Virgin, almost architectural in its power, is accompanied by a curious touch of timidity in the expression of the face: she is only the bearer of the Godhead, who is the Child in her arms, carried there not because He cannot walk, but because He is a Prince. His body is of superhuman proportions and the way in which He lies has in it something of the heroic. The Child is not giving a benediction but gazes unwaveringly at the people before Him, unlike ordinary children, and He has a fixity in His look which children do not have. His hair is dishevelled and on end, like a prophet's. At the bottom of the picture, the two child angels represent ordinary nature, as a foil to the superhuman. Has it been observed that the larger of them has but one wing? Raphael avoided the overlapping of a second wing for he did not want too massive an effect at the base, a licence which is all of a piece with others of the classic style. The picture has to be hung high up for the Madonna should be seen as descending, and, if hung too low, the best effect is lost. The frame which was added in Dresden is perhaps a little too heavy for it and the figures would gain by the removal of the big pilasters.[2]

The *Transfiguration* (Vatican). This picture really consists of two separate scenes, the Transfiguration in the upper part and the boy possessed of a devil below it, a combination of subjects which is obviously unusual and which was chosen by Raphael on this one occasion only, and this is his last word on the grand style in narrative painting (*Fig. 90*).

The Transfiguration has always been an awkward subject, since it demands

---

[1] The two female saints in Fra Bartolommeo's *God the Father*, of 1509, in Lucca (*Fig. 94*), are a prototype of this.

[2] Many good engravings exist of the *Sistine Madonna*, of which the first was F. Müller's (1815), a much admired masterpiece of the engraver's art which many even now consider the best of all the reproductions. The expression of the faces comes very close to the original and the plate possesses an incomparably soft and beautiful radiance. There is a copy of it by Nordheim. The next to essay the task was Steinla (1848), who first gave the top edge of the picture—the curtain-rod—correctly, but in spite of some improvement in details he did not reach the level of Müller's work. If any engraving can be compared to that it is J. Keller's (1871), who, with the greatest discretion in the means he employed, succeeded in catching the shimmer of the visionary apparition. Later generations felt that in doing this he had lost too much of the precision of form of the original, and so Mandel set to work, making a great attempt to capture the expressive quality of Raphael's drawing. He extracted from the picture an unexpected wealth of formal qualities, but at the expense of the magic of the whole, and in a few places, his very conscientiousness led him into ugliness. Instead of the misty vaporousness of the clouds he gives us a blurred mass of rain-clouds. Finally, Kohlschein quite recently adopted a new method of approach: he forced the lights, turning the shimmer into an artificial flickering and wilfully abandoning the effect at which Raphael aimed.

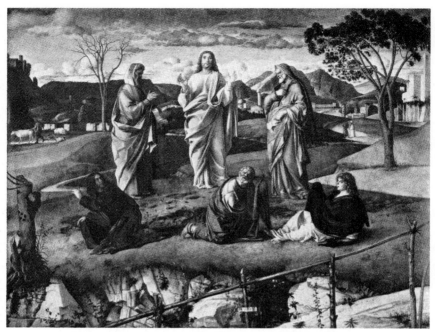

89. GIOVANNI BELLINI: *The Transfiguration*. Naples, Museum

three men standing together with another three at their feet half-reclining. With all its charm of colour and detail even so noble a picture as Bellini's in Naples (*Fig.* 89) cannot conceal the dilemma which the artist himself recognized, when he had to put at the feet of the radiant and transfigured Lord and His companions three little heaps of men representing the dazzled Apostles. There was, however, an older and more idealized type of iconography which did not show Christ as standing on the ground but raised in glory above the earth, and it was thus that Perugino represented the scene in the Cambio at Perugia. Obviously, there are many formal advantages to be gained from such a scheme, but there was never any question which type Raphael would choose; his heightened perception needed the miraculous. The gesture of the outspread arms he took over from earlier models, but the floating movement and the expression of ecstasy could not have been found anywhere else. Moses and Elias are swept up by the soaring flight of Christ and they follow Him, turned towards Him and dependent on Him, for He is the source of power and the centre of light and the others come only to the edge of the radiance which surrounds the Lord. The Disciples below complete the circle. Raphael created them on a much smaller scale in order to keep them closely bound to the earth and they are not independent entities with a disturbing life of their own but appear simply as

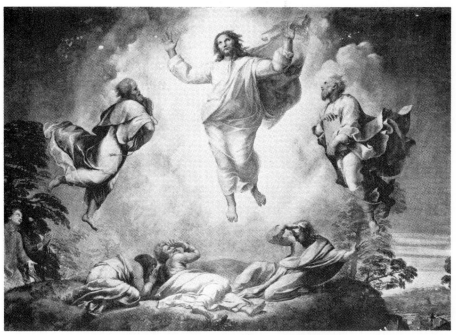

90. RAPHAEL: *The Transfiguration* (upper part). Vatican

necessary factors in the circle which the transfigured Lord has created around Himself, and it is only by contrast with these circumscribed figures that the floating figure gains a complete effect of freedom and independence. Had Raphael bequeathed nothing else to the world, this group alone would be a complete monument to his conception of art.

The Bolognese Academics desired to continue the traditions of the classic period, but even at that early date the feeling for mass and concentration had become completely blunted: Christ bearing down out of the clouds and addressing the Apostles, cramped between the seated and sprawling figures of Moses and Elias, and at the bottom, the Apostles themselves, of herculean size and vulgar in their exaggerated gestures and positions—that is Ludovico Carracci's picture in the Bologna Gallery (*Fig.* 91).

Raphael, however, was not content with the Transfiguration group by itself, but sought for a contrast, a marked counterpoint, and this he found in the story of the possessed boy which immediately follows the Transfiguration in St. Matthew's Gospel. This is the logical development of those principles of composition which Raphael had employed in the Stanza d'Eliodoro—in the upper part, peace, solemnity, celestial ecstasy; in the lower, the noisy throng and earthly wretchedness.

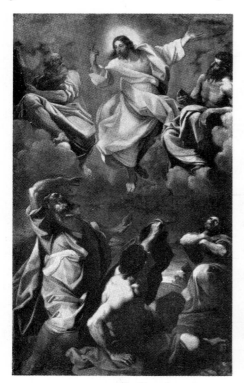

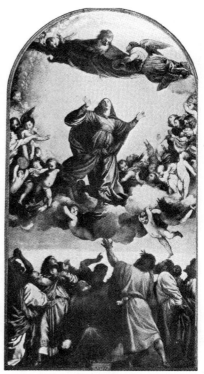

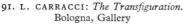

91. L. CARRACCI: *The Transfiguration.*
Bologna, Gallery

92. TITIAN: *The Assumption.*
Venice, S. Maria de' Frari

The Apostles stand there, closely packed together, confused in grouping and jagged in linear movement, the principal motive being a diagonal lane which is opened up through the crowd. The figures are considerably larger in scale than those of the upper part but there is no danger of their outweighing the scene of the Transfiguration for the lucidity of the geometry triumphs over all the din of the mob. Raphael left the picture unfinished at his death and many details of form are intolerable, while the colour of the whole picture is inimical to the effect, but the grandeur of the contrasts must have been his own conception.

Titian's *Assunta* (*Fig.* 92) was painted in Venice at the same time (1518), and here the plan and arrangement are different, although the principles are related. The Apostles in the lower half are grouped together in a solid block, where the individual loses all importance, forming, as it were, a base or plinth above which is the figure of the Virgin within a great circle, the upper edge of which coincides with the semi-circular top of the picture. It may be asked why Raphael, too, did not choose the rounded top for his picture, but perhaps he was afraid of exaggerating the ascending movement of Christ.

The pupils who finished the *Transfiguration* passed off their works under the name of their master in other places as well, and it is only very recently that any attempt has been made to free Raphael from this association. Strident in colour, ignoble in conception, theatrical in gesture and, above all, lacking in proportion, the products of Raphael's workshop must be accounted, for the greater part, among the most unpleasing pictures ever painted.

Sebastiano's rage, when he found such people blocking his way in Rome, is understandable enough. Sebastiano was a lifelong, bitter, rival of Raphael, but his talent was such that he had a right to be considered for the greatest commissions. He never quite freed himself from certain Venetian limitations, for even in 'monumental' Rome he continued to use the half-length scheme; he never attained to absolute mastery of the human body; he was also lacking in a fully developed sense of space, for his compositions are often muddled, crowded, and far from lucid. Yet his conceptions were truly great: as a portrait painter he was in the very first rank, and his historical pictures occasionally possess such expressive power that he can be compared with Michelangelo alone—indeed, we do not know how much he owed to Michelangelo. His *Flagellation* in S. Pietro in Montorio in Rome, and the *Pietà* in Viterbo are among the noblest creations of the golden age. The *Raising of Lazarus*, in which he sought to compete with Raphael's *Transfiguration* does not seem to me to reach the same level, for Sebastiano was better with a few figures than with a crowd, and perhaps he felt most certain of himself with half-length figures. The Louvre *Visitation* (*Fig.* 159) shows his aristocratic manner and the Raphael School version of the same subject in the Prado seems quite ordinary beside it, in spite of its large figures.[1] Again, the *Carrying of the Cross* by Sebastiano, in Madrid (replica in Dresden), may well surpass in its principal figure the suffering hero of Raphael's *Spasimo* in the Prado.[2]

If any one man may be named along with the two great masters in Rome it is Sebastiano. He gives the impression of a personality, destined to achieve the greatest things, which never fully developed—that he failed to make the most of his talents. He lacked the sacred passion for work, which made him the antithesis of Raphael whose most characteristic virtue was diligence, as Michelangelo recognized, and this praise of Raphael meant his power to take new strength from each new enterprise.

---

[1] This very feeble composition cannot possibly be based on a Raphael design; *cf*. Dollmayr, *op. cit.*, p. 344, as by Penni. J. Burckhardt's high praise for the spirit of the heads (*Beiträge*, p. 110) is incomprehensible to me.

[2] Not only is this celebrated picture not by Raphael's own hand, but even some of the final planning must have been entrusted to others. The principal motive, Christ looking back over His shoulder, is striking and certainly authentic Raphael, as is also the development of the procession as a whole, yet there are also weaknesses of drawing and grouping and obscurities in the composition which rule out Raphael's participation in the final version of the composition.

Chapter V : Fra Bartolommeo (1475-1517)

THE type of the monastic painter in the High Renaissance was Fra Bartolommeo, the great experience of whose youth had been to hear Savonarola preach, and to see his death. After that, he withdrew into the convent and gave up painting for a time, which must have been a hard decision for him to make; for in him, more than in others, one feels a need to preach in his pictures. He had not very much to say, but the purpose that inspired him was a noble one, for Savonarola's disciple cherished an ideal of powerful simplicity, by virtue of which he would strike down the wordly vanity and petty prettiness of Florentine religious art. He was no fanatic, no morose ascetic, for he sings songs of rejoicing and triumph: the works by which he must be judged are his votive pictures with serried ranks of saints around the enthroned Madonna, for in these pictures his message is clear and full of feeling. Weighty masses bound together by strict rule, grandiose contrasts of direction and a mighty rhythm in the movement of the whole—these are the elements of his style, that style which has its being in the wide echoing spaces of the churches of the High Renaissance.

By nature he had a feeling for the significant, for nobility of gesture, dignity in the cast of draperies, and for the splendour of a rhythmic contour. What can compare with the verve of his *St. Sebastian*, and where in Florence is there the compeer of the gesture of his *Resurrected Christ*? A strong physical sense was his safeguard against mere empty pathos, for his Evangelists are bull-necked men, and whoever is standing, stands unshakably firm, while those who grasp something do so with an iron grip. He demands the colossal as his normal scale, and, with the intention of getting the maximum plasticity, he intensifies the darkness of his shadows and backgrounds so much that, with the inevitable darkening of time, many of his pictures are now appreciated only with difficulty. He had only a half-hearted interest in the actual and the individual, for he was a man who cared for wholes, not details. His handling of the nude is superficial because he seeks only the general impressions of line and movement while his characterized types, though significant because of the sincerity behind them, have, after all, little more than generalised traits. These generalisations are tolerable because the poses and gestures are enchanting in themselves and because his personality shines forth from the rhythm of the composition. Only occasionally does he lose himself, as in the heroic seated Prophets: Michelangelo's influence led him momentarily astray, and in seeking to rival the power of movement obtained by that giant he became false and empty.

It is understandable that Perugino, because of his simplicity, was the most akin to him among the older men. There he found what he sought—disregard of subordinate detail, still spaciousness and restrained expressiveness; even his elegance of movement comes from the older man, with the addition of his own individual feeling for power and massiveness and firm outline, so that by comparison Perugino seems petty and mannered.

It is the province of a monograph to decide how far his broad painterly style, with its bold use of chiaroscuro and varied gradations of tone, derives from Leonardo. Such a monograph would also have to give a detailed survey of the effect produced on him by Venice, which the Frate visited in 1508: there he saw broad handling already fully developed, and in Bellini he found a sensibility and a perception of beauty which must have come as a revelation to him. We shall return to this point later.

* * * * *

It is not easy to predict Bartolommeo's future development from his *Last Judgement*, a work of the preceding century, formerly in Santa Maria Nuova and now in the Uffizi.[1] Only the upper part is by him, and it suffers from a diffusion of interest: the principal figure, that of the Saviour, is far too small, and in the row of seated saints leading into the depth of the picture the close crowding and the abrupt juxtaposition of the heads have a dry and old-fashioned appearance. Although it has been said with truth that this composition was a source of inspiration for Raphael's *Disputà*, yet a comparison of the two will also show very clearly what Raphael's original contributions were, and the nature of the difficulties he overcame. The lack of cohesion in the whole and the recession of the principal figure into the background are weak points which are still present in the first sketches for the *Disputà* and which were only gradually overcome. On the other hand, Raphael experienced no difficulty, from the very beginning, in developing clearly the rows of seated saints. He shared with Perugino a grasp of the general view of the whole and an ability to compose his figures in easy groups, whereas all the Florentines expect the spectator to distinguish one head from another amongst their closely packed rows.

One feels differently about the *Vision of St. Bernard* of 1506 (*Fig.* 93; Florence, Academy), the first picture painted by Fra Bartolommeo after he became a monk. It is not a very pleasing picture and its condition leaves much to be desired; yet it is an impressive picture. The vision is depicted in an unexpected way, unlike the gentle, shy woman of Filippino's picture, laying her hand on the pious man's book as she steps up to his desk; here it is a supernatural apparition sweeping down from above, wrapped in the solemnity of a great floating mantle and accompanied by a choir of angels pressing closely round and filled with awe and reverence. Filippino had painted girls, half-shy and half-curious, accompanying the Virgin on her visit; Fra Bartolommeo wants, not that the spectator

---

[1] [Now in the Museo di San Marco—*Trans.*]

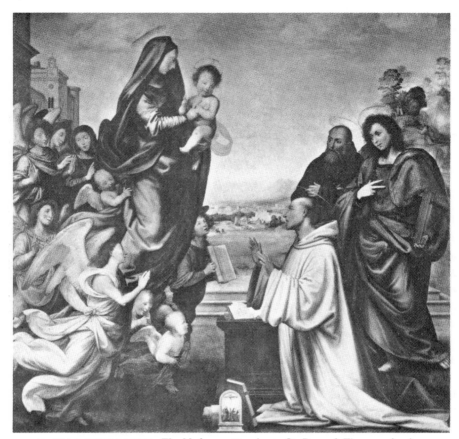

93. FRA BARTOLOMMEO: *The Madonna appearing to St. Bernard*. Florence, Academy

should smile but that he should be stirred to devotion. Unfortunately, his angels are so ugly that they interfere with the feeling of devotion. The saint receives the miracle with pious wonder, and this is so finely rendered that, by comparison, Filippino seems trite and even Perugino, in his picture at Munich, seems indifferent. The heavy, trailing, white robe has a new dignity of line, and the two saints behind St. Bernard are made to play their part in the emotional atmosphere, although the details of landscape and architecture have still an immature uncertainty, and the space as a whole is somewhat cramped so that the apparition has a rather heavy effect.

Three years later, the inspiration which gave rise to the *St. Bernard* burned strongly again in the picture of *God the Father with two kneeling female Saints* of 1509 (*Fig.* 94; Lucca, Academy), where St. Catherine of Siena in adoration repeats the earlier motive in a grander and more emotional form. The turn of the head, in *profil perdu*, and the more vigorous forward thrust of the body strengthen the feeling for mood already captured in the *St. Bernard*, just as the movement of the billowing folds of her dark habit makes a more effective translation of spiritual exaltation into terms of physical movement. The other saint, the Magdalen, remains motionless, holding out the box of ointment with a ritual gesture, and in her other hand she holds the end of her mantle high up before her, while her downcast eyes rest upon the congregation. This is an economy of contrast of the type which Raphael was to use later in the *Sistine Madonna*. Both figures kneel, but on clouds, not on the earth, although Bartolommeo enframes the whole between two pilasters and the eye is led into the depth of the picture over a quiet, flat landscape, a wonderfully solemn effect being obtained from the gentle line of the horizon and the great expanse of sky.

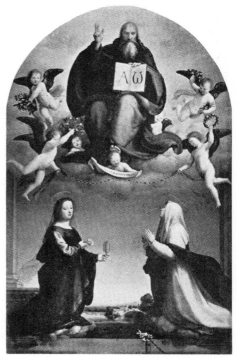

94. FRA BARTOLOMMEO: *God the Father and two Saints*. Lucca, Academy

One recollects coming across similar intentions in Perugino, but it is more likely that this is the reflection of impressions made upon him by the Venetians: in contrast to the agitated abundance of the Florentines this picture speaks clearly enough of the new idealism.

When Bartolommeo treats the normal *Madonna and Saints* type of picture, as for example, in the beautifully painted picture of 1508 in Lucca Cathedral,[1] his chief concern is once again the same as Perugino's—simplification of the total effect, obtained by plain draperies, quiet backgrounds and a mere cube for a throne—although he surpasses Perugino in his more vigorous movement, more plastic figures and less broken outlines, for his are rounded, flowing and avoid sharp intersections. How admirably the silhouettes of Mary and Stephen complement each other![2] There is an old-fashioned look about the way in which the surface is filled up more or less indifferently, but the new feeling for mass is seen

---

[1] The *putto* playing the lute is introduced into Florentine art here as a souvenir of his Venetian travels.

[2] Insensitive engravers, such as Jesi, place the Madonna higher up, from an arbitrary desire for 'improvement', thus spoiling the whole harmony. One example among many is the woodcut illustration in Woltmann-Wörmann's *Malerei*, based on the engraving.

in the placing of the standing figures close to the edge, while the whole is effectively framed between the two pilasters, distinguishing this picture from those earlier ones which allowed the eye to catch a glimpse of landscape between pilaster and edge of the picture.

Henceforward, the harmonies of his altar-pieces become even richer and more resonant and the grouping is composed in yet more sweeping rhythms. His crowds are subordinated to one leading motive, powerful blocks of light and dark are played against each other, yet, for all their rich variety, the pictures remain open and spacious. The fullest expression of this art is the *Mystic Marriage of St. Catherine* in the Pitti (*Fig.* 95), and the preparation for the *Patron Saints of Florence with the Virgin and Child and St. Anne*, in the Uffizi,[1] both of which were painted about 1512.

The space in both these pictures is closed and Bartolommeo used a dark background, for the spirit of the pictures would be spoiled by the diffusiveness of an open landscape, and requires the accompaniment of solemn, heavy architecture. To this end, he often uses a large, empty semi-circular niche as his architectural motive, a form the effectiveness of which he may have discovered in Venice: its richness lies in the shadows of the niche vaulting, and not in colour which is now disregarded, just as the Venetians themselves abandoned bright colours in the sixteenth century, in favour of neutral tones.

In order to obtain a varied outline for the figure-groups, Bartolommeo constructed a small flight of steps leading up from the foreground to the middle-distance, and this is the motive which, transformed into the grandest style by Raphael in the *School of Athens*, became absolutely indispensable in altar-pieces containing many figures. At the same time, the point of sight is placed low down in the picture, so that the rear figures come below the level of the nearer ones— a device which may be meant to represent the natural viewpoint of a spectator standing in the church. In any case, Bartolommeo's strongly accentuated compositions derive considerable advantage from this use of perspective, for the rising and falling of the rhythm are clearly marked. With all his richness, Bartolommeo never creates a confused or restless effect, for his pictures are constructed according to strict law and the true protagonists in the composition leap to the eye at once.

In the *Marriage of St. Catherine*[2] the figure in the right-hand corner is a very characteristic example of the sixteenth-century variety of movement which Pontormo and Andrea del Sarto made peculiarly their own—one foot on a step, one arm reaching across the body and the head turned in a contrasting direction.

---

[1][Later moved to S. Marco.—*Trans.*]

[2]The Mystic Marriage of St. Catherine with the Infant Christ is not the main motive of the picture, but the name may be tolerated to distinguish it from other pictures.

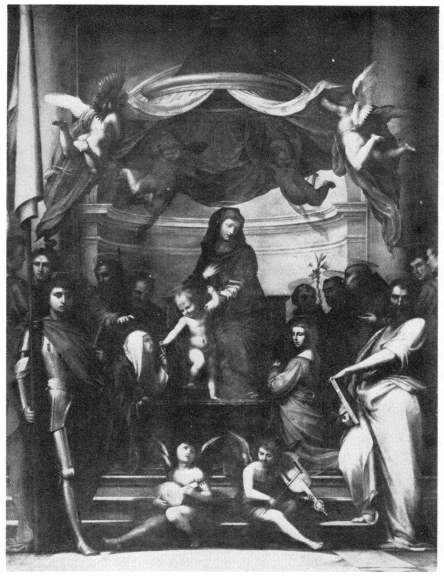

95. FRA BARTOLOMMEO: *The Marriage of St. Catherine*. Pitti

Every turn of the body, and the way in which the hands grasp the object they hold, show energy and decision, and the structure of muscles and joints has been studied with care. The arm bared to the elbow is an instance of this, and it follows closely the lead given by Michelangelo, although he would certainly have drawn this arm differently, for the wrist is not very expressive. The St. George on the opposite side is a happy contrast in his simplicity, while it was a novelty to the Florentines to see how gleaming armour could be made to emerge from a dark background. Finally, the group of the Madonna and Child is of the greatest sweetness, typical of the artist in its involved movement and soft flow of line; the Child handing the ring to the kneeling St. Catherine leads the movement downwards by this gesture, which links the group to the figures below.

Pictures of this kind, with their organic rhythms, their seriousness of approach to construction according to rule and proportion, and, above all, the plenitude of bold movement, made a great impression in Florence; here was a higher form of those qualities which had once been admired in Perugino's geometrically ordered *Lamentation* of 1494. Pontormo sought, not without success, to imitate the Frate's composition in his fresco of the *Visitation* (in the court of the Annunziata), where he places the principal group in front of a niche, sets strongly contrasted figures at the edges in the foreground, introduces the motive of the steps to fill the central space satisfactorily, and thus obtains a truly monumental effect, with the value of each individual figure increased by its connection with so significant a whole (*Fig.* 107).

The Besançon *Madonna* (*Fig.* 96) claims particular notice if only because of its fine St. Sebastian, splendidly flowing in action and painted with Venetian breadth, showing the combined influence of Perugino and Bellini. The light falls only on the right side of the body, which has the more vigorous movement, so that the whole figure gains greatly from the fact that the parts essential to the expression of movement are in the strongest light. Another important point about the picture is the subject, for the Madonna floats on clouds enclosed within an architectural interior from which the open air is seen only through a door in the background. This is idealism of a new kind: Bartolommeo may have wanted a dark background with half-light effects in depth, but he also created a new kind of spiritual contrast with the saints who stand on the ground. The spatial effect is adversely affected, however, and the open door contracts rather than increases it, but originally the picture was terminated at the top by a semi-circular *Coronation of the Virgin*, which may possibly have improved the general effect. This picture seems also to date from about 1512.

The emotional power of the Frate continues to increase until it reaches the pathos of the *Intercessory Virgin of Mercy* of 1515 in Lucca Academy (*Fig.* 97). The usual form of the *Mater Misericordiae* was a rectangle, greater in width than height, with the Virgin standing in the centre, her hands clasped in prayer, with the devout who have placed themselves under her protection kneeling to right and left beneath her outspread mantle. Fra Bartolommeo changes the form of the picture to a large upright with a semi-circular top. Mary stands

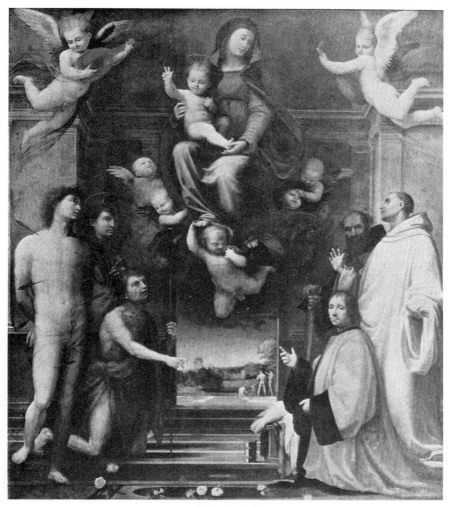

96. FRA BARTOLOMMEO: *Madonna and Child*. Besançon, Cathedral

raised above the earth, angels holding high her cloak, and thus she offers her intercession with a splendidly triumphant gesture, clear and urgent, with her arms spread apart and pointing, one upwards and the other downwards; and from Heaven Christ Himself, enveloped in a billowing mantle, grants her prayer. In order to give fluency to the Virgin's gesture, Bartolommeo had to raise one of her feet above the other, and the question was to find a reason for this unequal height. Without giving it another thought he calmly placed a block under the one foot to account for the movement, for the classic age found nothing disconcerting in such expedients, which would cause a public outcry nowadays.

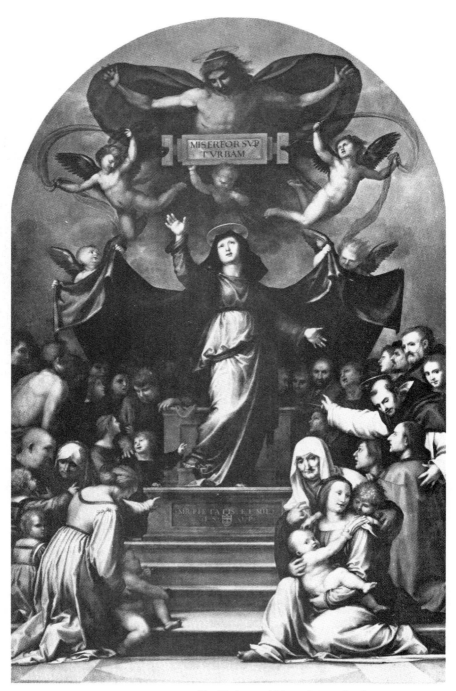

97. FRA BARTOLOMMEO: *The Madonna of Mercy*. Lucca, Academy

From the podium downwards the congregation is spread out towards the foreground over the steps, creating groups of mothers and children, people pointing and praying, which may be compared from the formal standpoint with those in the *Heliodorus*; yet this comparison has its dangers for it shows up the defect inherent in the picture—the lack of a co-ordinated movement which continues from part to part. Bartolommeo continually renewed his efforts to attain such a movement of masses but in this he seems to have reached the limits of his talent.[1]

A few years after the *Mater Misericordiae* Titian painted his *Assunta* (1518; *Fig.* 92), and a reference to this unique creation can scarcely be avoided, since the two motives are so closely

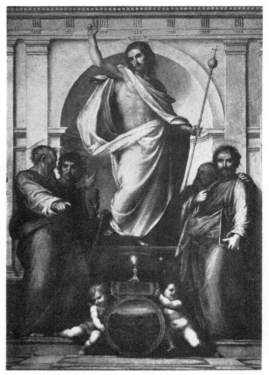

98. FRA BARTOLOMMEO: *The Risen Christ with the four Evangelists.* Pitti

connected; yet it would not be fair to measure Bartolommeo by Titian's standards. His importance for Florence was immense and the Lucca picture is an immediately convincing expression of the exalted ideas of that time. How rapidly such conceptions become debased can best be seen in a picture which has since become popular—Baroccio's version of the same theme, known as the *Madonna del Popolo*, in the Uffizi—which, as painting, is enviably bold and bright but is nevertheless already completely trivial in content.

The *Resurrected Christ*, of 1517, in the Pitti (*Fig.* 98), is akin to the *Mater Misericordiae*, but the uncertainties and imperfections have been eliminated so that this picture may be regarded as the Frate's most successful work; here he was now more tranquil. Yet the very restraint of the pathos in this mild and benedictory Christ has a more penetrating and convincing quality than violent gesticulation—'Behold, I live and ye shall live also!' Shortly before this time, Bartolommeo had been in Rome, and he may there have seen the *Sistine Madonna*,

---

[1] In the *Rape of Dinah*, Vienna, where the drawing goes back to Bartolommeo, the relationship to the *Heliodorus* is still plainer.

for the noble simplicity of the cast of the drapery is of a closely related type. The silhouette has an ascending threefold undulation, a splendid motive, which could be used with equal success in Madonna pictures, while the drawing of the upraised arm, with its clearly articulated joints, would have satisfied Michelangelo. The great niche recurs in the background, but it is overlapped by the figure of Christ and serves as a foil to Him, His figure being raised above the Evangelists by the pedestal on which He stands, an apparently obvious motive, which nevertheless was unknown to the Florentine Quattrocento, the first examples of its use occurring in Venice.

The four Evangelists are weighty figures of force and assurance; though only two of them are emphasised, for the pair at the back are completely subordinated to those in the foreground and are even assimilated to them in grouping, giving a good example of Bartolommeo's feeling for masses. The effect of the profiles and full-faces, and the erect and stooping postures, are most carefully calculated— the vertical of the full-face at the right does not derive its striking effect from itself alone, but draws its essential character from the formal context and architectural setting. In this picture everything is determined and increased by reference to its opposite, and the inevitability of the relationships can be felt.

Finally, Bartolommeo treated the group of mourners over the dead Christ, in the *Pietà*, with the most noble restraint of expression, as the best of his contemporaries did (*Fig.* 99; Pitti). The lamentation is subdued—just a gentle meeting of profiles as the Mother takes the dead hand and bends forward to kiss the forehead for the last time. There is no trace of the sufferings endured by Christ, the position of whose head is not that of a corpse, so that even here idealism prevails. The features of the Magdalen are almost invisible, as she throws herself in a passion of grief at the feet of the Lord, but the expression of St. John shows, as Jakob Burckhardt noticed, traces of his exertion in bearing the corpse— an unerringly dramatic touch.[1] In this way, the emotions represented are clearly distinguished and the exactly similar expressions which Perugino used are replaced by sharp contrasts which enhance each other's effect. The physical movements were subject to the same principle although the composition now lacks two figures, for a St. Peter and a St. Paul were once included in the picture,

---

[1]This observation remains true even if it be admitted that a mixture of physical and spiritual disquiet is unpaintable. In any case it is impossible to say which of the two causes is responsible for any part of the expression, nor is it here necessary, though it may be as well to recall the critical principle stated by Reynolds against the dilettanti writers of his day, 'who, not being of the profession, and consequently not knowing what can or cannot be done, have been very liberal of absurd praises in their descriptions of favourite works. They always find in them what they resolved to find. They praise excellencies that can hardly exist together; and above all things are fond of describing with great exactness the *expression of a mixed passion*, which more particularly appears to me out of the reach of our art.' [Reynolds, *The Fifth Discourse*, p. 115 of Fry's edition of the *Discourses*; the italics are Wölfflin's.—*Trans.*]

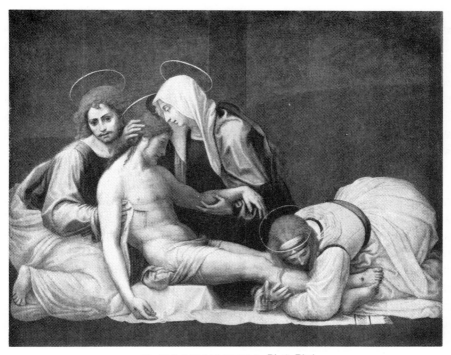

99. FRA BARTOLOMMEO: *Pietà*. Pitti

and we must think of them as bending down over the Magdalen, thus modifying her disagreeable silhouette.[1]

The lack of these figures leads to a displacement of the main accent: although there was certainly never any question of a symmetrical disposition of the masses, but rather a rhythmic freedom, yet the three heads do require some counterpoise, and the later addition of the base of the Cross is obviously wrong, for it is just this point which requires to be unaccented.

Compared to Perugino, who seemed so calm among his contemporaries (*cf. Fig. 51; Madonna and Child with Sts. Sebastian and John the Baptist*), Bartolommeo's line is yet more restrained and hieratic. The great parallel horizontals of the foreground serve to emphasise the simple relief-like arrangement of the figures, dominated by the two profiles, and Bartolommeo must have realized the benefit of introducing this calm note for he attains the same end in another way, by reducing the height of the group and transforming Perugino's steep triangle into a much lower one, obtuse-angled at the top. Possibly, too, the broad format of the picture was chosen with the same end in view (*cf. Fig. 54*).

---

[1]The figures once existed, but were taken out again: for a parallel completion of the group *cf.* Albertinelli's *Pietà* in the Academy, Florence.

Bartolommeo might have been able to go on working much longer, giving a calm and classic form to the whole range of Christian iconography. From his drawings, we get the impression that his imagination was easily stimulated into producing significant pictorial equivalents to which his hand could, with complete certainty, apply the rules for getting his effects; yet his effects are never the result of a mere application of rules, for they derive from the very fabric of his mind, which worked out the rules for itself. How little could be learnt in a purely academic way in his workshop can be seen by the example of Albertinelli, who was one of his most intimate associates.

Vasari called Mariotto Albertinelli (1474–1515) 'un altro Bartolommeo', and for a long time he was the latter's collaborator, yet his was a basically different temperament, lacking, above all, the conviction of the Frate. Very talented, he now and again attempted real problems, but was never able to develop a logical synthesis, and from time to time he dropped painting altogether and turned to inn-keeping.

The early picture of the *Visitation* (1503) shows him at his best (*Fig.* 100), for the grouping is pure and beautiful and in harmony with the background. The theme of mutual greeting is far from easy to tackle, especially the placing of the four hands into their proper positions. Not long before this, Ghirlandaio had essayed the theme in his picture in the Louvre, dated 1491 (*Fig.* 181); Elisabeth kneels and raises her arms while Mary soothingly lays her hands on her shoulders. In this way, one of the four hands disappears from view and the parallel lines of the Virgin's arms are lacking in felicity, so that one would not care to see the motive repeated. Albertinelli is at once richer and clearer, for the two women clasp their right hands while the disengaged left arms are differentiated, Elisabeth embracing her visitor and Mary humbly laying her hand on her breast. The kneeling motive is abandoned, for Albertinelli wished to bring the profiles into close juxtaposition, yet Elisabeth's subordination to Mary is clearly brought out by the hastened step of the elder woman and the inclination of her head, and this idea is still further

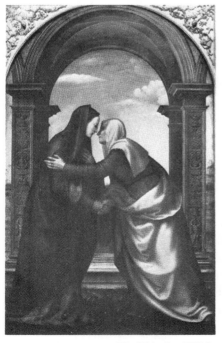

100. ALBERTINELLI: *The Visitation.* Uffizi

underlined by the shadow which the artist cast across her features, a significant detail which would not have occurred to anyone in the Quattrocento. The group is placed in front of an arcade which is undeniably Peruginesque in origin, as is also the effect of the airy background of open sky. Later artists would have avoided the view into the background at the edges of the picture and there are other traces of Quattrocento style in the draperies and the flower-strewn foreground.

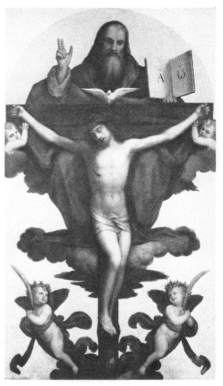

The great *Crucifixion* of the Certosa, of 1506, is also dependent on Perugino, but four years later he found a new form, the classic one, for the image of the Crucified in his *Trinity* (*Fig.* 101; Florence, Academy). All earlier artists separated the legs at the knees, although a finer result is obtained by subordination rather than co-ordination; that is, when one leg rests on the other. The next stage came when the movement of the legs was answered by a counter-movement of the head: if the limbs moved towards the

101. ALBERTINELLI: *The Holy Trinity.*
Florence, Academy

right, the head was tilted to the left and thus a theme which was apparently stiff and lacking in grace received a rhythmic interpretation which it has never since lost.

The interesting *Annunciation* (*Fig.* 102; Florence, Academy) is of the same year, 1510; it is a picture which gave the artist a good deal of trouble and is of importance in the history of stylistic development as a whole. It will be recalled how meagre a part was assigned to God the Father in Annunciation pictures— generally He appears as a small half-length figure somewhere up in the top corner, sending down the Dove. Here He appears at full length, centrally placed and surrounded by a ring of large-scale angels. These musician angels flying through the air involved a lot of hard work and the painter who, in a fit of ill-temper, gave up painting to keep a tavern, so that he should never have to listen to any more of the eternal talk about foreshortening, has here made a very respectable job of it. The celestial motive, especially, shows the beginnings of the Glorias of the seventeenth century, although everything here is still symmetrical and in one plane, whereas the later heavenly evolutions generally have a diagonal direction in depth.

The calm and aristocratic Virgin speaks of an increased sense of religious decorum, as she stands in her elegant pose, not turned towards the angel, but looking at him over her shoulder as she receives his reverent salutation. Without this picture Andrea del Sarto could never have created his *Madonna Annunciate* of 1512.

The picture is also interesting from a technical point of view, for it has a large dark interior, greenish in colour, as the background. The perspective takes account of the fact that it was destined to hang high up, but the steep fore-shortening of the cornice produces an unhappy effect in combination with the figure.

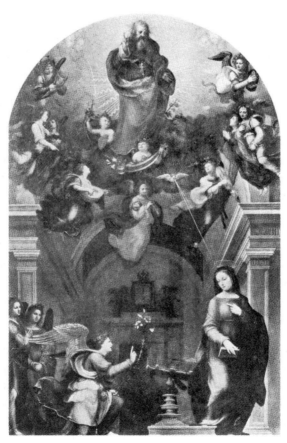

102. ALBERTINELLI: *The Annunciation*. Florence, Academy

CHAPTER VI : ANDREA DEL SARTO (1486-1531)

ANDREA DEL SARTO has been called superficial and soulless, and it is true that there are mediocre pictures by him and that in his later years he tended to sink comfortably into routine; he is the only one of the first-rate talents who seems to have had some defect in his moral constitution. Yet in every respect he was the refined Florentine, of the same race as Filippino and Leonardo, fastidious in his taste, a painter of an aristocracy of indolent bearing and noble gestures. He was a child of the world and even his Madonnas have a worldly elegance. He had no interest in vigorous movements or strong emotions and he scarcely ventures beyond quiet standing or walking poses, but within these limits he developed a ravishing sense of beauty. Vasari reproached him for his tameness and timidity, and for a lack of proper audacity, but one need only see a single example of the great 'machines' which Vasari himself was accustomed to paint to understand this judgement; yet even beside the powerful constructions of Fra Bartolommeo or the Roman School he does seem quiet and unsophisticated. Nevertheless, he was greatly gifted in many ways. He was brought up to admire Michelangelo, and there was a time when he could be accounted the best draughtsman in Florence. His handling of the joints of the body has a kick about it—if the colloquialism may be forgiven—which brings out their function with an energy and clarity which would be sufficient to ensure admiration for his works even if he had not combined his Florentine birthright of good drawing with a gift for painting which has scarcely been equalled in Tuscany. He paid no attention to a good many phenomena which have an attraction for the painter as such; for example, he does not seek to distinguish the textures of different objects, but there is a great charm in the gentle radiance of his flesh colours and in the soft atmosphere which envelops his figures. His perception of colour, as of line, has a soft, almost sleepy, beauty which makes him appear more modern than any other painter.

Without Andrea del Sarto Cinquecento Florence would be deprived of her festal painter: the great fresco of the *Birth of the Virgin* in the forecourt of the Annunziata (*Fig.* 106) gives us something which Raphael and Bartolommeo do not—the fine joy in being alive which men felt at the moment when the Renaissance reached its zenith. We would gladly have many more of Andrea's pictures of this kind of life and indeed he should have painted no others, but it was not entirely his fault that he did not become a Florentine Paolo Veronese.

1. The Frescoes in the Annunziata

THE traveller generally gets his first great impression of Andrea in the forecourt of the Annunziata where there are five scenes from the life of St. Philip Benizzi (*Figs.* 103–105) with the terminal date 1511, and the *Birth of the Virgin* and the *Three Kings* of 1514, all early works and serious subjects.

The frescoes are of a beautiful light tone, somewhat dry in the juxtaposition of colours in the earlier works, but Andrea's rich and harmonious modulations are already fully developed in the *Birth of the Virgin* (*Fig.* 106). The first two pictures are still loose and incoherent in composition, but in the third he introduces a severer treatment with a central accent and symmetrically developed sides. He drives a wedge into the crowd, causing the central figures to retreat, giving depth to the picture, which contrasts with the arrangement of the figures in lines along the edge of the foreground that Ghirlandaio, almost without exception, had continued to use. This centralised scheme is not new in historical pictures, but what is an innovation is the way in which the figures are linked by gestures. Instead of rows of figures one behind the other, the parts of the composition develop in an uninterrupted and logical sequence from background to foreground: it is exactly the same problem which Raphael set himself at the same time, but on a still greater scale, in the *Disputà* and the *School of Athens*.

The last picture, the *Birth of the Virgin*, marks Andrea's transition from a tectonic and severe style to a freely rhythmic one. The composition is based on a splendid forward curve which begins at the left with the women by the fireplace, reaches its maximum of movement in the figures of the walking women and dies

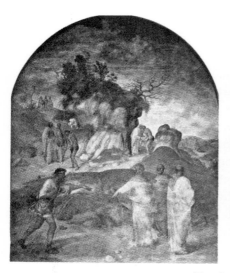 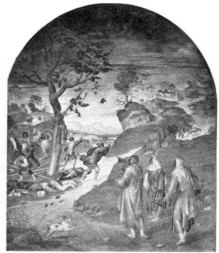

103–4. ANDREA DEL SARTO: *Two Scenes from the Life of St. Philip Benizzi.*
Florence, SS. Annunziata

away beside the woman in childbed. Certainly, the freedom of this rhythmic arrangement is quite different from the licence of the earlier loose style, for this is governed by law and the way in which the two standing women dominate and bind the whole picture together is scarcely conceivable as a motive before the sixteenth century.

As soon as Andrea changed over from his earliest style, with its loose juxtaposition of figures, to a more severe compositional form, he felt the need of architecture to aid his designs, to give coherence and unity to the whole and stability to the figures. This is the beginning of that perception of unity of space and figures which was, generally speaking, still unknown to the Quattro-cento which chiefly assigned the role of a pleasing and decorative enrichment to the architectural elements in a picture. Sarto was a pioneer in this respect, and nobody could maintain that his architectural proportions and relationships were very happy, nor can his embarrassment be concealed when he tries to deal with a space too great for his figures. On the whole, his architectural backgrounds are too heavy; when he puts an opening in the middle it has the effect of contracting rather than extending the space, and when he allows the spectator's eye to wander sideways into the landscape it is simply a distracting element. All the time his figures have a lost look about them, until he first arrived at a solution to this problem, as to others, in the interior of the room in the birth scene.

A comparison with Raphael shows how little Andrea was capable of rendering the dramatic content of a scene: his saint works his miracle with a gesture which is neither noble nor convincing, and the onlookers content themselves with

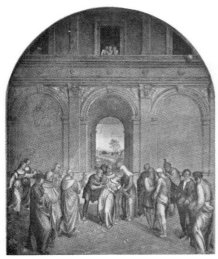 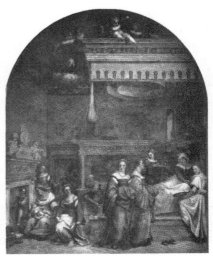

105. ANDREA DEL SARTO: *Scene from the Life of St. Philip Benizzi*. Florence, SS. Annunziata

106. ANDREA DEL SARTO: *The Birth of the Virgin*. Florence, SS. Annunziata

standing idly by with only the faintest expressions of astonishment. In the one case of a vigorous action, where the lightning strikes terror into the gamblers and scoffers, he puts these figures in the middle distance and makes them quite small in size when here, if anywhere, was the opportunity to show what he had learned from his studies of Michelangelo's cartoon of the bathing soldiers. His principal motives are full of repose, but it is worth the trouble to analyse the artist's intentions in detail, and here—where he had three times in succession to treat standing, moving, or seated figures and to develop them in a centralized scheme as parts of a composition which was to be symmetrical as a whole, though unsymmetrical in detail—here we may light upon some very beautiful motives, instinct with youthful sensibility. The simplicity often enough has the appearance of inexperience and timidity, yet we can well spare a moment from looking at figures which interest only by their *contrapposto*. Andrea obtains his full freedom in the *Birth of the Virgin*. No better interpreter of aristocratic nonchalance and indolent luxury has yet been found. The full rhythm of the Cinquecento lives in the figures of the two women in movement, and, at the same time, the woman in childbed was treated in a new and more splendid way. Ghirlandaio's flat position and stiff back now seem as dull and antiquated as the manner in which Masaccio[1] made her lie on her stomach must have seemed vulgar to the refined Florentines. The figure of the woman lying-in develops in a manner analogous to the recumbent figure on tombs—in both, there is now a twisting movement and a differentiation between the limbs.

From the point of view of varied movement, the most promising feature of a birth-scene is the circle of women who busy themselves with the child, for this offers a splendid opportunity for complicated curves and the creation of a web of movement incorporating the seated and bending figures. Sarto is still restrained in exploiting this theme, but later men tended to make it the principal subject of the picture, bringing the group of women into the foreground and thrusting the bed and the woman in it right into the background, so that the idea of a visit paid to the mother naturally disappears. Sebastiano del Piombo's imposing picture in S. Mariadel Popolo, Rome, is the first representation of this type, which became the generally accepted form in the seventeenth century.

At the top of the picture there is an angel swinging a censer, and, although the Seicento has accustomed us to the display of clouds in this place, yet we are surprised to find Andrea using the motive, for we are still too accustomed to the clear bright actuality of the Quattrocento to take such miraculous appearances for granted. Plainly, there has been a change of heart: men have gone back to idealism and think in terms of the supernatural. We shall find a similar change in

---

[1]Tondo in Berlin.

approach to the theme of the Annunciation.[1] In spite of this idealism, Andrea
did not abandon the Florence of his own
day in the furnishing of the room or
the costume of the women, for it is a
Florentine room of the latest style and
the costumes—as Vasari expressly says—
are those which were in fashion in 1514,
the date of the picture.

Because Sarto attained a freely rhythmic style in this birth-scene, it does not
mean that he regarded the more severe
and tectonic form of composition as
a preliminary stage which he could now
dispense with, for he returned to it in
another place, the cloister of the Scalzo.
The forecourt of the Annunziata itself,

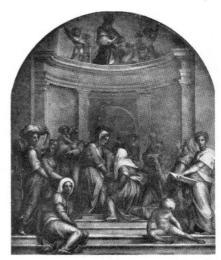

107. PONTORMO: *The Visitation.*
Florence, SS. Annunziata

however, contains an outstanding example of the type in Pontormo's *Visitation*
(*Fig.* 107), which was painted directly after Andrea worked there. Vasari was
quite right when he said that whoever wished to show his powers in this place,
alongside of Andrea del Sarto, would have to create something quite out of the
ordinary. Pontormo did this. His *Visitation* is imposing not only because of the
increased scale of the figures, but because it is an intrinsically great composition.
The centralised scheme which had been thoroughly tested by Andrea five years
earlier is here, for the first time, raised to the level of an architectonic effect. The
two women embrace on a platform raised on steps and set in front of a niche,
and by means of the steps, which come well forward, the subordinate figures are
arranged at a number of different levels, giving an animated rise and fall to the
line. The great articulating accents retain their dominance through all the play
of movement—the verticals at either side and, between them, a rising and falling
line which builds a triangle with the apex formed by the inclined bodies of
Mary and Elisabeth and with the angles of the base in the figures of the seated
woman at the left and the boy at the right. The triangle is not equilateral,
having a more sharply ascending line on Mary's side and a flatter one on
Elisabeth's, while the naked child at the bottom has not stretched out his leg
by chance, for he had to continue the line in this direction. All the parts are
interlocked and every single figure plays its part in the dignity and solemnity

---

[1]Andrea knew and used Dürer's work, as may be seen in other examples, and it is quite possible
that the angel here is derived from Dürer's *Life of the Virgin.* In any case, the artist must have been
glad of something which would fill up the superfluous space at the top.

of the all-pervading rhythmic theme. The dependence on Fra Bartolommeo's altar-piece is obvious; yet an artist of the second rank, borne along by the great age in which he lived, has here created a picture of real significance and influence.

After this, Franciabigio's *Sposalizio* seems thin and meagre in spite of its refinement of detail. We may pass it by.

2. The Frescoes in the Scalzo

IN a little colonnaded cloister of the Barefooted Friars (*Gli Scalzi*) Andrea del Sarto painted the history of the Baptist in monochrome, not in colour, and on a modest scale. Two pictures are by Franciabigio but the remaining ten and the four allegorical figures are entirely Andrea's work though not uniform in style, since the work dragged on for fifteen years, with many interruptions, so that here it is possible to follow almost the whole of the artist's development.

Grisaille painting had long been practised—Cennino Cennini says that it was used in places exposed to the weather, and it occurs also along with painting in full colour in places of minor importance such as parapets or the dark spaces between windows. The sixteenth century, however, seemed to take a certain pleasure in it for its own sake, a fact which is comprehensible in the context of the new style.

The little courtyard has a delightfully peaceful air and the unity of colour, the harmony between frescoes and architecture, the type of framing used for the fields, all combine to make a fitting setting for the pictures. No one acquainted with Sarto's work will seek for the significance of the frescoes in their representation of dramatic moments or events, for the Baptist is an uninspired preacher of repentance, the scenes of terror weak in dramatic effect, and we can hardly expect strong characterisation; but everything is perfectly lucid and full of fine movement, so that it makes a most instructive example of the way in which the interests of the period tended to concentrate more and more on formal qualities, assessing the merits of a history picture solely by its spatial composition. We shall discuss the pictures in the order in which they were painted.

1. *The Baptism of Christ* (1511: *Fig.* 108). This may be recognized immediately as the first of the series because of the way in which the figures are scattered about in the picture-space without filling it satisfactorily, leaving empty spaces. The figure of Christ is the best thing in the picture, extraordinarily subtle and sensitive in action and graceful in effect. The right leg bears no weight but both heels are brought together so that one leg partly hides the other, the contraction of the silhouette near the knees producing an uncommonly elastic effect. It is remarkable that the feet are not covered by the water but remain visible. This practice had always been current among a few minor idealising schools, but it is here adopted for the sake of plastic clarity, just as the baring of the hips is

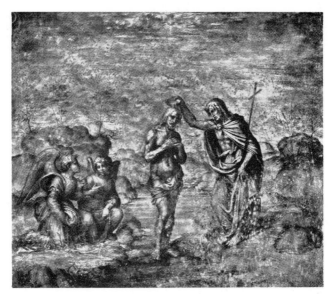

108. ANDREA DEL SARTO: *The Baptism of Christ*. Florence, Scalzo

necessary for lucidity since the older type of loin-cloth, tied horizontally, divided the body just at the point where the articulation needs to be stated most clearly. In this case, not only does the diagonal fall of the apron give the necessary distinctness, but it also furnishes, spontaneously, a line of contrast which is pleasing in itself. The hands of the Neophyte are crossed upon His breast, not clasped in prayer as was the earlier custom.

The figure of the Baptist is lacking in comparable subtleties, and the angularities betray some anxieties on the part of the artist, but the fact that he is shown standing still is an advance on Ghirlandaio and Verrocchio, who represented him in the act of stepping forward. The angels have a family likeness to the still more beautiful pair in the *Annunciation* of 1512.

2. *The Sermon of St. John the Baptist* (c. 1515; *Fig.* 109). This picture makes a totally different general impression because of the considerably increased bulk of the figures within the frame and the more compact filling of the picture surface. The compositional scheme suggests Ghirlandaio's fresco in Santa Maria Novella—the raised figure in the middle, and the arrangement of the circle of listeners with standing figures at either side are identical, as is also the twist of the preacher to the right. There is, therefore, much to be said for a close examination of the points of difference between the two (*cf. Fig.* 110).

Ghirlandaio represents the ardour of his preacher by making him appear to be moving forwards, where Sarto makes the only movement a twist of the figure upon its own axis, a pose at once less agitated and richer in potential movement.

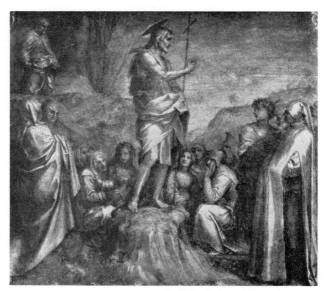

109. ANDREA DEL SARTO: *St. John the Baptist preaching.*
Florence, Scalzo

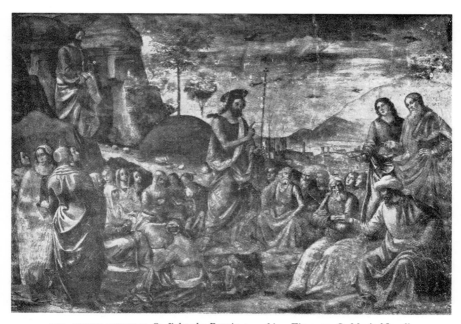

110. GHIRLANDAIO: *St. John the Baptist preaching.* Florence, S. Maria Novella

The marked contraction of the silhouette at the knees is here particularly effective. The old-fashioned rhetorical gesture with only the index finger outstretched now seems petty and trivial by comparison with the newer idea of the effectiveness of the hand as a single mass; and, where the earlier picture keeps the arm rigidly in one plane, the later work, with its freer gesture, gains in animation on account of the foreshortening alone. The expressiveness given to the limbs and the clarity of articulation throughout the figure make this a fine example of Cinquecento ideas on draughtsmanship.

Sarto has less space in which to put his audience, but all the same he contrives a more convincing effect of a crowd than Ghirlandaio, who shows a couple of dozen heads but whose general effect is confused since each is intended to be looked at individually. Andrea's figures at the edges, closing off the picture space, are monumental in themselves,[1] and the general effect is helped by the fact that the preacher is addressing people who are not visible in the picture.

The grandeur of Sarto's principal figure is to be explained not only by its relatively large scale, but also because every other element in the picture is calculated to lead up to it as the chief accent, even the landscape being composed with this in view. It provides a stop behind the preacher and an open space in front of him, so that he stands out as a freely silhouetted and tangible figure, whereas the same figure in Ghirlandaio's picture is not only planted in the crowd but also conflicts unhappily with the form of the background.

3. *The Baptism of the People* (1517; *Fig.* 111). A certain restlessness becomes perceptible in the style—the draperies are jagged and irregular, and the gestures overdone. The secondary figures, intended to enliven the severity of the scheme by adding the charm of the accidental, exceed their function. The fine nude youth seen from behind and glancing idly downwards is a highly characteristic Sarto figure.

4. *The Arrest of the Baptist* (1517; *Fig.* 112). This scene is also treated as a centralised composition, though little suited to the purpose. Herod and St. John do not face one another profile to profile; instead, the ruler is seated in the middle with the Baptist diagonally on his right and, on his left, the impressive figure of a spectator, seen from behind, to restore the symmetry. Since St. John is surrounded by the two gaolers, the balance of the picture requires some further counterpoise and this is obtained by introducing an unsymmetrical figure, that of the captain of the guard, emerging from the left background. The varied group of the actual arrest provides an extremely animated contrast to the massive calm of the single standing figure. Granted that this figure is little more than a tailor's dummy, nevertheless, such calculated contrasts represent an advance

---

[1]As is well known, the man with the long cowl, at the right, and the seated woman holding up her child are borrowings from Dürer.

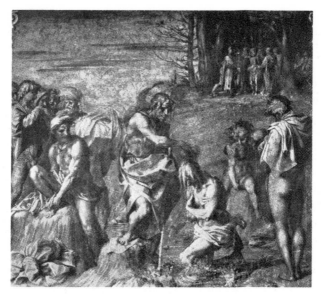

111. ANDREA DEL SARTO: *The Baptism of the People*. Florence, Scalzo

in Florentine art, for the earlier method was to balance the figures more or less equally in the space and to make their gestures equally uniform. In addition to this, the actual figure of St. John, fixing his eye with difficulty on Herod, is fine in itself; and if the gaolers could be a little more vigorous in action at least the mistake is avoided, into which others have fallen, of making them so violent that the principal figure is swamped.

5. *The Dance of Salome* (1522; *Fig.* 113). The earlier incongruous custom of uniting the scenes of Salome's dance and the bringing in of the head is dropped here and the dance forms a separate picture. Andrea seems to have taken a special delight in the theme and this dancing Salome is one of his finest inventions, enchantingly harmonious in movement, although the action is very restrained and the movement practically confined to the upper part of the body. The dancer is provided with a contrast in the form of the serving man who brings in a dish, turning his back on the spectator. The two figures are complementary and must be seen together, for it is the fact that the servant has advanced nearer to the centre than Salome, which gives full effect to the dramatic touch of her momentary pause. The style has become calmer again and the contours more fluent, while the whole is an admirable example of idealized simplification in the setting and in the suppression of irrelevant details.

6. *The Decollation of St. John* (1523; *Fig.* 114). One might well think that here, at least, it would have been impossible for Sarto to avoid the representation of violent physical action—the headsman swinging his sword was a favourite figure

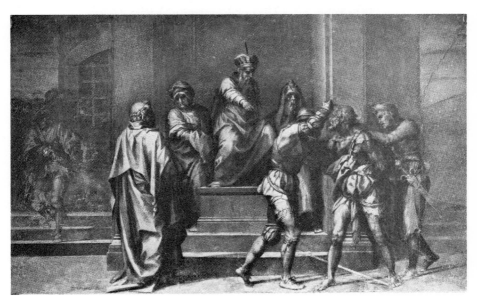

112. ANDREA DEL SARTO: *The Arrest of St. John the Baptist.* Florence, Scalzo

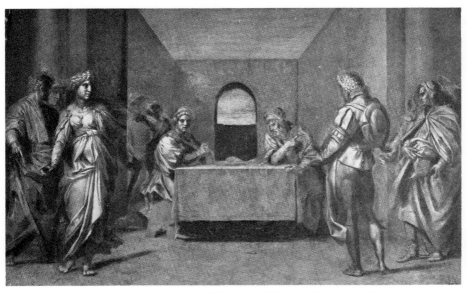

113. ANDREA DEL SARTO: *The Dance of Salome.* Florence, Scalzo

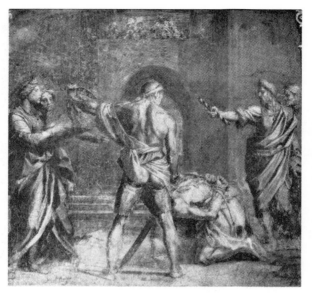

114. ANDREA DEL SARTO: *The Decollation of St. John the Baptist*. Florence, Scalzo

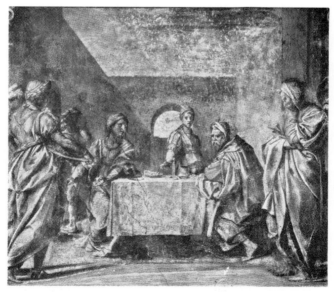

115. ANDREA DEL SARTO: *The Offering of the Head*. Florence, Scalzo

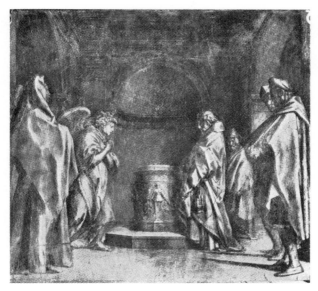

116. ANDREA DEL SARTO: *The Annunciation to Zacharias.*
Florence, Scalzo

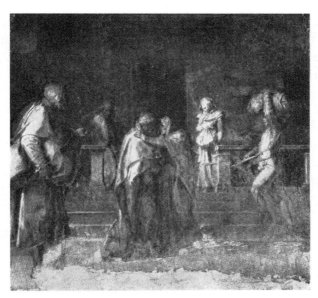

117. ANDREA DEL SARTO: *The Visitation.* Florence, Scalzo

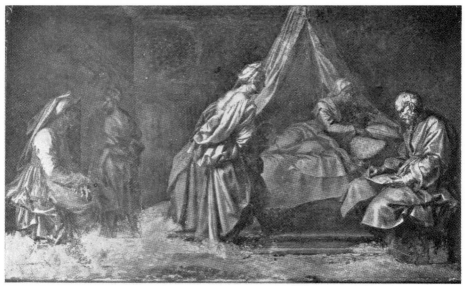

118. ANDREA DEL SARTO: *The Naming of St. John the Baptist.* Florence, Scalzo

among artists who sought movement for its own sake. Yet Sarto evaded the obligation: he does not show the actual beheading, but the quieter moment when the executioner lays the head on Salome's upraised charger. The headsman stands in the middle, his back turned and his legs astride, she is at the left and a captain is on the other side, so that the composition is again centralised. As far as possible, the victim is charitably hidden.

7. *The Offering of the Head* (1523; *Fig.* 115). The scene is again the banqueting hall, but this time the figures are closer together, for it is a narrower picture. The bearer of the head is as graceful as she was in the dance and her elegant, twisting movement contrasts with the frozen attitudes of the spectators, while all the animated action is concentrated in the centre and the sides are closed by pairs of figures.

8. *The Annunciation to Zacharias* (1523; *Fig.* 116). By now the artist was certain of his means. He had formulæ which would produce the desired result in any circumstances, and, relying on these, he allowed himself an ever-increasing sketchiness. The convention of the figures at the edges is used once more, while the apparition of the angel takes place in the background: silently he crosses his arms and bows his head to the priest who recoils in astonishment. Everything is suggested in a superficial way, but the absolute certainty of the mechanics of effect and the quiet solemnity of the architecture contrive to give a dignity to the whole which Giotto, whose sincerity was so much greater, would himself have found difficult to equal.

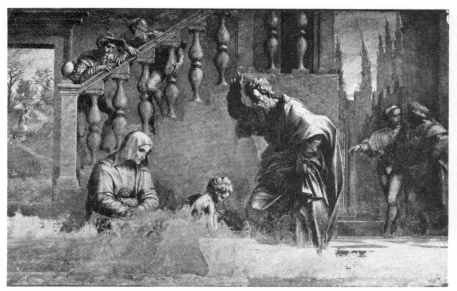

119. FRANCIABIGIO: *Zacharias blessing the Infant St. John the Baptist.* Florence, Scalzo

9. *The Visitation* (1524; *Fig.* 117). The symmetrical figures at either side are abandoned and the principal group of the two women embracing is placed diagonally, the diagonal determining the whole composition, for the figures form a quincunx, *i.e.* arranged like the five spots on dice. The architectural background introduces a feeling of calm by its orientation parallel to the picture plane.

10. *The Naming of the Baptist* (1526; *Fig.* 118). Once again there is a new scheme. The nurse with the new-born child stands in the centre of the foreground zone, facing Joachim seated at the edge of the picture, while there is a seated woman on the opposite side exactly corresponding to Joachim. Between the figures in the foreground, the mother in bed and a servant girl are inserted symmetrically into the second zone, the middle-distance. Vasari praises the picture highly and refers to a *ringrandimento della maniera*, but as far as I can see, there is nothing particularly new about the style, since all the elements had occurred before, and the particularly poor condition of the fresco does not even make us wish to see more of it: we can see all that Sarto, in this late period, thought fit to give.

The two pictures contributed by Franciabigio to this cycle both bear early dates. As the inferior artist, he does not emerge from the comparison with Sarto very favourably: to take only one of the two, the *Infant St. John receives his father's blessing* (1518; *Fig.* 119) has an antiquated effect because of the violent gesticulation of the father giving his blessing. Minor figures which are pretty enough in themselves, such as the boys on the staircase, are given too great

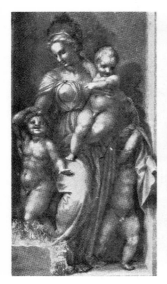
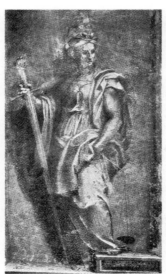
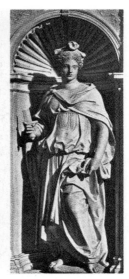

120. ANDREA DEL SARTO:
Charity. Florence, Scalzo

121. ANDREA DEL SARTO:
Justice. Florence, Scalzo

122. ANDREA SANSOVINO:
Justice. Rome,
S. Maria del Popolo

a prominence and, indeed, a more sensitive artist would never have brought in the big staircase at all—it is the only motive in the little court of the Scalzo which startles the eye. This fresco adjoins Andrea's earliest work, the *Baptism of Christ*, which it surpasses in size though not in beauty.

It has already been observed that the cycle of histories is interrupted by four allegorical figures, all by Andrea del Sarto, which imitate statues in niches. Once again the arts are drawing closer together, and there is scarcely a single major ensemble of paintings of this date which does not call upon sculpture, either real or imitated. The best of the figures here is probably the *Caritas* who bears one child in her arm and reaches down to pick up a second from the ground, and, in order to preserve her balance, she bends only the one knee while keeping a straight back (there is a similar group in the *Noah* on the ceiling of the Stanza d'Eliodoro). The *Justitia* is clearly derived from Sansovino's, in Santa Maria del Popolo, in Rome (*Figs.* 120–122), but one foot is raised in order to get greater movement.[1] The same figure recurs again in the *Madonna delle Arpie*.

---

[1]Quattrocento taste preferred the sword raised, Cinquecento preferred it lowered: Sansovino here represents the older style, Sarto the newer. The same may be said of St. Paul and his sword, and Paolo Romano's large statue, on the Ponte Sant' Angelo, is a representative of the older type.

3. Madonnas and Saints

THE falling off in sincerity of conception and in execution, perceptible in the Scalzo frescoes from about 1523 onwards, does not mean that the artist was tired of this particular commission, for the easel paintings of this period show the same symptoms. Andrea became indifferent, working to routine, relying entirely on the brilliance of his technique, and even where he appears to pull himself together his work still seems lacking in emotional warmth: the biographer can explain why this happened. His early works contain nothing which could have foreshadowed such a development and no better example could be found of the powers which originally animated him than the great *Annunciation* of the Pitti Palace (*Fig.* 123), which he must have painted in his twenty-fifth or twenty-sixth year.

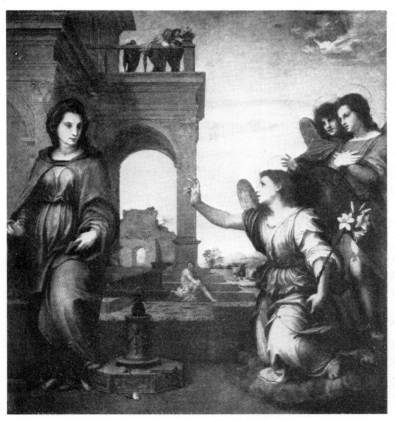

123. ANDREA DEL SARTO: *The Annunciation.* Pitti

Mary is noble and severe, as Albertinelli made her, but with a more sensitive perception of movement, while the angel is as beautiful as only Leonardo could have made him, with all the charm of youthful ardour in his head, bent forward and slightly on one side. He bows his knee as he stretches out his arm and greets the astonished Mary: this is a reverent salutation from a distance, not the impetuous rushing in of a schoolgirl as Ghirlandaio and Lorenzo di Credi made it. For the first time since the Gothic period the angel comes on clouds, for the miraculous is once again permissible in sacred pictures. The note of rapture is taken up and carried further by the two accompanying angels with curly hair and softly shadowed eyes.

Contrary to tradition, Mary is standing at the left and the angel enters from the right, and the reason for this may have been Andrea's desire to prevent the outstretched right arm covering the body, since it is only thus that the figure can be expressed with full clarity. The arm is bare—as are the legs of the accompanying angels—and the drawing clearly betrays the disciple of Michelangelo; in particular, in the way in which the left hand grasps the stem of the lily. The picture is not yet completely free from distracting detail, but the architecture in the background is excellent of its kind, and novel, giving firmness and cohesion to the figures, and in the same way the landscape echoes the principal movement.

The Palazzo Pitti contains a second *Annunciation*, of Andrea's late period (1528), originally a lunette, but now made up to a rectangle (*Fig.* 124), and together they form an antithesis of the beginning and end of his creative significance. Far exceeding the first in bravura of handling, this second *Annunciation* is empty of all expression, and this cannot be hidden beneath all the magical handling of draperies or atmosphere.

In the *Madonna delle Arpie* (*Fig.* 125), Mary appears as a mature woman and Andrea as a mature artist. This is the most aristocratic Madonna in Florence,

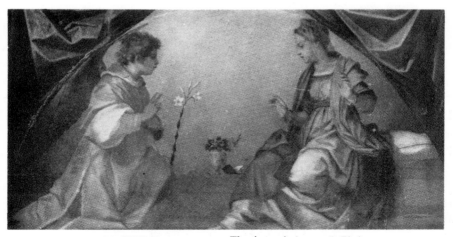

124. ANDREA DEL SARTO: *The Annunciation.* 1528. Pitti

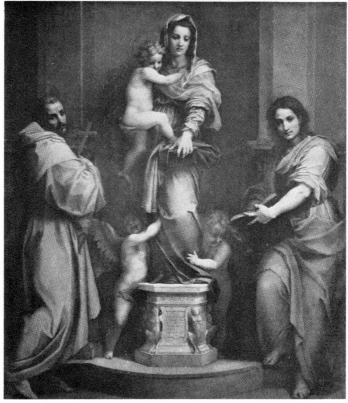

125. ANDREA DEL SARTO: *Madonna delle Arpie*. Uffizi

queenly in appearance and completely self-possessed, which makes her quite different from Raphael's *Sistine Madonna*, who does not think of herself at all. She stands like a statue on a pedestal, looking downwards. The Child hangs round her neck and she bears the heavy weight effortlessly on one arm, while the other reaches downwards and holds a book against her thigh. This, too, is a motive of the monumental style; there is nothing motherly or intimate about it, no genre-like toying with the book, just the ideal pose, for she can never have read or wished to read in this position. The way in which her hand extends over the edges of the book is a particularly fine example of the grand gestures of the Cinquecento.[1]

The attendant figures of St. Francis and St. John the Evangelist are both provided with a variety of movement and are kept subordinate to the Madonna in that they appear more or less in profile. Closely packed together, the figures form a complex unity and the variety of content in the group is reinforced by the

[1]Based on the example of the St. Peter in Raphael's *Madonna del Baldacchino*.

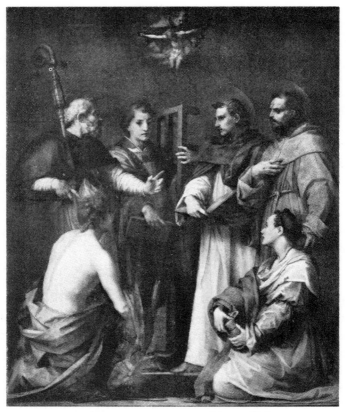

126. ANDREA DEL SARTO: *Disputà*. Pitti

spatial relationships, for there is not a superfluous inch of space and the bodies touch the edge of the picture, yet, surprisingly, there is no feeling that they are cramped. One reason for this is the pair of pilasters which lead the eye outwards at the top.

The richness of the actual painting is added to the plastic variety. Andrea seeks to deprive the eye of silhouettes, along which it might run, and to replace the coherence of contour with isolated, bright, surface planes. Here and there an illuminated fragment gleams out of the half-light and disappears again into the shadows. There is no longer any uniform development of planes in an even light and the eye is continually kept in pleasing movement, resulting in a feeling that the bodies really have a three-dimensional existence in space. This naturally triumphed over all earlier achievements of the style which kept to the one plane.

A still higher stage in the painterly style is reached in the *Disputà* in the Pitti (*Fig.* 126). Four men stand in conversation, involuntarily reminding us of Nanni di Banco's group in Orsanmichele; but this is no Quattrocento assembly of men standing unconcernedly together, it is a real disputation, where the roles can be distinguished. A bishop (Augustine?) is speaking, and the person addressed is St. Peter Martyr, the Dominican, whose refined and spiritual head makes all Fra Bartolommeo's types appear coarse. He listens attentively, unlike St. Francis, who lays his hand on his heart and shakes his head as if to say, 'Dialectics are not for me!' St. Laurence, as the youngest, expresses no opinion: he is the neutral foil and his role is the same as the Magdalen's in Raphael's *St. Cecilia*, with whom he also has in common the emphasised vertical. The stiffness inherent in a group of four standing figures is lessened by the addition of two kneeling figures in the foreground, on a lower level. These are Sts. Sebastian and Mary Magdalen, who have no part in the conversation, but are compensated by having the principal colour-accent, for Sarto gives them local colour and flesh tones while the men behind them are more restrained, with a good deal of grey, black and brown and with only a subdued glow of carmine right at the back (in the figure of St. Laurence). The background is quite dark.

From the point of view of painting and draughtsmanship this picture represents the high-water mark of Andrea's art: the nude back of St. Sebastian and the upturned head of the Magdalen are marvellous interpretations of the human form. And the hands—the delicate, feminine clasp of the Magdalen and poignant expressiveness of the disputants! Except for Leonardo, it seems as if no other artist treated hands as Andrea did.

There is a second picture of four standing figures, in the Uffizi (*Fig.* 127), which was painted about ten years later (1528) and which shows the continuation, and breaking up, of Andrea's style. Like all his later works it is bright in colour and tone, the heads loosely treated, but full of verve and vivacity in the handling and grouping.[1] It is patent that it had become easy for him to produce such brilliant effects, but the impression remains one of superficiality, and the *Madonna delle Arpie* had no worthy successors.

The newly-fashionable theme of the Madonna in Glory, or, rather, on clouds, must have been peculiarly acceptable to Andrea: he opens up the vault of Heaven and allows a great radiance to appear, while, in accordance with the taste of the time, he brought the Madonna on her clouds low down into the picture, into the very centre of the circle of saints grouped around her. The variations on standing and kneeling figures, the systematic arrangements of contrasted turns outwards and inwards, the upward and downward glances are more or less a matter of course by this time, but Sarto adds a new feature in the contrasts of light and shadow on the heads, some in full light and others in deep shadow; only he pays scarcely any heed to the source of light in the picture when he distributes these accents, for the general intention is to produce a marked

---

[1]There were originally two putti in the middle, but these have been cut out and hung separately.

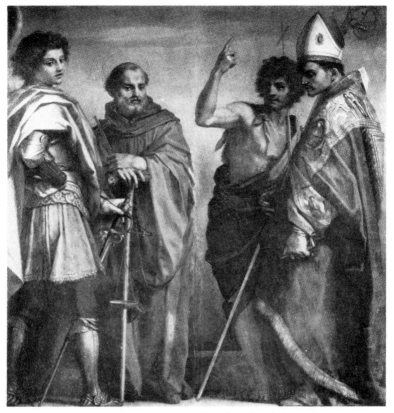

127. ANDREA DEL SARTO: *Four Standing Saints*. Uffizi

alternation over the picture surface. One soon notices the somewhat superficial application of a set of tested recipes, yet there is an undeniable impression of a certain inevitability which is due to Andrea's own temperament. The *Madonna with six Saints* of 1524 (Pitti) is a case in point (*Fig.* 128). There is no question of individual characters and the Madonna is, in fact, quite trivial. The two kneeling figures are repeated from the *Disputà* with the characteristic refinements of a practised hand, while the St. Sebastian may be based on the same model as the well-known half-length of the *Youthful St. John* (see below) but the treatment is so purely painterly that the contour is almost meaningless and the eye is held by the bright expanse of bare chest.

Finally, all the stops are pulled out in the great Berlin picture of 1528. The clouds are enclosed within an architectural setting, just as Fra Bartolommeo had already done; then there is a niche with its top cut off by the frame; a flight of steps with the saints disposed on them, so they can be clearly distinguished in depth, and the figures in the extreme foreground are made half-lengths, a

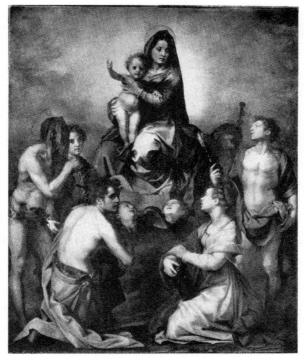

128. ANDREA DEL SARTO: *Madonna with Six Saints*. 1524. Pitti

motive which before this had been deliberately avoided in high art (*Fig.* 189).

What has already been said of Raphael's Holy Families holds good also of Andrea's, whose artistic aim was also to achieve the maximum richness and variety in a small space. He does so by using crouching or kneeling poses to get the figures near the ground, and then makes a knot of three, four or even five people against a background which is usually black. There is a whole series of pictures of this type and the good ones are those which first strike the spectator with an effect of natural movement so that he thinks of the formal problems only afterwards.

The *Madonna del Sacco* of 1525, in the cloister of the Annunziata, Florence (*Fig.* 129), occupies a special position, even in comparison with Raphael. A classic example of fully developed soft fresco technique in general and of the painterly treatment of drapery in particular, it has the additional merit of possessing an audacity in the arrangement of the figures which Andrea never again equalled. The Virgin is seated to one side, not in the centre, but the equilibrium is restored by the figure of St. Joseph opposite her, who, being further back in space, is perceptibly smaller as a mass, but compensates for this in the general balance of the picture because he is further removed from the central axis. The impression of monumentality which one receives at a distance is due to the few, and clear,

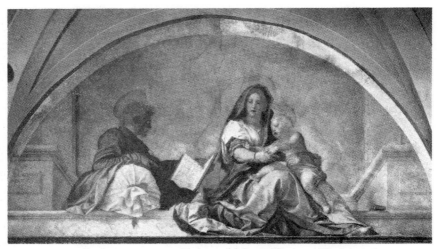

129. ANDREA DEL SARTO: *Madonna del Sacco*. Florence, SS. Annunziata

statements of major axes of direction and the extreme simplicity of the contours
is combined with great richness of form in the planes enclosed by them. The
magnificent, broad motive of the Madonna is due to the low position in which
she is seated, and her head, with its upward glance, will never lose its effectiveness, even though we tell ourselves that it is an extrinsic effect. The point of
sight is set very low down, corresponding to the facts of the situation, for the
fresco is over a door.

Among Andrea's single figures of saints the *Youthful Baptist* in the Pitti
(*Fig.* 130) enjoys world-wide fame, being one of the half-dozen pictures
invariably found reproduced in all the photograph shops during the tourist
season in Italy. It might not be uninteresting to enquire how long it has held this
position, and to what fluctuations of taste these accepted favourites of the public
are liable. The 'severe passionate beauty' celebrated in the 'Cicerone' disappears
at once when it is compared with Raphael's *St. John Baptist as a boy* in the
Tribuna (*Fig.* 168), but still he remains a handsome lad.[1] Unfortunately, the
picture has suffered badly, so that the intended painterly effect of luminous flesh
emerging from the darkness can now only be guessed at. The grasping hand and
the turn of the wrist are in Andrea's best manner and it is characteristic that
he seeks everywhere to break up the silhouette, allowing one side of the body to
disappear altogether. The swelling draperies, intended to counter the dominant
vertical, foreshadow the extravagances of the seventeenth century, while the
placing of the figure off-centre, with an empty space to the right, may be
compared with Sebastiano's *Violin Player* (*Fig.* 80).

[1]Sarto used the same model for the Isaac of the *Sacrifice* at Dresden, which was painted soon after
1520, and I believe he is also to be recognised in the *Madonna* of 1524.

This St. John has a sister in the seated *St. Agnes* in Pisa Cathedral, one of the master's most charming pictures, in which he seems, for once, to have attempted the ecstatic, although it is confined to a half-timid upward glance. Such states of great emotion were quite beyond his powers of expression, and it was a mistake to give him commissions for subjects like the Assumption, which he painted twice. Both pictures are in the Pitti, and, as might have been expected, they are unconvincing in expression and action: what can be said of an *Assumption of the Virgin* painted after 1520 which is still a mere seated figure? Even so, a worthier solution to the problem could surely have been found, but Sarto's rendering of prayer is as meaningless as

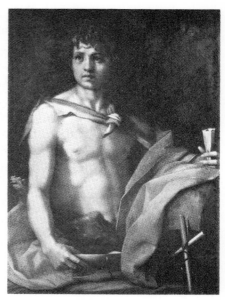

130. ANDREA DEL SARTO: *St. John the Baptist*. Pitti

the ridiculously embarrassed gesture with which Mary clasps her mantle on her lap. In both pictures he makes St. John the principal figure among the Apostles round the tomb, giving him that sensitive movement of the hands which is found in his early pictures. Yet the impression of conscious elegance is present to some degree and the Apostles seem only lukewarm in their astonishment. Nevertheless, this calm is preferable to the uproar of the Roman School as exemplified by Raphael's followers. The effects of light are calculated to produce a contrast between the radiant heavens and the darkened scene on earth. In the second and later picture, however, he left a bright rift open to the very bottom of the picture, and a greater master of movement, Rubens, followed him in this, since it is not a good idea to divide a picture of the Assumption by so strongly emphasised a horizontal.

The two kneeling saints in the earlier *Assunta* derive from Fra Bartolommeo and the motive was retained in the foreground of the later version; but, for the sake of contrast, one of the men—and he is an Apostle—is allowed to look out of the picture at the spectator during the solemn scene. This triviality is the beginning of those indifferent figures who look out of the foregrounds of seventeenth century pictures: artistic forms are already being debased into meaningless formulæ.

Of the *Pietà* in the Pitti Palace we will say nothing at all.

4. A Portrait by Andrea

ANDREA did not paint many portraits and, on the face of it, one would not credit him with any particular aptitude as a portraitist, but there are a few portraits of young men by him which attract by their mysterious charm. They are the two well-known heads in the Uffizi and the Pitti and the half-length in the National Gallery (*Figs.* 131, 132); they possess all the *noblesse* of Andrea's best manner and one feels that the painter had something out of the ordinary to express, so that it is not surprising that they have been held to be self-portraits. However, it can be stated with precision that they are nothing of the sort. The case is exactly paralleled by Hans Holbein the Younger, where the handsome, unknown youth early gave rise to a prejudice which is hard to eradicate. There is an authentic portrait of Holbein (a drawing in the collection of portraits of painters in Florence), but the logical conclusion that it excludes the others is rarely drawn because of the predisposition in favour of the more handsome man.

The authentic portraits of Andrea are to be found in the fresco of the *Procession of the Three Kings* in the forecourt of the Annunziata, as a young man, and in the collection of painters' portraits in the Uffizi, as an older man. These are absolutely certain identifications as Vasari speaks of both. The pictures mentioned above do not agree with these in features, and indeed, they do not seem to agree among themselves, for the London picture may perhaps represent

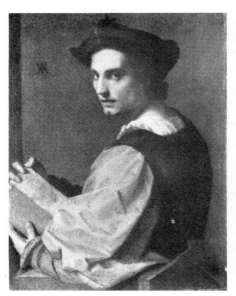

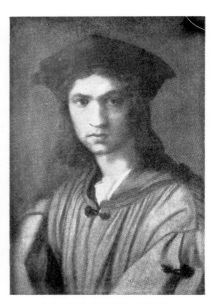

131. ANDREA DEL SARTO:
A Sculptor. London, National Gallery

132. ANDREA DEL SARTO:
So-called *Self-portrait.* Pitti

a different person from the Florentine ones. These latter can be reduced to one, in so far as they correspond line for line down to the details of the drapery: clearly the Uffizi example is the copy and the Pitti version the original which, though not undamaged, still shows the more sensitive handling and, accordingly, this will be the one spoken of here.

The head emerges from the darkness of the background, not sharply relieved against a black foil as is sometimes the case with Perugino, but, as it were, encompassed in the greenish half-light, and the highest light does not fall on the face but on a scrap of shirt accidentally displayed at the neck. The hood and collar are dull grey and brown in colour. The large eyes look calmly out of their orbits. With all its vibrantly painterly handling the effect of the whole is stabilised by the vertical position of the head, the simple, full-face view and the gentle fall of light which brings out exactly half the head and illumines exactly the necessary points. The head seems to turn with a quick movement and to be holding, just for a moment, the pose which gives absolutely pure vertical and horizontal axes, the vertical being continued right up to the peak of the cap. The simplicity of line and the reposeful masses of light and shadow unite with the clear definition of form of Andrea's developed style, with the bony structure clearly understood. The way in which the angle at the junction of nose and eye is brought out, the modelling of the chin, the indication of the cheek-bone are all strongly reminiscent of the style of the *Disputà*, which was clearly painted at about the same time.[1]

It may well be that this subtle and spiritual head is an ideal type, such as we find in sixteenth century art, and it would be pleasant to include it with the *Violin Player*, to which it is related both inwardly and outwardly, since both are portraits of artists. In any case, it is one of the finest examples of the high conception of the human form in the Cinquecento, the basic form of which is probably to be found in Michelangelo: the impression made by the mind which created the *Delphic Sibyl* is clearly recognisable here.

This portrait of Andrea's has a more Leonardesque pendant in the contemplative *Youth* in the Louvre (*Fig.* 133), an excellent work which has passed under a variety of names but is now, I think correctly, ascribed to Franciabigio, to whom is also given the *Portrait of a Youth* whose head is in shadow, of 1514, in the Palazzo Pitti. His left arm rests on a parapet with the hand upraised in the rather stiff and old-fashioned gesture which indicates speech.[2] The picture in Paris was painted somewhat later than this (*c.* 1520) and the last traces of

---

[1] This, in itself, is an argument against the 'self-portrait' hypothesis, for at the time when Andrea was painting in this style, he was no longer the young man portrayed here.
[2] The gesture is repeated in the principal figure of Franciabigio's *Last Supper* (Calza, Florence) and may, in the last instance, go back to the Christ in Leonardo's *Last Supper*, which Franciabigio knew and used.

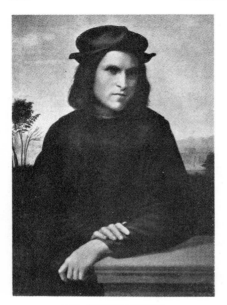

133. FRANCIABIGIO:
Portrait of a Young Man. Louvre

stiffness or timidity have disappeared. The youth, whose soul is stirred by some sorrowful emotion, gazes before him with downcast eyes, the characteristic mood being indicated most effectively by the sideways turn and slight droop of the head. Another personal touch is to be found in the listless gesture of the arms, one of which rests on the parapet, with the right hand laid on it, a motive not unlike that of the *Mona Lisa*, although here the movement is resolved into the expression of a fleeting moment, and the grand-manner portrait becomes transformed into a study of emotions, of genre-like charm. The spectator does not ask who it is, because his interest is held by the momentary emotion. The dark shadows in the eye-sockets are particularly effective in characterising the cloudy glance of melancholy; even the form of the horizon becomes a factor in the expressiveness, although the spatial effect is now discordant, since the picture has been enlarged on all four sides: our reproduction seeks to restore the original effect.

This pensive portrait has a peculiarly modern air about it, more sensitive and perceptive even than Raphael's *Self-portrait as a young man* in the Uffizi: the sentiment of the fifteenth century is always slightly obtrusive by comparison with the restraint in the expression of feelings of the classic period.

N O great artist has ever made so profound an impression on his immediate contemporaries as Michelangelo did from his earliest years, and it was the destiny of this most powerful and independent genius to have the longest span of life, remaining at work for more than a generation after the others had sunk into the grave. Raphael died in 1520, Leonardo and Fra Bartolommeo even earlier. Sarto lived until 1531, but the last decade of his life was the least important and it seems unlikely that he could have developed further even had he lived longer. Michelangelo never paused for a moment and he seems not to have reached the zenith of his powers until the second half of his life, when he created the Medici Tombs, the *Last Judgement*, and St. Peter's. From then on Central Italy knew only one kind of art, and Raphael and Leonardo were completely forgotten in front of the new revelations of Michelangelo.

1. The Medici Chapel

THE burial chapel in S. Lorenzo is one of the few instances known to art-history where the architecture and the figures are not only contemporary but were created with the specific intention of complementing each other. The whole of the fifteenth century possessed an isolating kind of vision which could appreciate beautiful details irrespective of their surroundings: in a state room, like the memorial chapel of the Cardinal of Portugal in S. Miniato, the tomb itself is an object which just happens to be there, but which could equally well be placed anywhere else without losing any of its effect. Even in the Julius Monument, Michelangelo would have had no control over the surroundings, since it was intended to be a building within a building. The façade of S. Lorenzo, which he was to make into an architectural and sculptural show-piece for the Medici family church in Florence, was the first project to contain the possibility of composing figures and architecture on a large scale and with calculated reciprocity of effect. The project fell through. Even if it had been carried out, the architecture could never have been more than a frame for the sculpture, and it was, therefore, artistically more satisfying when the new commission was given for a burial chapel, allowing the artist a space which not only permitted a freer arrangement of the sculpture, but also gave him complete control over the lighting. Michelangelo took this into account as an essential factor in his composition and arranged for the faces of *Night* and the '*Penseroso*' to be in complete shadow, an unprecedented effect in sculpture.

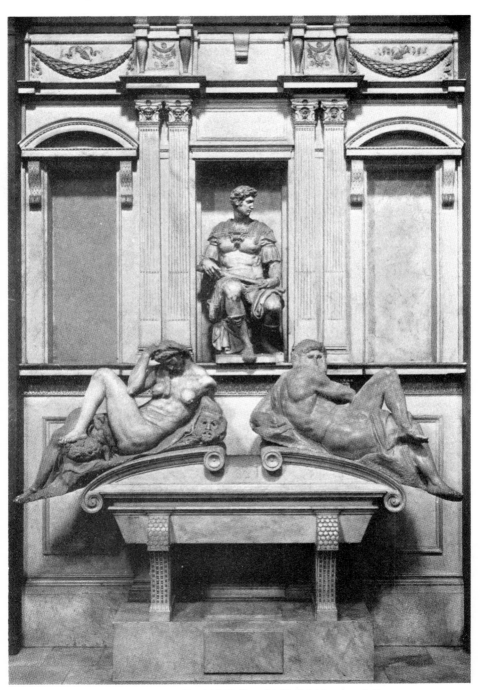

134. MICHELANGELO: *Tomb of Giuliano de' Medici*. Florence, S. Lorenzo

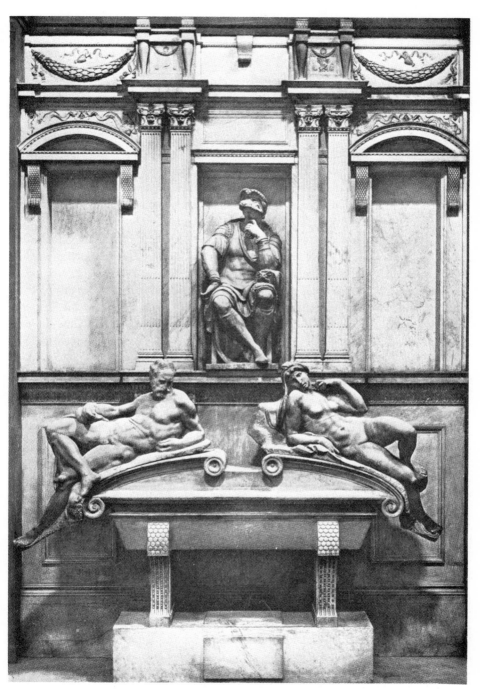

135. MICHELANGELO: *Tomb of Lorenzo de' Medici*. Florence, S. Lorenzo

The chapel contains the monuments to two members of the family who died young—Lorenzo, Duke of Urbino, and Giuliano, Duke of Nemours (*Figs.* 134, 135). An earlier plan, which provided for a more comprehensive representation of the family, was dropped. The scheme of the tombs consists of a grouping of three figures—the dead man, not sleeping, but a living, seated figure, accompanied by two recumbent figures on the steeply sloping lid of the sarcophagus. They represent the Times of Day instead of the Virtues which were formerly the customary guardians of the dead. This arrangement contains one peculiarity which is immediately noticeable: the tomb is not an independent piece of architecture with figures, standing in front of the wall-surface. Only the sarcophagus and its crowning figures stand free of the wall, while the hero himself is actually seated within the wall. Thus two elements, spatially disparate, are brought into a unified effect with the seated figure brought so low down that he comes between the heads of the recumbent ones. These latter bear the strangest relationship to their supports, for the lids of the sarcophagi are so narrow and steep that it seems the figures must slide down them. It has been suggested that perhaps the lower ends of the lids were intended to be completed by upturned terminal volutes which would provide a secure stop for the figures, as was actually done in the Tomb of Paul III in St. Peter's (a work which derives from Michelangelo). On the other hand, it is asserted that the figures would be prejudiced by this, losing their present elasticity and becoming insipid. In any case, it is probable that so abnormal an arrangement, which provokes the criticism of every layman, must go back to an author who could afford to take risks, and this leads me to believe that Michelangelo is responsible for the present design.[1]

These violations of the expected are not confined to the lower parts of the tombs, for there are dissonances in the upper part which, at first sight, are scarcely comprehensible. The figures are allowed to cut across the line of the cornice of the podium behind them with unprecedented recklessness, so that the sculpture appears in open contradiction to the architecture, which should be the master. This contradiction would be intolerable if it were left unresolved, but the resolution is provided by the third figure, which concludes the sequence, and is completely in harmony with its niche. From this we see that a triangular build-up of the figures was not all that was intended, for there is also a development in the relationships between the figures and the architecture. Whereas Sansovino's niches appear to enclose their figures in calm uniformity, there is here a dissonance which has to be resolved: it is the same principle as that in

---

[1]There is also some direct evidence for this in a drawing in the British Museum published by Symonds (Life of Michelangelo, I, 384) [B.M. 1859-5-14-822, Berenson No. 1495], which shows a figure on a similar type of lid, sketchily treated but quite distinct (*Fig.* 136).

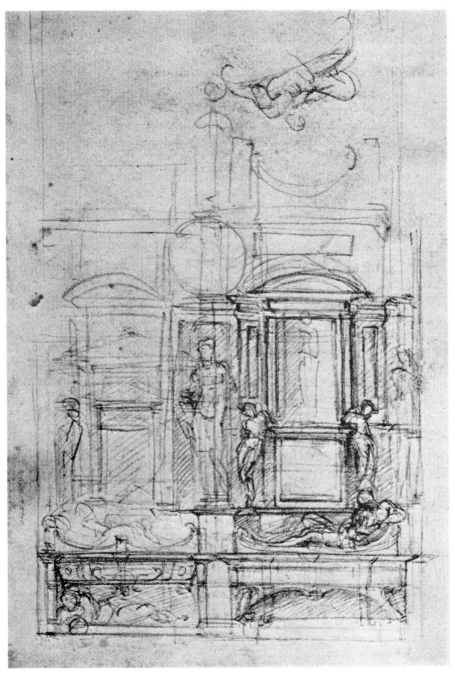

136. MICHELANGELO: Drawing. British Museum

the final version of the Julius Monument, where the compression of the central figure is relieved by the spaciousness of the fields on either side of it. Michelangelo worked out these new aesthetic principles on a huge scale in the outside walls of St. Peter's.[1]

The niches fit closely round the figures of the generals, leaving no superfluous space to weaken the effect, while the niches are so shallow that the statues project boldly. This is not the place to follow the chain of thought still further— to analyse, for example, the reasons governing the omission of a pediment over the central niche and the consequent shift of emphasis to the side ones. In any case, the architectural elements are governed by the primary intention of providing a favourable setting for the figures against small and subordinate architectural parts; and, indeed, this may provide the justification for the short lids on the sarcophagi, for the colossal figures which recline upon them are intended to look colossal. There is no other room in the whole world where sculpture speaks with such force. The whole architectural setting, with its slender panelling and restrained use of the third dimension, is entirely subordinated to the effect made by the figures.

It seems almost as if the figures were intended to appear too big for the room and it will be recalled how difficult it is to get far enough away to see them properly, how one feels hemmed in; what, then, are we to say on learning that four more figures of river-gods, lying on the floor, were to be included as well? The effect would have been oppressive, and it would have been an emotional effect which had nothing in common with the liberating beauty of the Renaissance.[2]

Michelangelo was not permitted to finish the work with his own hands—as is well known, Vasari is responsible for the present form of the chapel—but we may take it that we possess his essential ideas. Some of the architectural members are dark in colour, but otherwise the chapel is completely monochromatic, white on white, making it the first great example of the modern style which dispenses with colour.

The reclining figures of the *Times of Day* (*Figs.* 137–140) replace the customary figures of Virtues. Later artists used his type of figure to represent a Virtue, but the opportunities for characterizing the different times of day by varied poses were so much greater than those offered by the Virtues that this one fact alone would suffice to explain Michelangelo's decision, although he undoubtedly

---

[1] *Cf.* Wölfflin, *Renaissance und Barock*, 3rd ed., p. 43.
[2] The model for one of these river-gods has recently been found by Gottschewski in Florence, where it is now exhibited in the Academy (*cf.* the lucid account of the find in the *Münchener Jahrbuch der bildenden Kunst*, I, 1906). These figures on the ground had, however, no place in the present figure system, for they were projected when the upper parts were lighter and placed higher up.

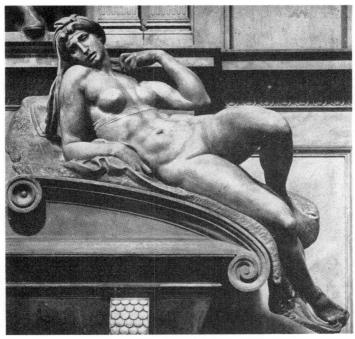

137. MICHELANGELO: *Dawn*. Florence, S. Lorenzo

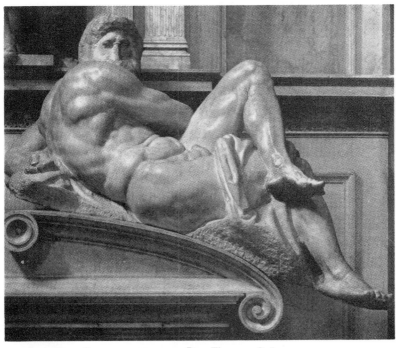

138. MICHELANGELO: *Day*. Florence, S. Lorenzo

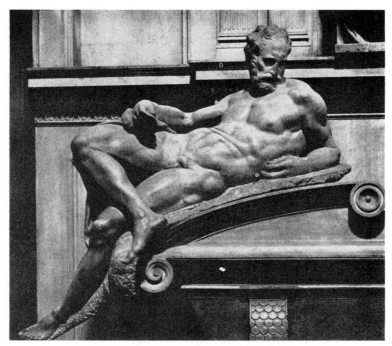

139. MICHELANGELO: *Dusk*. Florence, S. Lorenzo

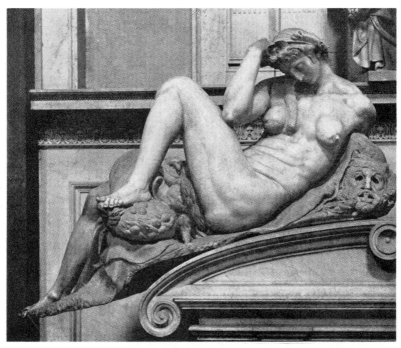

140. MICHELANGELO: *Night*. Florence, S. Lorenzo

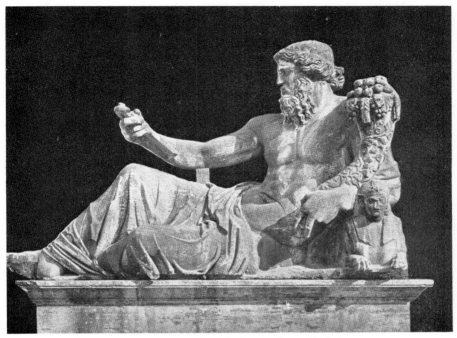

141. *The Nile*. Antique Sculpture. Rome, Capitol

started from the need for a reclining pose which would enable him to get his completely novel combination with the vertical of the seated figure.[1]

The ancients had river-gods, and a comparison between Michelangelo's figures and the two splendid antique statues for which he himself prepared a place of honour on the Capitol (*Fig.* 141), can throw a good deal of light on his own style. He takes over the motive and endows it with a richness which far surpasses all previous efforts: the twist of the body in the *Dawn*, as she rolls over to face the spectator, or the overlapping forms created by the upraised knee of the *Night*, have no equal anywhere. The figures are immensely stimulating because of the variety of planes and the major contrasts of axial direction, yet they remain at rest in spite of all this enrichment, and the strong tendency towards disintegration of the forms is countered by a still stronger will to create form. The figures are not only clear in the sense that all the essential facts are stated and the

---

[1]Those researches into the exact iconographical significance of the *Times of Day* are most likely to be successful which look to ecclesiastical texts for a foundation: Brockhaus has lately done this, though I cannot yet accept his conclusions. It is important not to overlook the position of the figures, on the sarcophagus which holds the corpse. Could there be a more powerful expression of the surrender of the body to mortality than these colossal figures representing the mutability of Time, which press down upon the tomb, kept down by the marked line of the cornice, entirely subordinate to the horizontal! And above them rises, freely, the vertical system with the image of the living 'immortal'.

principal axes made immediately obvious,[1] but the figures are contained within quite simple spatial boundaries: they are framed in space and arranged in strata, so that they can be apprehended as pure reliefs. It is extraordinary how *Dawn*, for all her movement, can be read as a single plane in this sense; her upraised left arm suggests a neutral background and everything in front of it lies in one plane parallel to it. Later artists learned movement by looking at Michelangelo and then attempted to outdo him, but they never understood his repose—least of all Bernini.

Recumbent figures permit the maximum effects of *contrapposto* because the limbs can be placed quite near to one another and yet be in contrasted movement. Formal problems, however, do not exhaust the possibilities of these figures, for they combine form with the strongest expression of a temperament in a particular situation. The weary man relaxing his limbs is a moving symbol of Evening, and seems himself to have reached the evening of life; or where, again, is there a more convincing rendering of awakening, heavy with sleep, than in the *Dawn*?

A change of feeling is perceptible in all these figures. The atmosphere is no longer one of freedom and joy as it had been in the Sistine Chapel, and all movement is heavier and slower; the bodies seem mountainously ponderous, animated only by fits and starts of the will.

The deceased are represented as seated figures, for the tomb is intended as a monument to the living man, not as a peaceful image of death, and there was a precedent for this conception in Pollaiuolo's Tomb of Innocent VIII in St. Peter's, although there the figure of the Pope giving a blessing is accompanied by another of the Pope stretched out in death. Michelangelo had to deal with two military commanders, and it may seem curious that he chose to represent them as seated, even seated in a rather indolent manner, which has a strongly personal quality— one in absorbed meditation, the other looking momentarily to one side, and neither of them in a pose characteristic of the soldier. The concept of aristocratic distinction had changed since the days when Verrocchio modelled his *Colleoni* and the type of seated general became so common later that it was retained even for so great a commander as Giovanni delle Bande Nere (Florence, outside S. Lorenzo). The actual treatment of the seated figures is interesting by comparison with the numerous earlier solutions of the problem which Michelangelo had already offered. The one can be referred to the *Jeremiah* of the Sistine Ceiling, the other to the *Moses*, but in both are characteristic alterations tending towards greater richness of treatment; for example, the *Giuliano* (with the marshal's baton) has a differentiation between the knees and in the placing of the shoulders. From this time onwards all seated figures were judged by these for sculptural

---

[1] The right arm of *Night* seems to have disappeared from view, but this is only an apparent disappearance—it is actually in the rough-hewn piece of stone above the mask.

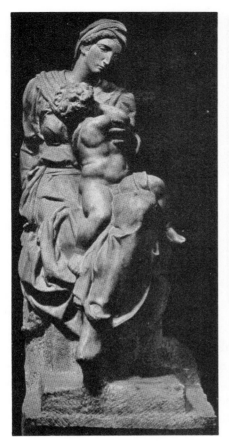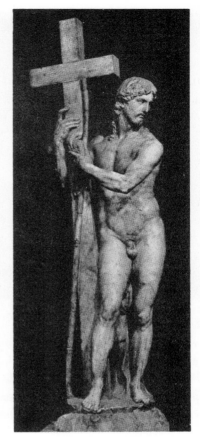

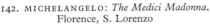

142. MICHELANGELO: *The Medici Madonna.*
Florence, S. Lorenzo

143. MICHELANGELO: *The Risen Christ.*
Rome, S. Maria sopra Minerva

value, and before long there was no end to the frenzied efforts to attract attention by throwing forward a shoulder, raising a foot, twisting a head—and, of course, the inner meaning necessarily got lost.

Michelangelo did not desire to render the personal characters of the two dead men and did not even bother with facial likenesses. Even the costume is ideal. Neither is there any inscription to explain the purpose of the monument, but this may have been intentional, since the Julius Tomb also lacks an inscription.

The Medici Chapel also contains another seated figure of a different kind—a *Madonna and Child* (*Fig.* 142). This group shows Michelangelo's style at its most mature, and it is the more valuable to us in that a comparison with an analogous early work, the Bruges *Madonna* (*Fig.* 21), makes his artistic development quite clear and leaves no possible doubt as to his intentions. It would be an admirable exercise, as an introduction to Michelangelo's art, to begin with the question of

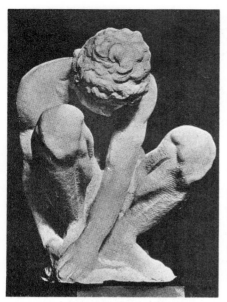

144. MICHELANGELO: *Crouching Boy*.
Leningrad, Hermitage

how much the Medici *Madonna* grew out of the one in Bruges. We should have to make it clear that the simpler possibilities are abandoned in favour of more complicated ones; how the knees are no longer ranged side by side, but one leg is crossed over the other; how the arms are differentiated, the one reaching forward and the other drawn back, so that the shoulders are different from all points of view; how the upper part of the body is bent forward and the head turned sideways; how the Child straddles His mother's knee, facing forward, but at the same time twisted back upon Himself and reaching out His hands to her breast. When the physical motives have been thoroughly mastered, there is the second consideration: how is it that, in spite of all this, the figure is so full of repose? The first quality—complete variety—is easily imitated, but the second—the appearance of unity—is extremely difficult. The group appears simple because it is lucid and can be taken in at a single glance, and it gives the impression of repose because the whole content is reduced to one compact, general form; the original block of stone seems to have been but slightly modified.

Perhaps the highest achievement in this direction was Michelangelo's *Boy* in the Hermitage, who crouches down and rubs his feet (*Fig.* 144).[1] The work has the appearance of a solution to a set problem, as though he had really set himself to produce the most complicated figure possible, while removing as little stone and altering the volume of the block as little as possible. This is how Michelangelo would have fashioned his version of the *Boy with the Thorn:* a pure cube, endowed with the maximum stimulus to plasticity.

The stylisations introduced into a standing figure, at this period, can be seen in the *Christ* in Santa Maria sopra Minerva, Rome (*Fig.* 143), which, unfortunate in its final execution, must be accounted as significant in its conception and important in the influence it exerted. It goes without saying that Michelangelo was no longer interested in draped figures and so he represented Christ as nude, not as the Risen Saviour with the banner of victory, but with

---

[1]Springer relates it, wrongly, to the Julius Monument and believes that it represents a conquered foe (*Raphael und Michelangelo*, II, 3rd ed., p. 30).

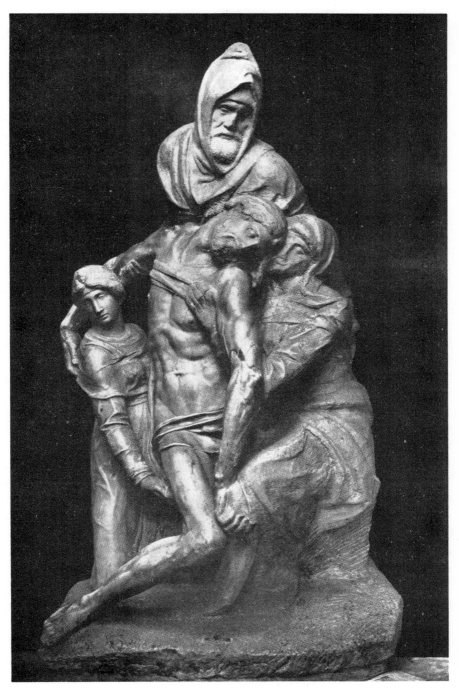

145. MICHELANGELO: *Pietà*. Florence, Cathedral

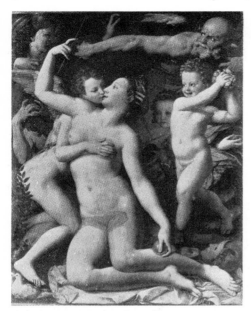

146. BRONZINO: *Allegory.*
London, National Gallery

the Cross, the Reed, and the Sponge, an arrangement which must have interested him by the disposition of the masses. The Cross rests on the ground and Christ supports it with both hands, giving rise to the important motive of the arm reaching across the chest, which, it must be remembered, was new; in the *Bacchus*, for example, such an idea would never have occurred. The direction of movement in the outstretched arm is intensified by the turning of the head in the opposite direction, and a further displacement is observable in the hips, where the left leg is drawn back but the chest is turned to the right. The feet are placed one behind the other, so that the figure, as a whole, has a surprising development in depth, which is, however, only really effective when seen (or photographed) from the normal aspect—the normal aspect being the one in which all the contrasts come into play simultaneously.

Michelangelo explored the possibility of obtaining still greater enrichment by a combination of standing and kneeling figures, as in the so-called *Victory* of the Bargello,[1] which is not a work to our taste but which had a special charm for the master's followers, as the numerous imitations of the motive testify. We may pass it over in order to consider only the last products of the master's plastic imagination, the various projects for a *Pietà*, the richest of which, with four figures, is now in Florence Cathedral, but was destined for his own tomb (*Fig.* 145).[2] The feature they all have in common is that the body of Christ is no longer disposed diagonally across His mother's knees, but is partly upright and collapsing at the knees, making a beautiful line quite impossible—but Michelangelo did not want a beautiful line. The last thought to which his chisel gave expression was to be the formless collapse of a heavy mass. The scheme was

---

[1][Now in the Palazzo Vecchio.—*Trans.*]

[2]As well as the well-known *Rondanini Pietà* in Rome, there is a similar unfinished work in the Castle at Palestrina which would repay close examination. (This observation, made in the first edition, led to nothing, but in the meantime the French made the discovery independently—*cf.* the well-illustrated article in the *Gazette des Beaux-Arts*, March, 1907, by A. Garnier, who strongly supports the authenticity of the piece). [The *Palestrina Pietà* has been exhibited in the Florence Academy since about 1940; the *Rondanini Pietà* was sold to the Brera, Milan, in 1952.—*Trans.*].

appropriated by painters and when one contemplates a similar group by Bronzino (*Fig.* 146), with an abrupt zig-zag of directions and a harsh compression of the figures, one can hardly believe that this was the generation which had its starting point in the age of Raphael and Fra Bartolommeo.

2. The *Last Judgement* and the Cappella Paolina

MICHELANGELO certainly did not embark upon the pictorial commissions of his old age with the repugnance with which he had formerly undertaken the Sistine Ceiling: he now felt the need to let himself go in great masses. In the *Last Judgement* (1534–41) he enjoyed the 'Promethean happiness' of realizing

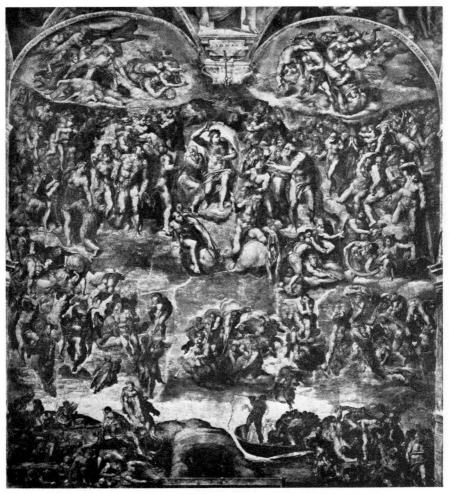

147. MICHELANGELO: *The Last Judgement.* Vatican, Sistine Chapel

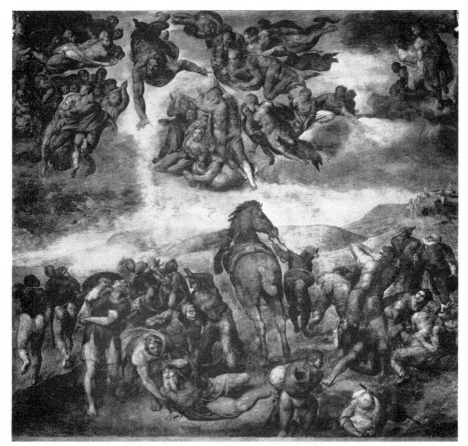

148. MICHELANGELO: *The Conversion of St. Paul.* Vatican, Cappella Paolina

all the possibilities of movement, attitude, foreshortening and grouping of the naked human form (*Fig.* 147). He wished to make these masses overpowering, to sweep the spectator off his feet, and he succeeds in his intention. The picture seems too big for the room; the one huge painting, without any frame, extends over the whole wall, blotting out all the earlier frescoes painted there. He did not even respect his own earlier frescoes on the ceiling: it is impossible to look at the two together without becoming aware of the violent discord.

The arrangement is most impressive in itself. Christ is placed high up in the picture, which contributes enormously to the effect, and He is shown in the act of springing up so that He seems to grow greater in size even as one looks at Him. Around Him is an awe-inspiring press of martyrs clamouring for vengeance: more and more of them surge forward, their bodies growing larger and larger— for the proportions are quite arbitrary—and the gigantic forms crowd together

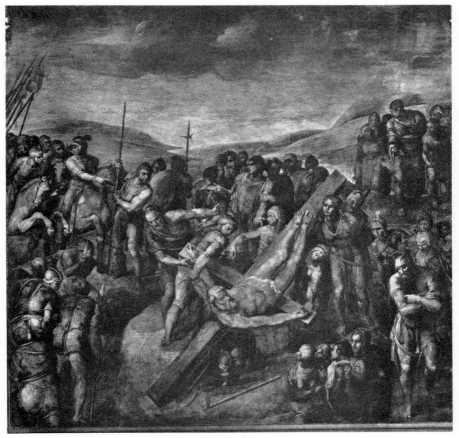

149 MICHELANGELO: *The Crucifixion of St. Peter*. Vatican, Cappella Paolina

to create unprecedentedly powerful masses, and only these masses count, for details no longer have any significance. The figure of the Virgin is completely dependent, attached to that of Christ, just as in architecture at this time the single pilaster was accompanied by a strengthening half- or quarter-pilaster. The main articulations of the picture are the two diagonals which meet in the figure of Christ. The gesture of His hand runs down through the whole picture like a flash of lightning, yet the effect is obtained optically, by the arrangement of the figures and not dynamically, by gesture. This line repeats itself on the other side of the picture, for it would have been impossible to give sufficient emphasis to the principal figure without this symmetrical arrangement.

In the Cappella Paolina, on the other hand, the histories painted in extreme old age, the *Conversion of St. Paul* and *Crucifixion of St. Peter*, break away from all symmetry and make a further advance towards formlessness (*Figs.* 148, 149).

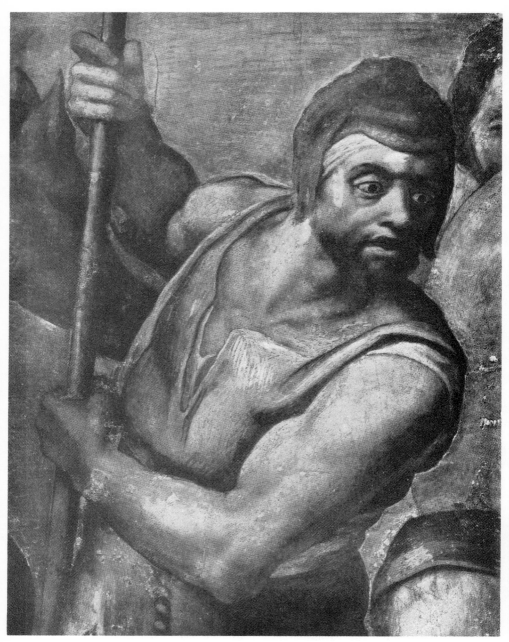

149a. MICHELANGELO: Detail from the *Crucifixion of St. Peter*. (Fig. 149)

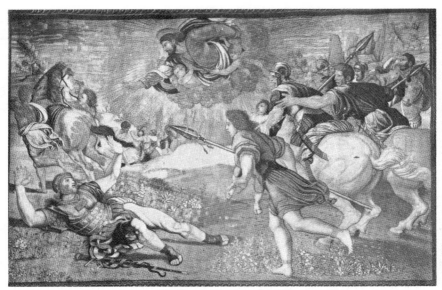

150. RAPHAEL: *The Conversion of St. Paul*. Tapestry. Vatican

The fresco fields end sharply up against the real pilasters, and half-length figures grow out of the bottom of the picture, all of which has certainly nothing to do with the classic style, but equally certainly it is not senile fumbling, for Michelangelo surpasses himself in the vigour with which the story is told. The conversion of St. Paul could not be more powerfully rendered than it is here: Christ appears high up in the corner of the picture, His radiance shining down on St. Paul, who stares out of the picture as he hears the Voice coming down from above and behind him. This tells the story once and for all, leaving the version given in the Raphael tapestries far behind; there, apart from details of movement, the principal effect is spoiled because the prostrate man has too comfortable a view of the wrathful God (*Fig.* 150). Michelangelo knew what he was doing when he set Christ above Paul—on his neck, as it were—so that He is invisible to the man below raising his head and listening, and one feels that this is indeed the blinded man with the Voice of Heaven echoing in his ears. The horse bolts out at the side of the tapestry; Michelangelo put his horse immediately beside Paul, but moving in the sharpest possible contrast of direction, and into the picture. The whole of this group is pushed unsymmetrically over to the left side and the one great line which descends steeply from the figure of Christ is flattened out and continued over to the other side. This is the final style, with harsh lines darting convulsively through the picture, heavy, lumpish masses and, next to them, yawning voids. The pendant, of the *Crucifixion of St. Peter*, is composed with similar shrill dissonances.

3. The Decline

NOBODY would wish to make Michelangelo personally responsible for what happened to Central Italian art; he was what he had to be, and he remains sublime even in the distortions of his ultimate style, yet his influence was formidable. All beauty came to be measured by the standard of his works, and an art which was the product of special and personal circumstances became the universal style. It will be necessary to look at this phenomenon—'Mannerism'—somewhat more closely.

From now on, everybody sought to obtain stupendous effects of mass, utterly rejecting Raphael's architectonic methods. Spaciousness and beauty of proportion became alien concepts; the feeling for the potentialities of a plane surface or spatial area became completely atrophied. Painters began to rival one another in the atrocious overcrowding of canvases, in a dissolution of forms which deliberately sought a contradiction between the amount of space available and the objects in it: it was not necessary to have a multitude of figures, for even a single head could be made to bear a disproportionate relationship to its frame, while in free-standing sculpture it was possible to set a colossal figure on a minute support (Ammannati's *Neptune* in the Piazza della Signoria in Florence).

Michelangelo's greatness was thought to lie in his richness of movement, and to work 'in Michelangelo's manner' meant to make great play with the limbs, which brings us into that world of multiple turns and twists where the uselessness of the action cries out to Heaven. Nobody knew any more what simple gestures or natural movements were. How fortunate was Titian's situation, if we think of his peaceful, nude female figures, by comparison with these Central Italians who had to rely on the most complicated poses to make a *Venus* interesting to their public! (As an example of this, the *Venus* in the Colonna Gallery (*Fig.* 151), ascribed to Vasari, may be compared to the prostrate figure of Heliodorus.) The worst of it is that they would have rejected sympathetic commiseration with some vigour.

Art became completely formalised and no longer paid any attention to nature, constructing motives of movement according to personal formulæ and making of the human body a purely schematic machine of joints and muscles. To stand in front of Bronzino's *Christ in Limbo*, in the Uffizi, is like looking at an anatomical museum: everything is anatomical pedantry and there is no trace of a straight-forward observation. The sense of texture in materials, an appreciation of the softness of flesh, or a feeling for the beauty of the surfaces of inanimate objects, all seem to have died out. Sculpture was the leading art and painters took to painting sculpture, blindly rejecting all the riches of their own art and beggaring themselves in the process. Such charming old subjects as the Adoration of the

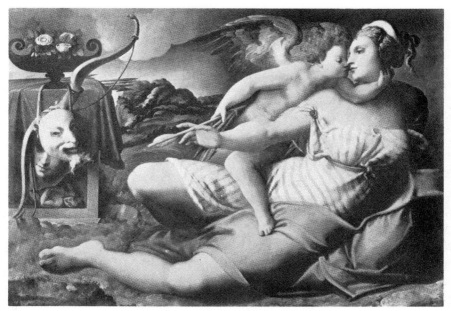

151. VASARI: *Venus and Amor*. Rome, Galleria Colonna

Shepherds, or the Three Kings, were now no more than pretexts for more or less perfunctory constructions of curves and universal nude bodies. When Pellegrino Tibaldi had to paint the shepherds who came from the fields to adore the Child, he produced a complete hotch-potch—athletes, Sibyls, and the Angels of the Last Judgement (*Fig.* 152). Every gesture is forced and the composition of the whole is ludicrously rigid; the picture looks like a travesty and yet Tibaldi was one of the best and most serious of his generation.

It may be asked what had happened to the festal splendours of the Renaissance, and why it was that a picture like Titian's *Presentation of the Virgin*, of about 1540, had become inconceivable in Central Italy? Men had lost all joy in themselves, they sought some general principle which lay beyond the actual world, and schematisation in art went hand in hand with a learned imitation of the antique. The differences between local schools disappeared and art ceased to have anything popular about it. In such circumstances there was no hope for it; it was dying at the roots and the unholy vanity of desiring to produce nothing but monumental works on the grand scale simply hastened the process.

It could not revive itself; salvation had to come from outside, and it was in the Germanic North of Italy that the spring of a new naturalism gushed out. Caravaggio makes an unforgettable impression on those whose perceptions have been dulled by the mediocrities of Mannerism, for he was the first to return to first-hand observation and to perceptions which he had made his own by direct

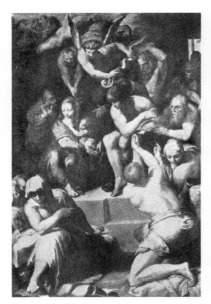
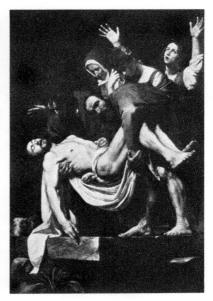

152. TIBALDI:
The Adoration of the Shepherds.
Liechtenstein Collection

153. CARAVAGGIO:
The Entombment of Christ.
Vatican Gallery

experience. The Vatican *Entombment* (*Fig.* 153) may not appeal by its subject-matter to many among the modern public, but there must be much in its favour if a painter like the young Rubens, who sensed such great powers within himself, found it worth his while to make a large-scale copy; and if we confine ourselves to a single figure, such as the weeping girl, we find a shoulder painted with such light and colour that all the false pretensions of Mannerism melt away like an unpleasant dream before this sunlit actuality. Once again the world is rich and joyous. Seventeenth-century Naturalism, and not the Bolognese Academy, was the true heir of the Renaissance, and one of the most interesting questions in art-history is why it was that, in the struggle between these two, Naturalism was doomed to succumb to the 'ideal' art of the Eclectics.

PART TWO

Chapter I : THE NEW IDEALS

IN the Campo Santo at Pisa, Benozzo Gozzoli painted a series of narrative pictures from the Old Testament,[1] including one of *Noah's Drunkenness* (*Fig.* 154). It is a typical Quattrocento narrative, full of detail, and showing the narrator's pleasure in representing the beginning and progress of the Patriarch's debauch as circumstantially as possible. He begins at the very beginning, 'It was a lovely afternoon in autumn and the grandfather took two of his grandchildren and went with them to watch the progress of the vintage . . .'

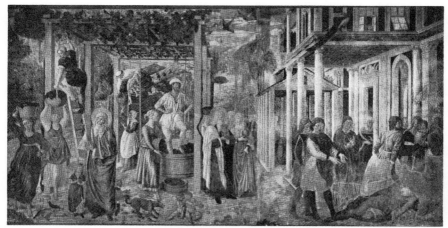

154. GOZZOLI: *The Drunkenness of Noah*. Pisa, Campo Santo

We see the labourers and the maids picking the grapes, filling the baskets with them and treading them in the vats. The whole scene is enlivened by the antics of some animals; birds perch near the puddles, and one of the children nervously watches a small dog, while his grandfather enjoys the pleasant scene. Meanwhile, the new wine has been pressed and is brought to the master for approval, his wife carrying the cup herself, while everybody hangs on his lips as he rolls the vintage critically round his tongue. His judgement must have been favourable, for the Patriarch now disappears into a retired arbour where there is a large cask of *vino nuovo*. Then the catastrophe occurs: the old man lies blind drunk outside the door of his gaily-painted house, indecently exposed. His children gaze at this strange transformation in profound astonishment, while his wife makes it her first care to drive away the maid-servants, who, rather unwillingly, cover their faces with their hands, one of them even peeping through her fingers in an attempt to catch another glimpse.

---

[1][These frescoes were almost entirely destroyed in the war of 1939–45.—*Trans.*].

Such a narrative does not occur after 1500, when the story is told with a minimum of figures, concisely and without any by-play, giving only the dramatic kernel of the story without any descriptions. The subject is taken seriously and genre-like embroideries are not tolerated, for the aim is to grip the spectator, not to amuse him. The emotions are the main preoccupation and the interest in humanity swallows up all the other things in the world.

In a Gallery where the Cinquecentisti hang side by side, the spectator's first impression is of monotony of subject-matter, for this art consists of nothing but the human body—large bodies which fill the whole of the picture-space, austerely excluding everything in the way of accessories; and what is true of easel pictures is equally true of wall-paintings. We are presented with a new race of men and art seeks effects which have nothing to do with intuitive joys in the many-sided variety of things.

I

THE Cinquecento set out with an entirely new conception of human greatness and dignity; movement became more sweeping and emotional sensibility deeper and more passionate. Human nature was perceptibly and universally elevated and

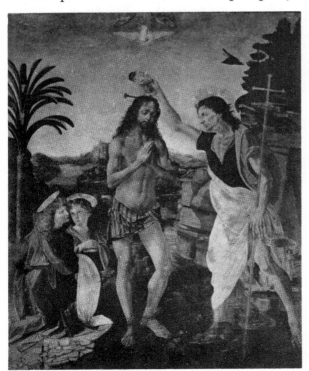

155. VERROCCHIO: *The Baptism of Christ*. Uffizi

a feeling for the significant, for the solemn and noble, began to crystallise in a way which makes the Quattrocento appear timid and limited in its range of gesture. In this way all expression was translated into a new language: clear, staccato notes became deep and sonorous harmonies and the world heard once again the splendid chords of a deeply emotional style.

When Verrocchio, let us say, depicts the *Baptism of Christ* (Fig. 155), the action takes place with a pressing haste, an anxious ingenuousness,

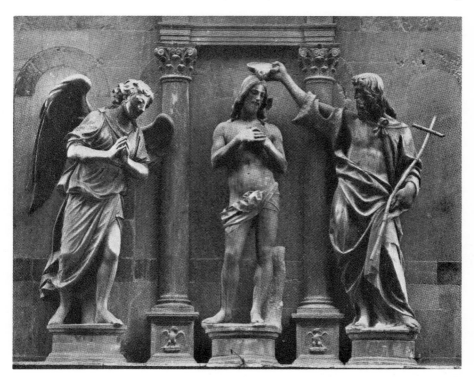

156. ANDREA SANSOVINO: *The Baptism of Christ*. Florence, Baptistery

which may seem worthy and honourable, but which the new race of men felt to be vulgar. If we compare Verrocchio's *Baptism* with Andrea Sansovino's group on the Baptistery (*Fig.* 156), we see that Sansovino has made something quite new of it. The Baptist is not arriving on the scene, he stands there quite calmly, his body turned to face us, not Christ, and only the vigorous turn of his head goes with the direction of his arm, fully extended and holding the vessel over Christ's head. There is no anxious following-up of the movement, no bending forward; the act is performed with ease and restraint, since it is a symbolic act and does not depend for its value upon a scrupulously exact performance. Verrocchio's Baptist follows the water with his eyes; Sansovino's lets his gaze rest upon the face of Christ.[1] There is a sketch by Fra Bartolommeo in the Uffizi for a *Baptism* which has exactly corresponding Cinquecento features. The same transformation takes place in the figure of Christ, who is now represented as a ruler and not as a poor teacher. In Verrocchio's picture He

---

[1] Sansovino's Baptist holds the vessel almost flat where earlier artists represented it up-turned, with archaic exactness. Even Giovanni Bellini, in his Vicenza picture of 1500, shows the water draining away to the last drop.

stands unsteadily in the brook with the water swirling around His thin legs, but a later age gradually did away with the standing in the water, since the every-day realism was worth sacrificing for the sake of greater clarity of appearance. But the standing posture itself is made easy and noble, as in Sansovino's elastic pose, with the leg which bears no weight moved out to one side. The result is a beautiful flowing line instead of an angular and jagged movement. The shoulders are drawn back although the head is sunk slightly forward; the arms are crossed on the breast, the natural development from the traditional motive of the hands folded in prayer.[1]

These are the grand gestures of the sixteenth century, but they are to be found as early as Leonardo, only quiet and sensitive, like his nature. Fra Bartolommeo is filled with the new pathos and a conviction that carries all before it like a gale: the prayer of his *Mater misericordiae* and the benediction of his *Risen Christ* (*Figs.* 97, 98) are inventions of the noblest kind. The ardour of prayer expressed in the whole form of the one and the impressive dignity with which Christ gives His blessing in the other, make all earlier efforts seem like childish games. Michelangelo was by nature not given to over-much pathos or rhetoric; his pathos is like the whisper of a mighty underground river, scarcely perceptible, but no one has ever equalled the force of his gestures—it is enough to quote the figure of the Creator from the Sistine Ceiling. Raphael completely absorbed the new spirit during the years of his maturity in Rome. What grandeur of perception animates the drawing for a tapestry of the *Coronation of the Virgin*, what a sweep in the gestures of giving and receiving! It takes a strong personality to keep these powerfully expressive motives under control and an instructive example of the way in which they can run away with the artist is furnished by the so-called *Five Saints* at Parma (engraved by Marcantonio, Bartsch 113; *Fig.* 157), a work of Raphael's school, in which the heavenly figures may be compared with the relatively timid group around Christ in the *Disputà* of Raphael's youth.

We have a literary parallel to this overdone pathos in Sannazaro's celebrated poem on the birth of Christ, *De partu virginis*.[2] The poet seems to have set out with the intention of avoiding the simplicity of the Biblical narrative as much as possible, embellishing the story with all the pomp and pathos he could contrive. From the outset, Mary is the Goddess, the Queen, and the humility of her '*Fiat mihi secundum verbum tuum*' is elaborated into a long bombastic speech which has nothing to do with the event as described in the Bible; she gazes up to Heaven

---

[1] A similar criticism could be made of Verrocchio's bronze group of the *Incredulity of St. Thomas*, on Orsanmichele. The motive of Christ baring the wound with His own hands, and watching His own gesture, is a mean one, and no later man would have treated the theme thus.
[2] The author is said to have spent twenty years in polishing it before its publication in 1526.

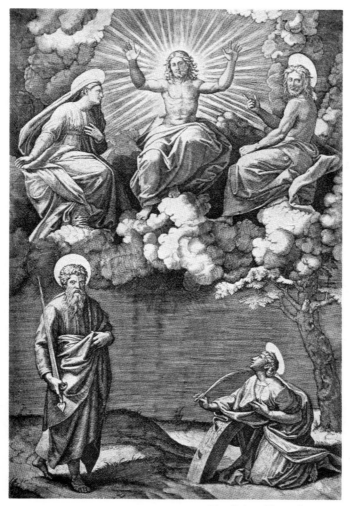

157. MARCANTONIO RAIMONDI: *Five Saints.* Engraving

'. . . *oculos ad sidera tollens*
adnuit et tales emisit pectore voces:
Jam jam vince fides, vince obsequiosa voluntas:
en adsum: accipio venerans tua jussa tuumque
dulce sacrum, pater omnipotens . . .'

The room is flooded with light. She conceives. Thunder is heard from a cloudless
sky

'. . . *ut omnes*
audirent late populi, quos maximus ambit
Oceanus Thetysque et raucisona Amphitrite.'

2

SIDE by side with the desire for ample, unencumbered forms there exists a tendency to minimize the expression of passion which is perhaps still more characteristic of the facial expressions typical of the century. It is this restraint which is meant when the 'classic repose' of the figures is quoted, and examples of it are easily found. At a moment of the most intense emotion, when Mary sees her Son lying dead before her, she neither weeps nor cries out; calm and tearless, unbroken by grief, she spreads out her arms and looks upward. Raphael drew her so, in an engraving by Marcantonio (*Fig. 158*), and Fra Bartolommeo painted her, without violence and without lamentation, pressing a kiss on the forehead of the dead Christ, who Himself bears no trace of His sufferings. Michelangelo, still greater and still more restrained than the others, had already depicted the scene in this way in the *Pietà* of his first Roman period (*Fig. 20*).

When Mary and Elisabeth, great with child, embrace in a *Visitation*, it is the meeting of two tragic queens; a slow, solemn, silent greeting (*Fig. 159*; Sebastiano del Piombo, Louvre) and no longer the cheerful, hasty running up to one another with the friendly young woman gesturing to her old cousin and telling her not to stand on ceremony. Similarly, in scenes of the Annunciation, Mary is no longer a girl gazing in pleased alarm at her unexpected visitor, as we find her in Fra Filippo, Baldovinetti or Lorenzo di Credi; nor is she a meek young woman with the downcast eyes of a candidate for confirmation; she is completely composed,

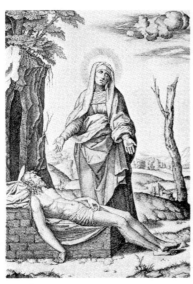

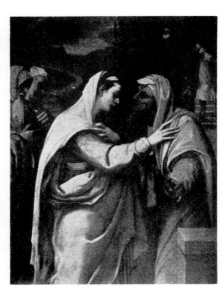

158. MARCANTONIO RAIMONDI:
Pietà. Engraving after Raphael

159. SEBASTIANO DEL PIOMBO:
The Visitation. Louvre

and, bearing herself like a princess, she receives the angel like a great lady who is schooled never to show surprise.[1] Even the emotion of motherly love and tenderness is subdued—Raphael's Roman *Madonnas* are quite different from those of his earlier period. The Virgin had become a great lady and it was no longer suitable for her to press the Child to her cheek, as she does in the *Madonna della Casa Tempi* in Munich. A distance is maintained between them and the *Madonna della Sedia* shows her as the proud, rather than the loving, mother, who is oblivious of the outside world; and if the *Madonna of Francis I* shows the Child throwing Himself towards His mother, it should be noted how little she advances towards Him.

3

THE conception of good breeding which still prevails in the West was first set out in Italy in the sixteenth century, and a great many gestures and movements disappear from pictures because they were felt to be too commonplace. We feel a distinct sense of moving into another class of society and a bourgeois art is transformed into an aristocratic one which adopts the distinctive criteria of demeanour and feeling prevalent among the upper classes, and, accordingly, the whole Christian cosmos, saints and heroes, had to be re-styled into aristocrats. Then it was that the gulf between the popular and the noble was fixed. St. Peter, in Ghirlandaio's *Last Supper* of 1480 (*Fig.* 13), gestures with his thumb towards Christ, a gesture of the people, which High Art forthwith rejected as inadmissible. Leonardo was fastidious for his day, but even he occasionally offends against a pure Cinquecento taste: I should imagine a case in point to be the gesture of the Apostle at the right of the *Last Supper* (*Fig.* 12a), laying one hand on the table, palm upwards, and about to smack the back of the other hand down on to it. This is an expressive gesture, which, even now, is common enough and easily comprehensible, yet the high style rejected it along with others. It would take us too far if we attempted to analyse completely this process of 'purification', even in a restricted number of cases, so a few examples must stand for many.

When the head of the Baptist is brought to the table at Herod's feast, Ghirlandaio shows the King bowing his head and pressing his hands together, audibly lamenting, but to the new generation this seemed unkingly and Andrea

---

[1]Leonardo blames a contemporary of his for representing the Virgin as thrown into such a flutter by the angelic message that it looks as if she wanted to jump out of the window. Albertinelli and Andrea del Sarto were probably the first to strike the true note of the Cinquecento, although they were anticipated by Piero della Francesca's *Annunciation* at Arezzo. The most grandiose version of the subject is Marcello Venusti's picture in the Lateran, the conception of which betrays the mind of Michelangelo. There are repetitions in S. Caterina ai Funari, Rome, and elsewhere, and a drawing in the Uffizi (Berenson, No. 1644: 'I see no reason why it should not be given to Venusti').

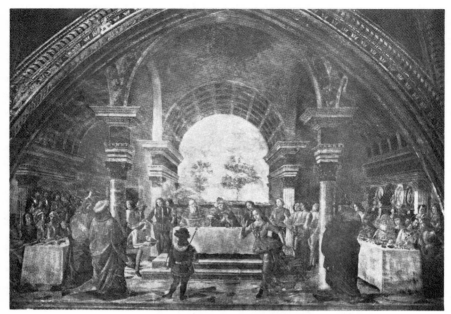

160. GHIRLANDAIO: *The Feast of Herod*. Florence, S. Maria Novella

del Sarto shows Herod's arm outstretched, languidly warding off the sight and signing for it to be taken away (*Figs.* 160, 115). When Salome is dancing, Filippo or Ghirlandaio make her leap around the room like an impetuous schoolgirl, but the gentility of the sixteenth century required more moderation from a princess, who should dance only slow measures; and thus it was that Andrea painted her.

Generalised ideas were formed of noble posture in sitting or in walking. Zacharias, the father of St. John, was a simple man, but the way in which Ghirlandaio depicts him seated with one leg balanced on the other knee as he writes the name of the newborn child, was not good enough for the hero of a Cinquecento history picture.

The true aristocrat is easy in bearing and movement, neither striking an attitude nor stiff as a ramrod in order to make his presence felt; he appears as he is, for he is always presentable. Castagno's heroes are, for the most part, vulgar bravos and no gentleman would wish to look like that: even the type of the *Colleoni* in Venice must have seemed ostentatious to the sixteenth century. The women in Ghirlandaio's birth-scenes march in, bolt upright, to pay their visits in a fashion which a later age would have considered slightly middle-class, since the great lady should have an easy, almost negligent, deportment.

If Italian written testimony to these new ideas is desired, it can be found in Count Castiglione's 'Cortegiano', the handbook of the accomplished gentleman

(1516), which expresses the views current at the Court of Urbino, and Urbino was then the meeting-place of everyone in Italy who had pretensions to rank and culture, the recognized school of politeness. The phrase for elegant and aristocratic nonchalance is '*la sprezzata desinvoltura*'. The Court was dominated by the Duchess, who was celebrated for her unpretentious nobility: it was the '*modestia*' and '*grandezza*' of her speech and gestures which made her regal. We learn a good deal about those things which were held to be compatible, or otherwise, with the dignity of a nobleman.[1] Again and again it is emphasised that his essential characteristic is a restrained gravity, '*quella gravità riposata*' that marks the Spaniard: it is said—and this is clearly something new—that it is unseemly for a gentleman to take part in quick dances ('*non entri in quella prestezza de' piedi e duplicati ribattimenti*'), and similar advice is given to the ladies, to avoid all violent movement ('*non vorrei vederle usar movimenti troppo gagliardi e sforzati*'). Everything must have '*la molle delicatura*'.

This discussion of what is, and what is not, becoming, is naturally extended to cover speech, and, if Castiglione still allows considerable freedom, we find a more severe master of ceremonies in the more popular book on etiquette, 'Il Galateo', by Della Casa, which even takes the old poets to task; and the sixteenth century critic professes surprise that Dante puts words which belong to the tavern into the mouth of Beatrice.

In the sixteenth century, the universal search was for restraint and dignity of demeanour, and men became serious in the process of searching, so that the Quattrocento must have seemed like a wanton and heedless child to the men of the new generation. They must have thought, for example, that it was incomprehensibly naive to permit two laughing boys to swagger about with shields on a tomb, as happens on Desiderio's Marsuppini monument in Santa Croce. The proper thing was to have mourning putti, or, better still, large figures of the Virtues in grieving attitudes, since you can hardly expect children to be serious.[2]

4

ONLY the truly relevant is now allowed to find its way into pictures: in Quattrocento history pictures there are numerous genre or idyllic features which have little to do with the real theme, but their lack of sophistication charms the modern spectator, as we have already seen in discussing Gozzoli's *Noah*. It scarcely occurred to painters to aim at the creation of a concentrated impression,

---

[1]For example, it is better for a nobleman to be moderately good at chess than an expert player, lest it be thought that he had devoted too much study to the intricacies of the game.
Here, too, we find what is probably the first expression of modern false modesty—if you wish to praise yourself, do so in a roundabout way, as though accidentally mentioning your own merits.
[2]Mourning putti occur in Rome as early as the fifteenth century, since Rome was always more ceremonially serious than Florence. Monuments with cheerful children, though very young ones, are part of the unrestrained ease which recurs in the seventeenth century.

for they wished to entertain their public with a wealth of incident. In Signorelli's fresco at Orvieto of *The Blessed receiving their Heavenly Crowns*, there are angel-musicians in the sky, one of whom is tuning his instrument, quite calmly absorbed in his task even at this most solemn moment and in so conspicuous a position. He might well have thought to do it earlier.[1]

In the Sistine Chapel Botticelli painted the *Exodus of the Jews from Egypt*. The exodus of a nation, how heroic a scene! Yet what is the principal motive? A woman with two small children, the elder of whom is trying to lead his rebellious, tearful, younger brother, who is rebuked for hanging on his mother's arm. This is very delightful, but who among the later men would have had the courage to intro-duce this incident from a family Sunday afternoon walk into such a subject as this? In the same chapel Cosimo Rosselli depicted the *Last Supper*, introducing a still-life of large, polished, metal jugs and dishes into the foreground, and nearby he painted a dog and a cat frisking about, with yet another little dog standing on its hind legs and begging. Naturally, all religious feeling is com-pletely lacking in the picture but nobody took offence; and the painter was working in the private chapel of the Head of Christendom.

There have been individual artists, such as the great Donatello, who had a feeling for the historic moment as a unity. His narrative scenes are by far the best of the fifteenth century, but for other artists it was extraordinarily difficult to concentrate, to abandon the merely entertaining, and to take the presentation of an event seriously. Leonardo lays it down that a painted history ought to make the same emotional impression on the spectator as he would have felt if he had been present at the actual event,[2] but this was not likely to have much effect while whole crowds of people were tolerated in pictures, who simply stand about or look around them without having any part in the action. Giotto made every person in his pictures take part in some way suited to them, either actively or by showing sympathy or interest, but the Quattrocento at once introduced those silent choruses of figures and tolerated them in pictures because interest in the representation of living things and of personal characteristics had become stronger than interest in the action and the relations between the characters represented. Often the man who commissioned the work, and all his relatives, wished to be represented in the story; or it would be merely local celebrities, who could be honoured in this way by their fellow-townsmen, without being required to play any particular part in the picture. Leon Battista Alberti did not hesitate expressly to seek this honour for himself in his treatise on painting.[3]

---

[1] Even in votive pictures we find an angel sitting isolated at the foot of the throne, engaged in tuning his lute (Signorelli, Carpaccio), and we again ask ourselves what kind of religious feeling could tolerate such irrelevancies in devotional pictures.

[2] *Trattato*, ed. Ludwig, No. 188 of the Italian-German edition.

[3] *Kleinere Schriften*, ed. Janitschek, p. 162–3. [Leoni's English translation of 1726, *Three Books of Painting*, p. 27.—*Trans.*].

When studying the fresco cycle on the walls of the Sistine Chapel, one is struck, time and again, by the indifference of the artist to the subject-matter; how rarely it occurs to him to emphasise the protagonists; how, more or less, the conflict between different interests everywhere threatens to swamp the essential with the inessential. Has any lawgiver ever had a more inattentive audience than Moses in Signorelli's fresco? It is almost impossible for the spectator to understand the situation represented. Botticelli, at least, would seem to be the man to give a vehement emotional rendering of the uproar of Korah's rebellion, in which whole groups were involved in the passions aroused, yet even in his picture the flare-up of excitement soon dies out in rows of stolid bystanders.

It must have created a deep impression when the Raphael tapestries of the *Acts of the Apostles* first appeared alongside these Quattrocento histories, for these are pictures which treat their subjects really seriously, where the stage is cleared of all unnecessary figures, and which display a vigour of dramatic animation that immediately grips the spectator. Paul preaches at Athens and his audience consists, not of static figures with characterized heads, but of people whose features show exactly how each individual reacts to the sermon, and to what extent he is able to follow it. When some strange event occurs, such as the sudden death of Ananias, everyone who witnesses it recoils with the most eloquent gestures of astonishment or horror; while the whole population of Egypt could have been drowned in the Red Sea without a Quattrocento painter representing a single Jew as excited about it.

It was reserved for the sixteenth century, not to discover the world of human emotions, the great passions which sway the mind, but to exploit them artistically; and this art has as one of its principal characteristics a strong interest in the psychology of events. The Temptation of Christ was a theme admirably adapted to the spirit of the new age; a theme of which Botticelli had not been able to make anything, filling his fresco of it with a mere representation of a ceremony. Inversely, where painters of the Cinquecento had to deal with subjects lacking in drama they often went astray and imported emotions and sweeping gestures into subjects which do not require them, into, for example, idyllic scenes of the Nativity of Christ. Naive enjoyment of descriptive detail in painting ceases with the sixteenth century and the pleasure of indulging oneself with the wide world and the many things it contains dies away. When a Quattrocento artist had to paint an Adoration of the Shepherds he would introduce anything and everything, as we may see in Ghirlandaio's picture of this subject in the Academy of Florence (*Fig.* 161).[1] The animals are painted with minute care—the ox and the ass, a sheep and a goldfinch. Then there are

---

[1][Now replaced in the Sassetti Chapel, Santa Trinità, for which it was painted.—*Trans.*].

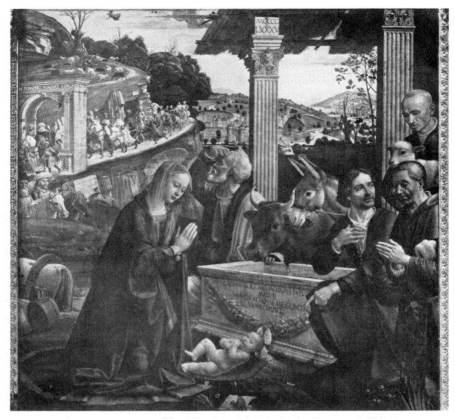

161. GHIRLANDAIO: *The Adoration of the Shepherds*. Florence, S. Trinità

flowers and stones and a smiling landscape, and, in addition, we are shown the family luggage—a shabby old saddle lying on the ground with a small cask of wine beside it, and, for the archæologically inclined, the painter gives some extra ornamental pieces: a sarcophagus, a couple of antique pillars, and a triumphal arch in the background, brand new, with a golden inscription on a blue frieze.

This kind of entertainment for a spectacle-loving public is entirely foreign to the great style. We shall speak later of the way in which the eye sought gratification elsewhere; here it must suffice to say that the interest must be concentrated exclusively on the actual event depicted in a history picture, and that the deliberate attempt to obtain the principal effect by means of significant and emotionally expressive action automatically excludes mere visual pleasure in gaily coloured miscellanies. This means also that the diffuse narratives of the Life of the Virgin, and similar subjects, had to experience a severe compression.

5

EVEN portraits tended to become slightly dramatised in the sixteenth century. Here and there, indeed, attempts were made, from the time of Donatello onwards, to get beyond a mere description of the passive model, yet these were exceptions to the general rule of representing the model exactly as he looked while sitting for his portrait. Quattrocento portrait heads have an inestimable simplicity, lacking any intention to stress personal idiosyncrasies; yet compared with the classic portraits they seem, as it were, unconcerned. The Cinquecento required a specific expression, which should show immediately what the sitter is thinking about or what he wishes to say. It was not sufficient to show what the permanent structure of the face was like: a momentary aspect of the free life of the spirit had to be depicted too. For this reason, every painter now sought to discover the most significant aspect of his sitter's character, human dignity was more respected and we get the impression that the generation which arose on our side of the dawn of the sixteenth century was one which possessed greater powers and more sensitive perceptions. Lomazzo, in his treatise, laid down the rule that the painter should disregard any imperfections in his sitter and should emphasise and heighten the grand and admirable features in his portraits. This is a later theoretical formulation of that which the men of the classic age had done of their own accord—'al pittore conviene che sempre accresca nelle faccie grandezza e maestà, coprendo il difetto del naturale, come si vede che hanno fatto gl'antichi pittori'.[1] It is obvious that this predisposition involved considerable risk of distorting individual traits and forcing the personality of the sitter into a scheme of expression which was foreign to it. However, it was not until after the great period that the Epigoni succumbed to this danger.

This more exalted conception of humanity may have some relevance to the fact that the number of commissions for portraits was now smaller than formerly; obviously artists could not be expected to portray any and every face. It is said of Michelangelo, indeed, that he regarded it as a degradation of art to imitate any earthly thing in its individual limitation, unless it were of supreme beauty.

6

IT was inevitable that this spirit of increased dignity should affect both the conception and representation of supernatural beings. Religious feeling might express itself in the one way or the other, but the social advancement of the sacred personages was a consequence entailed by non-religious premises. Attention has already been drawn to the way in which the Virgin Annunciate

---

[1]Among others he cites Titian, who had brought out in his *Ariosto* 'la facundia e l'ornamento' and in his *Bembo* 'la maestà e l'accuratezza' (Lomazzo, *Trattato della Pittura*, ed. of 1585, p. 433).

becomes aristocratic and reserved: the shy maiden becomes a queen, and the Madonna with her 'Bambino' who, in the fifteenth century, might have been any respectable housewife from the next street, becomes noble, stately and unapproachable. She no longer smiles on the spectator with laughing eyes, nor is she the Mary who casts down her eyes shyly and modestly, nor the young mother who has eyes only for her child: she now appears, grand and assured, before the eyes of the devout like a queen who is accustomed to seeing people kneel before her. This character is variable, being sometimes a rather worldly greatness, as in Andrea del Sarto, and sometimes a heroic exaltation above the world, as in Michelangelo; but, in every case, the transformation of the type is to be observed.

Likewise, the Christ Child is no longer a merry and playful child who has dug a seed out of a pomegranate and offers it to his mother (Filippo Lippi), nor is He a laughing little rogue whose small hand gives a blessing which no one could take seriously—when He does smile, as in the *Madonna delle Arpie* (*Fig.* 125), it is directed towards the spectator in a not very pleasing coquetry, for which Andrea del Sarto is responsible; but usually He is serious, very serious, as Raphael's Roman pictures testify. Michelangelo, however, was the first to represent the Child in this way, without imposing un-childlike attitudes—such as blessing— upon Him. He gives us a truly natural boy, whether sleeping or waking, but He is a joyless Child.[1]

Botticelli clearly represents the Quattrocento prelude to this interpretation, for he became more and more serious with increasing years, and in this he offers a vigorous protest against the smiling superficialities of a Ghirlandaio. Nevertheless, he cannot be classed with the typical artists of the new century, for although his Madonna is serious enough in appearance, she is a depressed and sorrowing creature, lacking grandeur, and his Child is not yet the Ruler of the World. Unless I deceive myself, the increasing variety of representations of the Madonna with the Child at her breast has some connection with the change of ideals, for it is possible that the Cinquecento thought such a scene lacking in dignity. It is true that Bugiardini painted a *Madonna del Latte* (Uffizi); but he makes the Virgin point to her breast as though saying to the spectator, 'This is the breast which fed the Lord'. The same painter, in his *Betrothal of St. Catherine to the Infant Christ* (Bologna Gallery), does not represent the Child as unable to understand the significance of the ceremony, but rather the opposite, for the small boy is fully aware of the situation, and His upraised finger would seem to be exhorting the modest bride.

---

[1] German art, in its best period, has an analogous emancipation of the Christ Child from the un-childlike function of giving a benediction. The Child in Holbein's Darmstadt *Madonna* stretches out His left hand in a gesture which is no longer a blessing.

A complete change in the outward form of the picture accompanied the change of inward meaning. Formerly, all the treasures of the world were heaped about the Virgin's throne, and our Lady herself was adorned with all the splendour of fine stuffs and precious ornament. Brightly patterned Oriental carpets were unrolled, marble parapets gleamed white against the blue sky, Mary was enclosed in leafy bowers or a heavy purple hanging swept down from above, patterned in gold, sewn with pearls and lined with costly ermine. With the sixteenth century all this gay variety disappears at once. There are no more flowers and carpets, no rich ornament on the throne, and no delightful landscape; the figure dominates everything, and, if any architecture is introduced, it is some massive, simple motive, and from the dress all profane ornament is excluded. The Queen of Heaven must be represented with simplicity and nobility. Whether this change is the expression of deeper piety I do not enquire: there are some who hold the opposite view, that a careful avoiding of the profane indicates uncertainty of religious conviction.[1]

An analogous elevation of the types takes place in the attendant saints: it is no longer permissible to fall back upon types taken at random from the street to stand around the throne of the Madonna. The fifteenth century was quite ready to accept from Piero di Cosimo a St. Anthony who was a doddering old man with spectacles perched on his nose and none too clean a habit. Other artists had aimed higher, but the sixteenth century insisted on an imposing appearance; not necessarily an idealized type, but the painter must have exercised selection in his choice of models. We need say nothing of Raphael, whose characterizations are incomparable, but even Andrea del Sarto in his more superficial moments never presents us with the low or vulgar, while Fra Bartolommeo concentrates all his powers in the never-ending attempt to achieve expressive power in his male saints.

More could be said of the links between the members of what might be called the household and Mary and her Child; for example, how St. John, formerly the playmate of the Infant Christ, becomes filled with reverence and kneels down in adoration—but we will confine ourselves to some remarks on the subject of angels, as represented in the new century.

The Cinquecento took over from its predecessor two types of angel, the child and the adolescent girl-angel; the most charming examples of the latter, as everyone will recall, being in the pictures of Botticelli and Filippino. They are sometimes introduced as candle-bearers, as in Botticelli's Berlin tondo, where one of them gazes up at the flickering flame with a naively stupid look on her

---

[1] Others may comment on the share in these events which is to be attributed to Savonarola's influence: there is some risk of making too much depend on this one personality. The whole question has to do with a general, and not an exclusively religious, phenomenon.

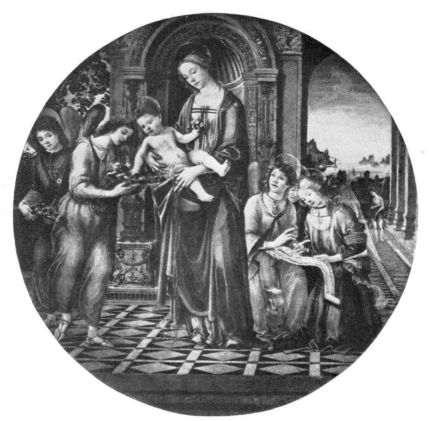

162. FILIPPINO LIPPI: *Madonna and Child with Angels*
Florence, Corsini Gallery

face; or they are allowed to linger near the Child, carrying flowers or singing, as in the exquisitely sensitive early picture by Filippino in the Corsini Gallery, reproduced here as an example (*Fig.* 162). Shyly, and with downcast eyes, one of the maidens offers a basket of flowers to the Christ Child, and while He rolls over in delight and takes hold of the present, two other angels sing from music with heartfelt seriousness, although one glances up for a moment and a smile steals over her face. Why did the sixteenth century never return to such motives? The new angels lack the charm of youthful timidity and they have put aside their ingenuousness: to some extent they now share the regal state, and they bear themselves accordingly. The spectator must not be allowed to smile.

To represent angels in flight, the Cinquecento reverts to the old, stately sweep which was known to Gothic art. The arabesques and flowing draperies of these incorporeal forms had ceased to have any meaning to the realists of the fifteenth century, who craved for plausibility of movement and who replaced sweeping flight by walking or running on small supporting clouds; and thus arose those agile girlish figures who are neither beautiful nor dignified, but who kick up their bare heels very convincingly. Attempts were soon made to render flight by a swimming movement, involving much kicking of the legs, but it was the mature style which first discovered means of expressing that measured and stately passage through the air which has since become usual.[1]

The main thing to be noted about the child-angels is that they, too, are permitted to share the childish qualities of the Bambino. Nothing more is required of them than that they should be children, although, according to circumstances, they may reflect something of the general exalted and sustained sentiment. The impression made by the putto with the tablet in the *Madonna di Foligno* (*Fig.* 84) is more serious, even though he is not praying, than, for example, that made by the two little naked boys in Desiderio's Tabernacle in S. Lorenzo, for ardently as they approach the benedictory Christ, it is yet impossible to regard the scene as anything but light-hearted. Venetian pictures have familiarised us with the youthful musicians who sit at the feet of the Madonna, playing guitars or other instruments with skill and vigour, but the Cinquecento found this unsuitable as well, and the musical accompaniment for a sacred meeting was entrusted to older hands, to preserve the purity of sentiment. The most popular example of the truly childish putti of the new century is to be found in the two figures at the foot of the *Sistine Madonna* (*Fig.* 87).

7

GIVEN the manifest tendency to secure greater respect for altarpieces and to loosen the all too close bonds which bound the Heavenly and the earthly together, it is not to be wondered at that the miraculous was immediately taken up and represented not only by aureoles and nimbi but also by events presented in an idealised way, which, formerly, had been depicted in the most realistic and circumstantial way.[2]

---

[1]The medieval flying figures come directly from the antique. The Renaissance invention of the running type was an unconscious reversion to the form of flight with which the earliest Greek art began, known to archæology as the 'bent-knee type' (as in the *Nike* at Delos, which may be compared with the illustration of Benedetto da Maiano's *Angel*, on p. 11). The more expressive type, derived from the motion of the swimmer, continued for a while in antiquity alongside the other (*cf.* Studniczka, *Die Siegesgöttin*, 1898, p. 13) and there are parallels for this in modern art. Perugino's *Assumption* in the Academy at Florence shows both types side by side; and, while Botticelli and Filippino make their angels erect, one can still find the old running angel in contemporaries, as *e.g.* occasionally in Ghirlandaio. Signorelli, more than any other Quattrocento painter, probably attained the most perfect form of the new scheme (Orvieto frescoes), and Raphael's *Disputà* depends on him. Later, foreshortening and increased movement were added, as well as flight into, or out of, the depth of the picture. Examples of this are readily available in the *Four Sibyls* of Santa Maria della Pace or the *Madonna del Baldacchino*.

[2]In the Quattrocento there were artists like Francesco Cossa of Ferrara whose implacable sense of reality was such that he could never bring himself to represent the Angel of the Annunciation with a normal halo of light, but stuck a plate of brass on his head (picture in Dresden).

Fra Bartolommeo was the first to represent the apparition of the Madonna to St. Bernard as a descent from Heaven, and Andrea del Sarto followed him in that he made the Angel of the Annunciation approach on clouds, in support of which he could also adduce Trecento prototypes. Andrea's *Birth of the Virgin* (1514) shows angels on clouds pressing into an everyday room where the birth has taken place (*Fig.* 106) and while the Quattrocento preferred to imagine the Madonna on a solid throne from the end of the fifteenth century we may find Mary again raised up into the skies—a 'Madonna in Glory'—and this old-fashioned scheme was translated into a momentary apparition, in an unexpected and unique way, in the *Sistine Madonna*.

8

THIS stressing of the supernatural aspect of the subject to be represented brings us to the more general question of the relation to actuality of the new art. For the fifteenth century, the supreme object was actuality—realism. Beautiful or not, in a *Baptism* Christ must be shown with both feet submerged in the water of the brook. Once or twice, it is true, an idealist from one of the provincial schools had disregarded this injunction and represented the feet of the Lord as standing on the surface of the water, as in Piero della Francesca's picture in London; but this was not permissible for a Florentine. Yet this idealization slipped in quite naturally with the new century, and so it was with other things. Michelangelo's *Pietà* (*Fig.* 20) shows the Virgin as quite youthful and he remained unmoved by any protests. The too-small table in Leonardo's *Last Supper* (*Fig.* 12) and the impossible boats in Raphael's *Miraculous Draught of Fishes* (*Fig.* 69) are further examples, showing that the new ideals no longer regarded actuality as the decisive factor and were prepared to accept the unnatural if it helped the artistic effect.

When people speak of the idealism of the sixteenth century, however, they usually mean something different—a general refusal to be bound by limits of place, time or the individual—and this antithesis of idealism and realism is thought to represent the essential difference between classic and Quattrocento art. The definition is not apt. It is probable that at that time no one would have understood these concepts, which would be relevant only in the seventeenth century, when these antitheses first began to emerge as such: at the time of the transition into the Cinquecento it was a question rather of intensifying the older art than of disavowing it.

Fifteenth-century Biblical scenes are never treated in the realistic way adopted by modern painters who wish, as it were, to translate the historical event into terms of modern life: the intention was to produce the most plausible and tangible impression possible, and, to this end, motives drawn from contemporary everyday life were employed, but always with the proviso that they could be modified as and when it seemed necessary. Conversely, the sixteenth century did not idealize in the sense of avoiding contact with actuality and seeking monumentality at the expense of clear characterization: its flowers grew from the old soil, but they were bigger. Art was still a clarification of everyday life, but it was felt that the greater demand for dignity of presentation could only be satisfied by a selective choice of types, dress and architecture which were hardly to be found in actuality.

It would be completely misleading to attempt to identify classicism with the imitation of the antique. It may well be that the antique speaks more audibly to us in works of the Cinquecento than in those of the older generation—we shall come back to this in another connection later—but in intention, the artists of the classic period had essentially the same approach to antiquity as the men of the Quattrocento.

IT is necessary to go into some details and we may begin with the way in which the localisation of the subject is treated. We know that Ghirlandaio devoted a good deal of space in his pictures to architecture: does he show us Florence? Certainly we get glimpses, here and there, down one of the narrow streets of the city, yet all his courts and halls are imaginary; they are architectural fantasies which were never built, for his sole concern was to produce an effect of splendour. The sixteenth century retained this point of view, differing only in their idea of splendour. Extensive prospects of cities and landscape panoramas dropped out of use, not because of a search for indeterminate and generalised impressions, but because these things ceased to be of special interest. The *ubiquité* of French classicism is not yet to be found here.[1] It is true that concessions to idealism in the setting are made, which strike us as peculiar. A story such as the Visitation, where we expect to see the entrance to a house, Elisabeth's home, is represented by Pontormo in such a way that the stage is set with nothing more than a large niche with a flight of steps leading up to it (*Fig.* 107). Yet we must recollect that Ghirlandaio in his *Visitation*, in the Louvre (*Fig.* 181), used a great arch as background, which does not help to elucidate the scene in any way; but we may say in a general fashion that our Northern ideas on these subjects should not be allowed to influence our judgement, for the Italians have a faculty for taking the human being as something quite independent of his surroundings, and for disregarding these surroundings, which we find difficult to understand since we always regard a figure as intimately connected with its situation. For us,

---

[1]Raphael, indeed, did allow a Ferrarese to paint a detailed landscape in the *Madonna di Foligno* (which does not represent Foligno). The *Madonna of Monteluce* [in the Vatican] shows the Temple at Tivoli, and many other examples will suggest themselves.

a mere niche deprives a *Visitation* of its convincing and life-like quality, even though we appreciate the gain in formal effectiveness; for the Italians, any background will do so long as the figures speak. The generalisation of the scene—or, as we would say, the lack of realism—can never have been felt by Pontormo with anything of the force which we are disposed to feel.[1]

It is a still higher degree of idealism which leads to the placing of the Madonna on a pedestal, as if she were a statue: this, too, is a concession of the great style to formal effect and must not be judged by Northern conceptions of 'intimacy' of religious feeling. Here, too, the Italian is able to disregard the disturbing effect which the motive, considered in cold blood, is bound to have; and he maintains the same attitude in cases where, for the sake of a motive of movement, a cube or some such object is placed without explanation as a support for a foot.

LEONARDO took the opportunity to warn the artist against the use of modern costumes, since they are mostly aesthetically unhelpful, good enough for tombs,[2] and he advises the use of antique drapery, not for the sake of an antique appearance but simply because it shows off the body to the best advantage. In spite of this, Andrea del Sarto risked painting his fresco of the *Birth of the Virgin* (1514) (*Fig.* 106) as a completely modern picture of a social occasion, and in this he was perhaps more consistent than any of his predecessors, for even Ghirlandaio continually mixed antique-ideal motives with contemporary dress, and the custom continued afterwards. The *Life of the Virgin* series in Siena by Sodoma and Pacchia show similar classic elements in pictures of modern life. The single example of the Raphael frescoes in the Stanza d'Eliodoro is quite sufficient to show that the aesthetic of that time was quite untroubled by scruples as to whether the monumental style would be compatible with the everyday and contemporary, or whether the histories should be transposed into a higher order of reality, such as the antique. These scruples did not arise until later, when the classic style was already declining.

What does surprise us is the use of the nude and half-nude: here, actuality seems to have been sacrified to artistic ideals, to the creation of an ideal world, and yet it is not difficult to show that the Quattrocento had already introduced nudes in history paintings and had even, in the person of Alberti, prescribed it in theory.[3] One would never have encountered a naked man, such as the one sitting on the church steps in Ghirlandaio's *Presentation in the Temple*, in the

---

[1] Every foreigner must have noticed how often the Italian stage shatters the dramatic illusion. In this sense we have to accept the historically irrelevant characters introduced by Pontormo and others into their pictures—a practice which began long before the sixteenth century.

[2] *Trattato*, Ludwig's Italian-German ed., No. 451.

[3] L. B. Alberti, *Della Pittura* (ed. Janitschek, *Albertis kleinere kunsttheoretische Schriften*, p. 118–9) [English ed. of 1726, III, p. 18].

Florence of that day, for all its freedom of manners; but no one thought of finding fault with it in the name of realism. A picture like the *Fire in the Borgo* cannot therefore be said to have broken essentially with the Quattrocento tradition—it is simply that the Cinquecento gives more nude forms.

Above all, allegorical figures had to accommodate themselves to it—they lost one garment after another, and the tombs of prelates by Andrea Sansovino show the unhappy *Fides* seated in an antique bathrobe; the meaning of the bare body is quite impossible to guess. This indifference towards the significance of a figure is inexcusable, but these allegories had never, even in earlier times, been local or familiar types. The exposition of naked limbs becomes positively unpleasant in sacred pictures—I am thinking of Michelangelo's *Madonna* tondo in the Tribuna of the Uffizi, although the example of this heroine must not be taken as typical of the age. Only it is true to say that, if any one man may be held responsible for major changes in the history of culture, that man was Michelangelo, who brought about the generalised heroic style and caused place and time to be disregarded. In every way, his idealism was of the most powerful and unbounded sort: through him, the world of actuality was disrupted, and he took from the Renaissance its fine joy in itself.

THE decisive factor in the question of realism and idealism is neither costume nor locality, and all the romancing of the fifteenth century is just a harmless game with architecture and dress: the really striking effect of actuality depends on the individual character of the faces and figures in the picture. Ghirlandaio may please himself in the accessories he shows us, and in a picture like *Zacharias in the Temple* (Santa Maria Novella) we say at once, 'This place, where these people are standing, must be Florence'. Does one get the same impression from a sixteenth-century picture? It is obvious that portrait heads are rarer, and one feels much less impelled to enquire the name of this or that person represented. The interest in individual character, and the power of portraying it, have not disappeared—think of the portrait groups in the *Heliodorus* frescoes (*Fig.* 65) or of Sarto's pictures in the Annunziata (*Figs.* 103–106)—but the time was past when no one could think beyond a life-like portrait head, and to make each head an object of interest in itself was sufficient justification for its existence in a historical subject. As soon as the subject was taken seriously, and the rows of apathetic spectators were banished, the situation was changed fundamentally: the interest in individual character now found a formidable rival in the representation of emotions, a problem which, from time to time, superseded the interest in character. The action of the body can be so interesting that one scarcely bothers with the head. The figures acquire new value as compositional factors and become important in the building up of the whole, as simple indications of the forces engaged in the architectonic construction, without any great significance in themselves; and these formal effects, unknown to the earlier generation, automatically lead to a merely superficial characterization. Similar kinds of generalised heads of very little individuality can be found throughout the whole of the fifteenth century—there are scores in Ghirlandaio—and there is no question of a fundamental cleavage between the old and the new art which made the latter disregard the individual as such. Heads which look like portraits occur less frequently, but it is not the case that the classic style demanded a generalised and ideal type of humanity. Even Michelangelo—who again adopts a position of his own—has a number of heads which look drawn from life in the earlier Sistine frescoes; for example, in the *Deluge* (*Fig.* 31). After this, Michelangelo began to lose interest in the individual; while Raphael, who in the first Stanza seldom went beyond generalisation, came to be more and more interested in it. Yet we must not believe that the two had simply changed places—the mature Michelangelo does not give us the universality of the sub-individual, but of the super-individual.

It is another question whether the individual was conceived and represented in the same way as earlier. That eager desire to possess oneself of nature down to the tiniest detail of a fold, and the joy in the actual for its own sake, had exhausted themselves. The Cinquecento sought the grand and the significant in its picture of humanity, and it thought its end attained by simplification and the suppression of inessentials: if it overlooked certain things it was not because of any flagging of the eye, but, on the contrary, because of a greatly intensified perceptive faculty. Nobility of vision is an idealization from within and has nothing to do with prettifying embellishments—the idealization from without.[1]

It may reasonably be assumed that even in the great period artists occasionally felt dissatisfied with what was offered by nature. It is very difficult to discuss these feelings and it would be rash indeed to venture upon a positive generalisation either way as to the difference between two epochs such as the Quattrocento and Cinquecento. There are hundreds of stages in the conscious transformation of the model, once the artist takes it in hand. Raphael, at the time when he was working on the *Galatea*, expressed himself to the effect that he could do nothing with models, but relied entirely on a conception of beauty which came spontaneously to him.[2] It so happens that we have documentary evidence for Raphael's idealism, yet surely Botticelli would have expressed himself in the same way, and is his *Birth of Venus* (*Fig.* 174) any less of a creation of the imagination

---

[1] Lomazzo's *Trattato*, 1585, p. 433, has this passage on the methods employed by the great masters in their portraits: '*Usavano sempre di far risplendere quello che la natura d'eccellente aveva concesso loro*' i.e. the good qualities of the sitters.

[2] Guhl, *Künstlerbriefe*, 2nd ed., I, p. 95 [an English translation is given by Müntz in his *Raphael*, London, 1882, p. 490—*Trans.*].

alone? Ideal figures and ideal heads occur even in the 'realistic' Quattrocento, and everywhere we find that the distinctions are only gradually made, yet it is obvious that there is a much larger proportion of idealization in the sixteenth century, since the aspirations of that age are incompatible with the close intimacy with ordinary life maintained by the previous century. It is important to note that, at the very moment when art was discovering for itself a more exalted kind of beauty, the Church also sought an increase of dignity for the principal persons of Christian belief. The Madonna must no longer be an ordinary respectable sort of woman, who might live in the next street; she had to cast off all traces of her human origin and social station. Now, once again, there were men capable of conceiving the ideal: Michelangelo, the greatest of all naturalists, was also the greatest idealist. Equipped with all the Florentine gift for individual characterization, he was at the same time the man who could most completely renounce the outside world and create solely from his own conceptions: he created his own world and it was his example—though not his fault—which chiefly led to the lack of respect for nature which was shown by the next generation.

Finally, we must observe in this connection that the Cinquecento had an increased desire to contemplate the beautiful. This is a desire which is subject to change and there are times when it almost completely disappears

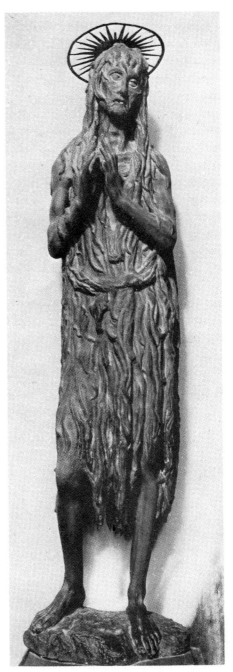

163. DONATELLO: *St. Mary Magdalen.*
Florence, Baptistery

in face of other interests. The antecedent art of the Quattrocento also had a beauty, a beauty of its own, which it only rarely sought to express because there was a much more urgent desire for the purely expressive, characteristic and vital. Once again, Donatello is the example to invoke: the master who created the bronze *David* of the Bargello (*Fig.* 2) could also delve insatiably into ugliness and was prepared to make even his saints disagreeable in form, because his sole aim was a convincing vitality, and, under the impression created by this vital quality, his public would ask no questions about beauty and ugliness. The *Magdalen* in the Baptistery (*Fig.* 163) is 'an oblong, emaciated monster' (Cicerone, first edition) and *St. John the Baptist* (marble in the Bargello) is a withered ascetic, not to mention the figures on the Campanile. Towards the close of the century, however, beauty begins to break through and in the Cinquecento there begins that general recasting of types, which not only substituted a more exalted conception in place of a humble one, but also rejected certain forms altogether because they were not beautiful.

The Magdalen is the beautiful sinner and not the emaciated penitent, while the Baptist takes on the strong and virile beauty of a man brought up in the wind and the rain, without a trace of privation or asceticism. The youthful St. John, however, is represented as the type of a perfectly beautiful boy and, as such, he becomes a favourite figure of the age (*Fig.* 168).

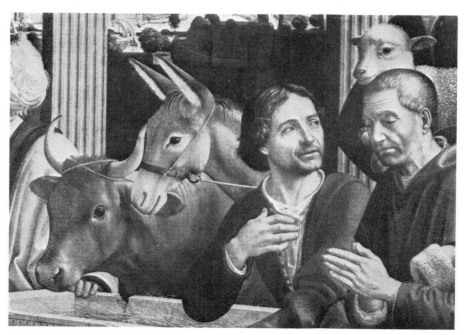

Detail from Fig. 161

Chapter II : THE NEW BEAUTY

WHEN we speak of a new style arising, the first thing which occurs to us is that there has been a transformation in the architectural sense, but if we examine it more closely we find that the change is not confined to the environment of man—major or minor architectural features, furniture or costume—but that man himself has changed even in his outward, bodily form; and the real kernel of a style is in the new outlook upon the human body and in new ideas about deportment and movement. This conception of style is a much more weighty one than that which obtains nowadays, when styles change like fancy dresses being tried on for a masquerade. However, this uprooting of style dates only from our own century and we have really no longer any right to talk of styles, but only of fashions.

The new corporeality and the new movement of the Cinquecento become perfectly clear if we make a comparison between a picture like Sarto's *Birth of the Virgin* of 1514 (*Fig.* XII) and a Ghirlandaio fresco of a similar subject (*Fig.* 164). The actual gait of the women has changed entirely; instead of a stiff mincing it is a composed and dignified motion—the tempo has slowed to *andante maestoso*. There are no longer any short, sharp twists of the head or single limbs, but only slow and easy movements of the body, and instead of sprawling and angular

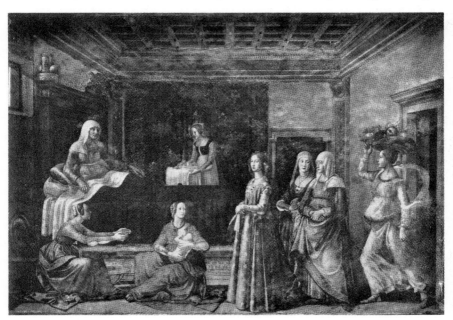

164. GHIRLANDAIO: *The Birth of St. John the Baptist*. Florence, S. Maria Novella

gestures there are easy and sustained rhythmic curves. The spare bodies of the early Renaissance, with their bony and emphatic joints, cease to represent the ideal of beauty—Sarto shows rounded and well-developed figures, splendid and sensual, the broad nape of the neck emerging from the heavy folds of dresses which sweep the ground, where Ghirlandaio's are short, stiff dresses with tight-fitting sleeves. The clothes, which here expressed rapid and nimble movement, later by their very fullness have a retarding effect.

I

In the second half of the fifteenth century, movement was rendered in an elegant and often precious way. When the Madonna holds the Child she often thrusts out the point of her elbow and extends the little finger of the hand which fastidiously grasps Him. Ghirlandaio was not much given to subtleties, but he completely assimilated this mannerism, and even an artist of Signorelli's powerful temperament made concessions to the taste of the age, seeking graceful-ness in an unnatural refinement. The Madonna, as she adores the Child, does not simply put her hands together, but allows only the two first fingers to touch each other while the others stand apart.

Sensitive persons like Filippino seem to shrink from the very thought of grasping an object firmly, and, if some saintly monk is supposed to hold his book, or the Baptist his cross, the lightest of touches has to suffice. Raffaellino del Garbo or Lorenzo di Credi are just the same—with conscious elegance St. Sebastian presents his arrow, held between two fingers, as if he were passing a pencil. The act of standing sometimes becomes a sort of swaying, dancing movement, a form of tottering which produces a most unpleasant effect in sculpture, as in Benedetto da Maiano's *St. John* in the Bargello, which is not above reproach in this respect. One looks with real longing for the firm tread of the next generation: even Michelangelo's reeling *Bacchus* stands more firmly on his feet.

An epitome of this preciosity of taste in the later Quattrocento is the 'Verrocchio' picture of the *Archangels* (Florence, Academy)[1] which may be coupled with the *Tobias* in London (*Fig.* 165).[2] In face of this mincing kind of movement, we feel involuntarily that an old decorative style is breaking up and we are witnessing the phenomenon of a collapsing archaism.

Firm, simple and natural movement returns with the sixteenth century. Gestures are more restrained and petty decorativeness, artificial stiffness and swagger are all overcome. Andrea del Sarto's *Madonna delle Arpie* presents an

---

[1][Now in the Uffizi.—*Trans.*]

[2]The attribution to Verrocchio is now abandoned in favour of Francesco Botticini. [N.G. Cat., 1951, Follower of Verrocchio.] For the style, compare with the very singular works by Pollaiuolo in St. Peter's, the tombs of Sixtus IV and Innocent VIII, where the female figures compete in unnaturalness with the worst Baroque.

entirely new spectacle, standing firmly and strongly on her feet (*Fig.* 125), and we can almost believe that she is capable of carrying the heavy Child on the one arm alone. The way in which she props the book against her thigh, laying her hand across the edges of it so that one large and coherent form results, is again in the most splendid Cinquecento style. In every case, movement is rendered with greater force and energy: take, for example, Raphael's *Madonna di Foligno* (*Fig.* 84). Who would believe that we have to go back as far as Donatello in order to find another arm and hand which grasps as firmly as St. John does here?

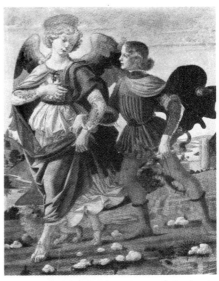

165. 'VERROCCHIO': *Tobias and the Angel.* London, National Gallery

In the fifteenth century there is often something indecisive about the twist of a torso or the turn of a head, as if men were shy of strong expressiveness; but now, once again, there returns a joy in the powerful movements of a strong temperament, and a head swung round or a pointing arm is suddenly possessed of a new strength. One feels a heightened physical vitality, and, indeed, the mere act of looking at something is endowed with an energy previously unknown and the sixteenth century is once again able to depict a keen and powerful gaze.

The Quattrocento enjoyed the highest degree of charming movement in agile, hurrying figures: not for nothing is this motive to be found in all the artists of the time. The angel hastens with his candle, and the servant-girl, bringing wine and fruit from the country to the woman in childbed, rushes in at the door, her clothes blown by the wind into crisp, rippling folds (*Fig.* 166). This figure, so highly characteristic of the age, has its Cinquecento counterpart in the woman carrying water in the *Fire in the Borgo* (*Fig.* 167): the contrast between the two figures embraces the whole difference between two conceptions of form. This woman carrying water, striding along, calm and erect, her strong arms bearing the load, is one of the most splendid creations of Raphael's mature and virile sense of beauty. The kneeling woman with her back turned, in the foreground of the *Transfiguration,* is from the same family, and if we also compare the similar figure from the group of women in the *Heliodorus* we have a standard by which to judge the development in Raphael's last style towards strength and powerful simplicity of line.

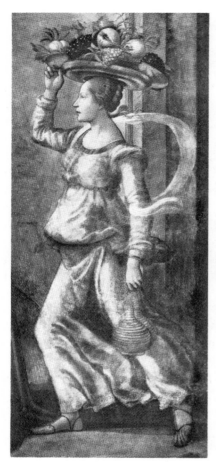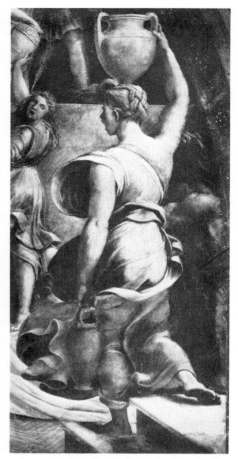

166. GHIRLANDAIO: Detail from the 167. RAPHAEL: Detail from the *Fire in the*
Birth of St. John (Fig. 164).   *Borgo*. Vatican

On the other hand, the taste of the new age found nothing more intolerable than immoderate tension and constrained movement: Verrocchio's horseman, Colleoni, has energy enough, and iron strength, but that is not beauty of movement. Notions of aristocratic ease meet the new ideal of beauty, expressed in an easy flow of line: in Count Castiglione's 'Cortegiano' there is a note on the subject of riding which may well be quoted here. It is to the effect that a man should not sit primly and stiffly in the saddle *'alla Veneziana'* (the Venetians were thought poor horsemen), but perfectly easily; *'disciolto'* is the word used. Of course, this only counts for a man without armour, for a lightly clad man can easily sit his horse where heavy armour makes it necessary almost to stand upright—'in the one case the knees are bent, in the other they are kept stiff '[1]—

[1]Pomponius Gauricus, *De Sculptura* (Brockhaus ed. p. 115).

but for artistic purposes, from now on, only the first of these positions was employed.

Perugino had earlier shown the Florentines how to render a soft and graceful movement, for, in his day, his motive of a figure standing with the weight on one leg and the other flexed loosely sideways, with a corresponding tilt of the head in the opposite direction, was something quite novel in Florence. The Tuscan idea of grace was more angular and unwieldy and although many artists attempted to employ his motive none of them had quite his sweetness of movement or gentle play of line. The sixteenth century, however, abandoned the motive entirely:[1] Raphael, who had revelled in it as a young man, never uses it in his later works. One can well imagine the scorn which Michelangelo would have poured on such poses. The new poses are more compact and more restrained in outline, and, quite apart from its sentimentality, Peruginesque beauty no longer sufficed because it failed to satisfy the new taste for mass. Separation and isolation of parts were no longer wanted; concentration and firmness of general form were required. For this reason, a whole series of hand and arm movements were recreated, and, for instance, the arms crossed over the breast in prayer became a characteristic motive of the new century.

2

IT seems as if all at once a new kind of human body grew up among the Florentines. Rome had always possessed the full, heavy forms which were the new ideal, but they may have been rarer in Tuscany: in any case, artists painted as if Quattrocento Florence had no models of the kind which Andrea del Sarto later portrayed in his pictures of Florentine women. Early Renaissance taste preferred the undeveloped form, slim and agile, and the angular grace and springy lines of youth possessed a greater charm than the ripeness of womanhood or the full physical development of manhood. The girl-angels of Botticelli and Filippino, with their sharp articulations and skinny arms, represent the ideal of youthful beauty, and this astringency is not modified even in Botticelli's group of the Graces dancing, although they represent a maturer age. The sixteenth century had a different opinion on this matter: even Leonardo's angels are softer in form, and how much difference there is between a *Galatea* by Raphael or an *Eve* by Michelangelo and the Venuses of the late Quattrocento! The neck, formerly long and slender and set like an inverted funnel on the sloping shoulders, becomes round and short, on broad, strong shoulders. Elongation of the form is abandoned, and all the limbs are made fuller and more powerful. Beauty is once more seen in the rounded torso and broad hips of the antique ideal, and

---

[1]It is still retained in the figure of Christ in Andrea Sansovino's *Baptism* (begun in 1502), but it is already modified (*Fig.* 156).

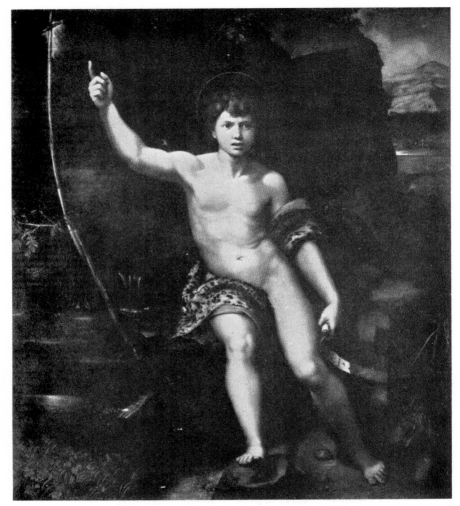

168. RAPHAEL: *St. John the Baptist preaching*. Uffizi

the eye seeks large and coherent planes. The Cinquecento counterpart of Verrocchio's *David* is Benvenuto Cellini's *Perseus* (*Fig.* 183): the lean and supple boy is no longer considered beautiful, and when, in spite of that, it is necessary to represent an adolescent, the artist gives him roundness and fullness. Raphael's *St. John the Baptist* as a boy preaching (*Fig.* 168: in the Tribune) is an instructive example of the way in which nature was disregarded in order to give mannish forms to the body of a boy.

The beautiful body is clear in its articulation. The Cinquecento had such a feeling for structure and such a desire to express the inner form that all details became insignificant by comparison—idealization began early here and was very marked in effect, so that the parallel between Lorenzo di Credi's nude model in the Uffizi[1] and Franciabigio's ideal figure in the Borghese Gallery (more probably by Andrea del Brescianino) is instructive in more than one respect (*Figs.* 169, 170).

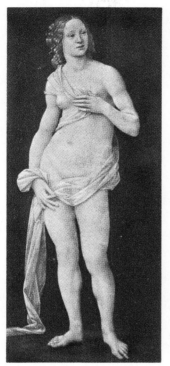 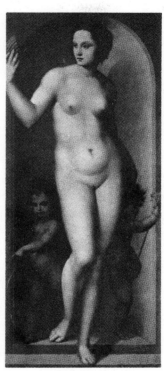

169. LORENZO DI CREDI: 170. 'FRANCIABIGIO': *Venus.*
Venus. Uffizi   Rome, Galleria Borghese

Heads become broad with large planes and accented horizontals: a firm chin and full cheeks are admired and even the mouth must not be small and neat. Although there was once no greater beauty in a woman than to be able to show a high, smooth forehead ('*la fronte superba*', says Poliziano), and the hair was even plucked out in order to conform to the canon,[2] the Cinquecento thought a low forehead the more desirable form, since it was thought to give an air of greater repose to the face, and the eyebrows, too, were given a flatter and more even line. We no longer see high, arching brows, such as we find in Desiderio's busts of girls, where their laughing and wondering faces have the brows raised

---

[1] The drawing for the head of this figure, we may note in passing, is in the Albertina and was published in *Handzeichnungen alter Meister*, III, 327.
[2] *Cf.* the note on the *Mona Lisa*, p. 30.

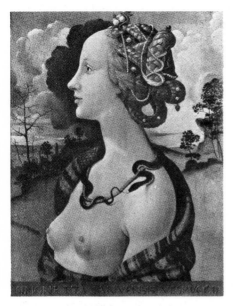

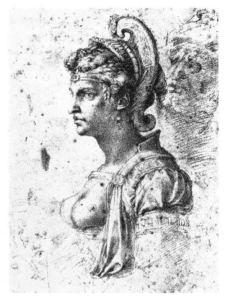

171. PIERO DI COSIMO:
La bella Simonetta. Chantilly

172. 'MICHELANGELO': So-called
Vittoria Colonna. Drawing. Uffizi

higher still, suggesting the lines from Poliziano's *Giostra*, that they all show

'*nel volto meraviglia*
con fronte crespa e rilevate ciglia'.

In the same way, the pert, tip-tilted nose may once have had its admirers, but now it has gone out of fashion, and the portraitist will go to great trouble to smooth out the unruly line and to adjust the form into a placid, even shape. What we call a noble shape of nose, such as we appreciate in antique statues, is an ideal which was revived for the first time in the classic age.

Beauty is that which gives an impression of calm and power, and the concept of 'regular beauty' may date from this period, with which it is in perfect accord. What is meant by this is not merely a complete symmetry between the two sides of the face, but a clarity, and, as it were, a legibility, and a consequent relationship of proportion between the parts of the face, which is difficult to define in words but shines out at once from the general impression. Portrait painters took good care to emphasise this regularity and the second generation of the Cinquecento required still more from its painters in this respect: Bronzino's undeniably fine portraits have faces which have been polished and smoothed to the last degree.

Pictures speak louder than words here, and a good parallel can be obtained by putting Piero di Cosimo's *Simonetta* side by side with the so-called *Vittoria*

Colonna of Michelangelo,[1] for both are ideal figures which epitomize the tastes of two epochs (*Figs.* 171, 172).

There could be no sixteenth century series to compare with the Florentine busts of girls from the fifteenth century: the Cinquecento Gallery of Beauties consists of very womanly women—the *Donna Velata* of the Pitti, the *Dorothea* in Berlin, the *Fornarina* of the Tribuna, Andrea del Sarto's magnificent women in Madrid and Windsor, and so on. Taste has turned in favour of women with ampler charms.

3

THE playful fancy of the fifteenth century unleashed all its caprices in the treatment of hair, and painters created magnificent coiffures with an infinite wealth of festooned garlands and varied tresses, sprinkled with precious stones and enlivened with ropes of pearls; but we must distinguish between these fantastic elaborations and the hair-styles which were actually worn—and they were capricious enough. The tendency was towards division and separation, towards the decorative detail, in contrast to the later taste which preferred the hair as a single mass of simple form, and even in decoration precious stones were not left as single flashes in the hair but assembled into a harmonious form. The loose and waving form was rejected in favour of firm unity: the floating ringlets, so common in Ghirlandaio and his contemporaries, which fall on to the cheek and cover the ear, disappear at once as a merely pretty motive, compromising the clarity of the whole. The ear, an important point in the structure of the whole, must be clearly visible. The hair on the forehead is brought into a simple line over the temples, with an enclosing function, whereas the Quattrocento did not want to see this, and deprived the forehead of its natural frame, increasing its size beyond its normal limits. The older style tends to emphasise the verticality of this arrangement still further, by putting a jewel on the top of the head, where Cinquecento breadth preferred a strong horizontal as a boundary.

And so the stylistic inversions proceed. The long, slender neck of the Quattrocento beauty, which had to appear unencumbered and supple, required different ornaments from those of the massive sixteenth-century forms: there is no more play with single jewels suspended from threads, but these are replaced by heavy chains, and the closely fitting, light necklace becomes pendent and heavy. To sum up, men sought the weighty and the measured, and joy in fantastic creation was forced into the path of strict simplicity. Indeed, there were even voices raised in favour of natural disorder in the hair, which claimed that the skin was more beautiful in its natural state (*palidetta col suo color nativo*) than when made

---

[1] Michelangelo's authorship was first contested—and rightly so—by Morelli, but it does not affect the argument.

up with red and white cosmetics, so that a woman only changed colour in the morning when she put it on. It was Count Castiglione who said that, and it is a significant reaction from the gaudiness and artificiality of late Quattrocento fashions.

We must at least observe, in this connection, that among men the previously tousled hair was smoothed into a simple outline. It is no accident that the portraits of Credi or Perugino show the hair stirred by a gentle breeze, for the elaborate style demanded this. Sixteenth-century portraits all show the hair brushed into smooth and ordered masses. The beard was generally allowed to grow in the sixteenth century—for it underlines the impression of dignity. Castiglione leaves it to each man to decide for himself, although when he sat to Raphael he wore a full beard himself.

Costume provides a still clearer indication of the new ideas; for clothing is the direct expression of prevailing ideas on the human body and its movements, and it was inevitable that the Cinquecento should turn to soft and heavy materials, pendent and puffed sleeves and sweeping trains such as we see in Andrea del Sarto's *Birth of the Virgin* of 1514 (*Fig.* XII), which, as Vasari expressly states, depicts the fashion of the day. It is not our intention to analyse the motives in detail: the decisive factor is the universal desire for fullness and weight in clothing, the stressing of broad lines and emphasis on the hanging or trailing, which all retarded movement. Conversely, the fifteenth century accentuated freedom and mobility of movement. Short, closely-fitting sleeves which left the wrist free; no luxuriant masses, but a trim elegance; a few small slashes and ribbons on the lower part of the sleeve, otherwise nothing but a few narrow hems and seams. The Cinquecento desired weightiness and rustling fullness, rejecting complicated cutting and small, single motives, and figured stuffs disappeared before the heavy, deep folds of the skirt. Costume is based on the calculation of large surface contrasts and only those stuffs are employed which can be used for large effects, not materials which have to be looked at closely. Botticelli's Graces have their breasts covered with a sort of network of threads (*Fig.* 7), but these are archaic subtleties which were as incomprehensible to the new generation as the flutter of ribbons, veils and similar gauzy objects. The sense of touch demanded satisfaction in a different way, by a firm grasp of objects, rather than a caress with the fingertips.

4

FROM this point of view we may glance at architecture and its Cinquecento transformations. Like dress, this is a projection of man and his sense of solidity on to the outside world: in the spaces which this sense creates for itself, in the form of ceilings and walls, an age expresses itself as clearly as in the stylisation of the human body and its actions, setting forth its ideals and its standards of value. The Cinquecento had a particularly strong feeling for the relation between man and architecture, for the resonance of a beautiful space. It could scarcely think of existence apart from an architectonic concept and a basis in terms of architecture.

Like everything else, architecture becomes heavy and serious, constraining the gay mobility of the Early Renaissance to a more measured tread. The multiplicity of gay ornaments, the wide arches, the slender columns, all disappear and are replaced by heavy and restrained forms, solemn proportions and grave simplicity. Spacious echoing rooms are needed for the grand ceremonies which are now sought for in preference to mere amusements; and solemnity of effect can be compatible only with the strictest adherence to rules and canons.

Ghirlandaio provides us with a mine of information about interior decoration in late fifteenth-century Florence. The room in the *Birth of the Baptist* (*Fig.* 164) probably gives a fairly exact picture of a patrician house, with its pilasters in the corners, continuous cornice, coffered wooden ceiling with gilt ornaments, and the colourful tapestry hung unsymmetrically on the wall. Furniture stands about, disposed either for use or decoration, but without any regard for regular arrangement: whatever is beautiful, must be beautiful anywhere.

By contrast with this, the typical Cinquecento room is cold and bare, for the gravity of the architectural forms outside affected interior decoration as well, and there are no more effective details and picturesque corners, for everything is architecturally stylised, not merely in form but also in decoration and fittings. Gay colours are completely abandoned. This is the picture we see in Andrea del Sarto's *Birth of the Virgin* of 1514 (*Fig.* 106). Monochromatic treatment is connected with the greater efforts made to obtain nobility of effect: restrained colours and neutral tones, which do not attract attention, are found preferable to obtrusive or gaudy colours. Count Castiglione says that the gentleman should normally dress in unpretentious dark colours: only Lombards go about in bright colours and slashed clothing and if anyone tried to do so in Central Italy he would be taken for a lunatic.[1] Brightly coloured hangings disappear along with striped girdles and oriental shawls, for the taste for them now seems childish.

Colour was also banished from architecture with any pretensions to grandeur, disappearing entirely from the façade and undergoing the severest limitation in the interior. The view that the noble must necessarily be colourless held sway

---

[1] It was only a step from here to the adoption of Spanish dress. Sympathetic appreciation of the Spanish character—*grave e riposato*—is frequently to be found in Castiglione, who thought the Spaniards more nearly akin to the Italians than the French were, with their mercurial temperament.

for a long time, and, as a result, many old monuments suffered so that we have to reconstruct the image of the Quattrocento from comparatively fragmentary remains. The architectural backgrounds of a Gozzoli or a Ghirlandaio are of great help to us in this, even though they cannot be taken absolutely literally in matters of detail. Ghirlandaio had an almost insatiable taste for bright colour— blue friezes, yellow strips on pilasters, variegated marble pavements—and yet Vasari praised his simplicity because he abandoned the use of gilt ornaments in his pictures.[1]

The same is true of sculpture. We have already mentioned (p. 67-8) a major example of Quattrocento polychromy, the tomb by Antonio Rossellino in S. Miniato; another example was once Desiderio's Marsuppini Tomb in Santa Croce, which now stands in characterless whiteness, although close examination reveals traces of colour. It would be a worthy task in our age of restoration to take this damaged sufferer in hand and allow it to shine once again with all its old joyfulness. It does not take much colour to get a colouristic effect: a few touches of gold alone will suffice to remove the colourless look of white stone, the appearance of contrast between it and the surrounding colours of the world. The *Madonna* relief by Antonio Rossellino, in the Bargello (*Fig.* 4), and the *St. John* by Benedetto da Maiano, are treated in this way, not heavily gilt, but gaining a colourful shimmer from a few touches in the hair or the garment of skins. Gold goes naturally with bronze, and there exist also some particularly fine combinations of bronze and marble with gold; for example, the Tomb of Bishop Foscari in Santa Maria del Popolo, Rome, where the bronze figure of the dead man lies on a marble cushion decorated with golden ornaments.

Michelangelo broke away from colour effects from the very beginning, and as a result everyone else forthwith began working in monochrome: even terracotta, which seems specially adapted to the charm of paint, loses all colour, as may be well seen in the work of Begarelli. I cannot endorse the judgement, often repeated, that modern lack of colour in sculpture is due to the ambition to imitate antique statues. The rejection of colour was determined upon before any archæological purist could have thought of this idea, and such far-reaching changes of taste are not as a rule determined by historical considerations. The Renaissance saw the antique as coloured as long as it used colour itself and in all cases where antique monuments were introduced into pictures they were treated as polychromatic; from the moment when the desire for colour ceased, the antique was seen as white, but it is wrong to say that it gave the initial impulse.

---

[1] Gold lasted longer among the Umbrians than the Florentines and it is interesting to observe its gradual disappearance from Raphael's works in the Vatican.

5

EVERY generation sees in the world that which is congenial to it, and the fifteenth century must obviously have had entirely different standards of visual beauty from those of the sixteenth century, since it saw the world with different eyes. Poliziano's 'Giostra' has a passage describing the Garden of Venus which is a compendium of Quattrocento sensitivity to beauty: he speaks of the sunny groves and the spring of clear water, he names the many lovely colours and the flowers, going from one object to another and describing them at length without fear of wearying his audience, and with the most delicate perception he speaks of the little green meadow:

> . . . *scherzando tra fior lascive aurette*
> *fan dolcemente tremolar l'erbette.*

In the same way, a flowery meadow was, for the painter, a collection of purely individual existences, every one with its own vital sentiment, which he could share. It is said of Leonardo that he once painted a bunch of flowers in a vase with astonishing art[1]: I quote this one case as an example of many strivings by painters of that time. Glancing lights and reflections on jewels, cherries, metal utensils, were all observed with a new delicacy of perception, which grew out of fifteenth-century Netherlandish pictures. A specially precious taste was evinced by giving St. John the Baptist a glass cross with metal rings: painterly delights could be afforded by leaves with light glancing off them, glowing flesh and light cloudlets against a blue sky, and, in every case, the most intense brilliance of colour was sought after.

The sixteenth century no longer knew these joys. The juxtaposition of gay and beautiful colours had to give way to strong shadows and the desire for spatial effects. Leonardo mocks at painters who did not want to sacrifice beauty of colour to modelling, comparing them to orators who use fine phrases without any meaning.[2] Quivering blades of grass and the flicker of light on crystal are no longer the concern of Cinquecento painting, which lacked a close-up vision, realizing only grand actions and major effects of light and shade. And this is not all. The interest in the outside world is increasingly confined to figures alone: we have already seen how altarpieces and histories concentrate on their own special effects and cease to cater for a general delight in the visible world, where formerly the altarpiece had been a place for assembling every beautiful object under the sun. Narrative pictures were the work, not of only history painters, but of men who were also architectural, landscape and still-life painters. Such

---

[1]Vasari (ed. Milanesi), III, p. 25. This was in a *Madonna*. Venturi cites the passage in connection with Lorenzo di Credi's tondo in the Borghese Gallery (No. 433).
[2]*Trattato*, Ludwig's Italian-German ed., No. 236. The increased use of shadow effects in architecture (and sculpture) must also be borne in mind as inimical to colour.

interests now became incompatible with one another. Even where the intention is neither dramatic nor solemn and religious, in purely idyllic scenes or unemotional representations of secular or mythological subjects, it is the beauty of the figures which swallows up almost every other consideration. To which of the great men would one entrust Leonardo's glass of flowers? When Andrea del Sarto treats any such subject he dashes it off in a purely superficial way, as if he were afraid of compromising the purity of the monumental style;[1] and yet we occasionally find a beautiful landscape in his works. Raphael, potentially at any rate, was probably the most versatile of them all as a pure painter, yet he produced very little in this line. All the means were still available, but it seems that there was a tendency to concentrate exclusively upon figure painting and to look down upon everything non-figural: it is significant that it was a North Italian, Giovanni da Udine, who was employed in Raphael's workshop on picturesque details. Later still, it was the Lombard, Caravaggio, who caused a veritable storm in Rome with just this subject—a vase of flowers: it was the sign of a new art.

When a Quattrocento painter like Filippino paints *Music* (picture in Berlin; *Fig.* 173) as a young woman adorning the swan of Apollo while the wind blows her mantle about with all the blithe *coloratura* of the Quattrocento style, the picture, with its putti and animals, water and foliage, has all the charm of a Böcklin mythology; but the sixteenth century would have emphasised the statuesque motive alone. The feeling for nature as a whole becomes more and more limited and there is no doubt that this was bad for the development of art, for the High Renaissance worked within such narrow limits that there was an ever-present danger of self-exhaustion.

The change of taste towards plasticity coincides, in Italian art, with the approach to antique beauty and there is a tendency to explain both these phenomena as having been produced by the same cause—deliberate imitation of the antique—as if the picturesque beauties of the world had been abandoned in favour of the antique statues. However, we must not base judgements on analogies drawn from our own century, with its historical approach to such matters. If Italian art, at the zenith of its powers, shows a new creative impulse, it can only be explained as a development from within.

6

To sum up, we must speak once more of this relationship to the antique. Popular opinion has it that the fifteenth century did indeed look at the monuments of antiquity, but that they forgot all about such foreign elements when

---

[1]There is now a distinction between monumental and non-monumental: quite different stylistic criteria are valid for the little Cassone pictures.

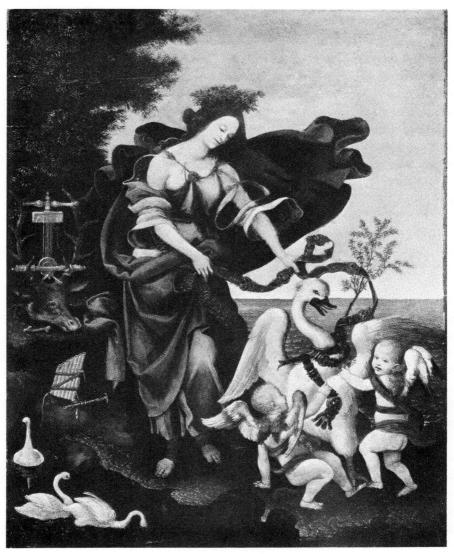

173. FILIPPINO LIPPI: *Allegory of Music*. Berlin

they came to their own work, whereas the sixteenth century, less strongly gifted with originality, could never rid itself of the impression made by antiquity. This is a tacit assumption that both ages looked at the antique in the same way, but it is just this assumption which is controversial. If the Quattrocento eye observed aspects of nature which were not seen by the Cinquecento, it is a psychological consequence that, in front of the antique, the same factors in the object perceived will not make themselves equally prominent to both consciousnesses. It is always the case that a man sees only what he is looking for, and it requires long training, such as we have no right to assume existed in an artistically productive age, before this naive kind of vision is overcome, since it is not merely a question of what is reflected on the retina, but what is actually observed. It is, therefore, more correct to suppose that, given a similar desire—to be 'antique'—the fifteenth and the sixteenth centuries were bound to have different results since each understood the antique in a different way: that is to say, each sought its own reflection there. If, therefore, the Cinquecento appears to us as the more antique it must be because its own inner life had become more akin to that of antiquity.

Architecture shows this relationship most clearly, for no one doubts the sincere intention of the architects of the Quattrocento to restore the 'good ancient style', and yet there is very little likeness between their works and those of the ancients. The attempts of the fifteenth century to master the Roman language of form make it seem that the antique was known to them only from hearsay: the architects took the ideas of column, arch and cornice, but the way in which they shaped the individual members, and fitted them together as elements of a larger whole, makes it seem difficult to believe that they had ever seen Roman ruins. Yet they had seen them, admired them, studied them, and were quite convinced that they were creating an antique impression themselves. The façade of S. Marco in Rome is copied from the arcades of the Colosseum, yet in the essential thing, the proportions, it is quite different—that is, Quattrocento—but this was not done with the intention of emancipating the building from its prototype but because it was thought that one could build in this way and still be antique. Architects borrowed the letter of the formal system, but remained independent in spirit. It is an instructive study to take, for example, the antique Triumphal Arches, which were above ground and available for imitation in both the earlier and later periods, and to observe how the Renaissance held aloof from the classical example offered by the Arch of Titus and seized upon archaisms which have analogies with the Augustan buildings at Rimini, or still further afield, until such time as they had become classic of their own accord.[1]

The same is true of antique figures. With unerring feeling, artists took from these admired models only those things which they themselves understood, that is, those things which they had already mastered for themselves; and we may even say that the repertory of antique sculpture, which included examples both of mature and over-ripe styles, not only had no effect on the course of the stylistic development of modern art, but that it did not even lead to any premature developments. When the Early Renaissance takes up an antique motive it

---

[1] *Cf.* H. Wölfflin, *Die antiken Triumphbögen, eine Studie zur Entwicklungsgeschichte der römischen Architektur und ihr Verhältnis zur Renaissance*, in *Repertorium für Kunstwissenschaft*, XVI, 1893.

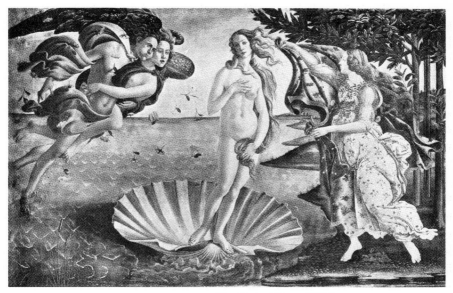

174. BOTTICELLI: *The Birth of Venus*. Uffizi

is fundamentally altered before it emerges again in the work of art: a treatment which is exactly the same as that accorded to the antique in such periods of marked stylistic development as the Baroque and Rococo. In the sixteenth century, art reached a level where, for a short time, it saw the antique face to face, on equal terms; and this was the result of its own inner development, not the consequence of a deliberate study of the fragments of antiquity. The broad stream of Italian art followed its own course, and the Cinquecento was as it had to be, with or without antique sculpture. Its beauty of line did not come from the *Apollo Belvedere*, nor did classic repose come from the *Niobids*.[1]

It takes some time to accustom oneself to seeing the antique in the Quattrocento, but there can be no doubt of its presence: when Botticelli undertook mythological subjects he wished to recreate the appearance of the antique. Strange as it may seem to us, his *Venus* poised on the sea-shell, as much as his *Calumny of Apelles*, is intended to depict these subjects in the same way as a painter of antiquity would have painted them, and his *Primavera*, with the goddess of Love in a red dress patterned with gold, with the dancing Graces and the flower-scattering Flora, was reckoned a composition in the antique spirit. The Venus on her shell bears little enough resemblance to her antique sister and Botticelli's group of the Graces is entirely different in appearance from the antique group, but there is no need to assume an intentional desire to distinguish himself from the antique on Botticelli's part, for he did no more than his

[1] In any case, the Florentine *Niobids* were still unknown at the beginning of the sixteenth century.

contemporaries and colleagues in architecture did when they put up their arcades with thin columns, wide and airy arches, and rich decorative detail, thinking they were imitating the antique.[1]

Had there arisen a Winckelmann at that time to preach the 'calm greatness and noble simplicity' of antique art, he would have found no one to understand him. The early Quattrocento was far nearer this ideal, but the earnest attempts of a Niccolo d'Arezzo and a Nanni di Banco, or even of a Donatello, were not renewed. Movement was sought after, variety and decoration were prized, the whole sense of form had altered radically; yet no one thought that touch had been lost with the antique, for it was the antique which provided the finest models of movement and fluttering draperies, and the monuments of antiquity were an inexhaustible treasury of decorative details suitable for furnishings, clothing and buildings.[2] No better way could be thought of than to fill backgrounds with antique buildings, and so great was the enthusiasm for these monuments that the Arch of Constantine in Rome, for example, where it was actually present before the eyes of everybody, was time and again introduced into frescoes, and not once only, but twice in the same picture. True, it was not shown in its actual state, but as it ought to be—painted in colours and gaily rigged up. In every case where an antique scene was represented the effect sought was of a fantastic, almost fairy-tale, splendour, and, at the same time, men did not look for gravity in the ancient world, but for cheerful serenity. Naked people with brightly coloured sashes, lying in the grass, were pleasing things, and could be called Mars and Venus. There was nothing statuesque and marmoreal for there was, as yet, no question of renouncing multi-coloured variety, gleaming flesh and flowery meadows. As yet, there was no feeling for the *gravitas* of the ancient world; men read the ancient poets, but with a different accent, and the pathos of Virgil died away in unheard echoes. Those noble passages which have impressed themselves on the memory of later generations, such as the words of the dying Dido, *et magna mei sub terras ibit imago*—for these the perceptions of men were not yet sharp enough. We believe we can safely speak in this way, in view of the illustrations which were made of the ancient poems, the whole tone of which is so totally unlike anything we should expect. How easy it was to create an antique impression, we can gather from Vespasiano's charming description of the humanist Niccolò Niccoli at table.[3] The cloth was of the finest white linen, and set with rich bowls and antique vessels, while he

---

[1] In Verrocchio's relief of the death of one of the Tornabuoni family (from the tomb in Santa Maria Novella, now in the Bargello) we can see the antique treatment of a contemporary scene. Frida Schottmüller discovered the antique prototype; cf. *Repertorium*, XXV, p. 403.
[2] According to Vasari, Filippino was the first to cram large numbers of antique motives into his pictures.
[3] Quoted by J. Burckhardt in his *Civilization of the Renaissance* [Phaidon ed., 1944, p. 129], and more recently in his *Beiträge (Die Sammler)*, p. 332, note.

himself drank only from a crystal goblet. '*A vederlo in tavola*', cries the enchanted narrator, '*così antico come era, era una gentilezza*'. The little picture is sensitively drawn in an archaic way and it fits in perfectly with Quattrocento conceptions of antiquity; but how unthinkable in the sixteenth century! Who would have called it 'antique'? Above all, who would have spoken of eating in such a context?

The new conceptions of human dignity and beauty operated of themselves to bring art into a new relationship with classical antiquity. At once the two tastes met and it is an understandable result that now, for the first time, the eye learned to pay attention to matters of archæological exactness in the reproduction of antique figures. Fantastic costumes disappeared and Virgil was represented as a Roman poet instead of an oriental wizard, and the old gods are given back their proper form and attributes. The antique was now seen as it really is, and the ingenuous approach disappeared; but from this moment the antique became a danger and contact with it became ruinous to the weaker men, once they had eaten of the tree of knowledge.

Raphael's *Parnassus* (*Fig.* 64) affords a most instructive contrast with Botticelli's *Primavera* (*Fig.* 7), giving a fair idea of the new conception of an antique scene, and, in the *School of Athens*, we encounter a free-standing figure of Apollo which has a genuine air. The question here is not whether the figure was (or was not) based on an antique gem;[1] what is important is that we are immediately impelled to think of an antique. For the first time, antique statues are reproduced in a really plausible way: the modern sense of line and mass has been developed to such a pitch that it bridges the centuries. It is not only the representation of human beauty which is affected, but there is also, once again, an appreciation of the solemn quality of antique drapery (indications of which had already appeared in works of the early Quattrocento), and the dignity of antique presentation, the nobility of restrained gesture, were again perceived. The scenes from the Æneid in Marcantonio's *Quos Ego* engraving form an instructive contrast to Quattrocento illustrations. The age had become sensitive to statuesque qualities and this tendency to see primarily in terms of plasticity was bound to lead to a complete saturation in antique art.

Nevertheless, all the great masters remained independent in their attitude to experience, or else they would not have been great; the taking over of individual motives, or the stimulus provided by this or that prototype, is no evidence to the contrary. It is possible to regard the antique as a factor in the education of Michelangelo or Raphael, yet it is no more than a secondary factor. The risk of losing originality was greater for sculptors than painters—Sansovino, right at the beginning of the century, in his splendid tombs in Santa Maria del Popolo, had made a start in the direction of a thorough-going imitation of the antique, and,

---

[1] It is almost certainly right to refer it to the Medicean gem of *Apollo and Marsyas*.

compared to older works like Pollaiuolo's tombs in St. Peter's, his style has the effect of a proclamation of a neo-Roman art. Yet Michelangelo, by himself, was able to ensure that art did not go astray in the blind alley of an assimilative antiquarian classicalism. In the same way, the antique played an increasingly large part in Raphael's environment, yet his greatest achievements were always independent of it.

It must always be borne in mind that the architects never lent themselves to the exact reproduction of ancient buildings, though the Roman ruins must have spoken more potently than ever before. Men understood their simplicity now, having themselves overcome the unbridled desire for decoration: they could grasp their massiveness, having arrived at analogous proportions themselves, and now a more perceptive eye desired exact measurements of them. Excavations were made, and Raphael revealed himself as half an archæologist. Men had passed one stage in their own development, and they could now also distinguish different periods in antique work,[1] yet in spite of this sharpened insight, the age remained true to itself and 'modern', and from the fruits of archæological studies the Baroque was to spring.

---

[1] In this connection *cf.* the so-called Raphael Memorandum on the excavations in Rome (printed in Guhl, *Künstlerbriefe*, I, and other books [*e.g.* Fischel's *Raphael*, I, 1948, p. 201]), and also Michelangelo's astonishing critique of the building periods of the Pantheon, which, so far as I can see, tallies with the results of the most recent researches (Vasari, Milanesi ed., IV, 512, in the *Life of Andrea Sansovino*).

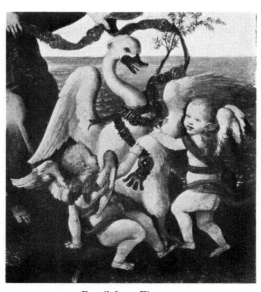

Detail from Fig. 173

Chapter III : THE NEW PICTORIAL FORM

T HIS final chapter must deal with the new methods of presentation, by which we mean the way in which a given object is made into a visual image suitable for use in pictorial form, in the sense in which the concept of 'pictorial form' is applicable to all the visual arts.

It is obvious that the new feelings for mass and movement, as already expounded, must make themselves felt as conditioning factors in the form of a picture; that the concepts of repose, grandeur, and importance in the impression to be made by a picture will emerge as the decisive elements, irrespective of the actual subject depicted. This does not exhaust the underlying causes of the new pictorial form, for others come into play, independent of the preceding diagnoses and definitions, and which cannot be deduced from them; causes without relation to feelings and states of mind, but which are simply the results of a more complete cultivation and education of the eye. These are the real artistic principles—on the one hand, clarification of the visible object and simplification of appearances, and, on the other, the desire for ever greater variety of content within the field of vision. The eye desires more, because its powers of absorption have been significantly increased, but at the same time pictures have become simpler and more lucid, in so far as the objects represented have been better prepared for the eye. And there is yet a third factor—the capacity to see parts collectively and simultaneously, the power of grasping the variety of things in the field of vision as a single unit, which links up with a type of composition in which every part of the whole is felt to have its necessary and inevitable place within that whole.

These are matters which can be treated only in one of two ways: either at very great length or else very briefly, that is by speaking, as it were, in headlines, for a moderate length would be more likely to bore the reader than enlighten him. I have chosen the shorter way, which alone is suitable to the framework of this book. If, therefore, this chapter seems rather inconsiderable, the author may be permitted to remark that, nevertheless, it was not quickly written and that it is probably an easier task to collect running quicksilver than to catch and fix the different impulses which go to make the concept of a mature and complex style. The novelty of the attempt must serve as an excuse—at any rate, a partial excuse—if this section is more than usually lacking in those things which make for easy reading.

1. Repose, Spaciousness, Mass and Size

THE pictures produced in any one generation have, considered as a whole, as individual a pulse-beat as the works of any one master. Quite independently of the subject depicted, the line may flow restlessly and hastily, or with measure and calm; the planes may be so filled that they appear cramped, or the objects may be so disposed as to appear easy and surrounded with space; and the modelling may be petty and jerky or broad and connected. After what has already been said about the new beauty of the Cinquecento, in its feeling for the body and its movements, it is to be expected that the pictures themselves would become calmer, more massive and spacious. A new relationship is established between the space represented and the objects which are disposed within that space, the compositions become more impressive and weighty, and in contour and modelling we perceive the same serenity, the same reticence, which are inseparable from the new beauty.

I

THE contrast leaps to the eye, if we put the *Madonna with the book,* a youthful work of Michelangelo's, beside a similar tondo relief by Antonio Rossellino, who may be taken as typical of the older generation (*Figs.* 4 and 23). In the latter we have glittering diversity; in the former, a simple style based on large planes: it is not just a question of leaving things out and simplifying the subject-matter— this has already been discussed—but of the handling of the planes themselves. When Rossellino enlivens his background with the flicker of light and shade in his rocky landscape and adorns the flat plane of the sky with little wisps of frizzy cloud, it is simply a continuation of the style in which the head and hands are also modelled. Michelangelo first looked for the major planes in the human form and then related them to each other, and, in doing this, the question of how to treat the remainder solved itself. The same principles hold good for painting: here, too, the delight in caprices and in multiplicity of small surface undulations ceases and gives way to a desire for large, still, masses of light and shade. In music, the direction would be *legato.*

The stylistic change is, perhaps, still more clearly visible in the handling of line. Quattrocento line has a somewhat abrupt intricacy, for the draughtsman's main interest is in form in movement, and, unconsciously, he overdoes the movement in the silhouette, the hair and in every detail of form. The shape of the mouth, with the full curves of the lips, is one which the Quattrocento made peculiarly its own, and a Botticelli or a Verrocchio sought with an almost Düreresque energy to give a convincing representation of the movement inherent in parted lips, the curve of the lips themselves and the swing of the outline

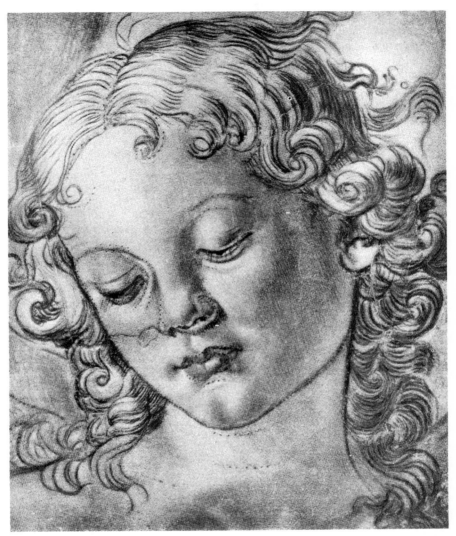

175. 'VERROCCHIO': *Head of an Angel*. Drawing. Uffizi

defining their contour. In the same way, the nose, with its cartilages giving it the greatest variety of forms, became one of the favourite features of the fifteenth century. The movements of the wings of the nostrils were modelled with the deepest interest, and scarcely any of the Quattrocento portraitists could forego showing the holes of the nostrils.[1]

---

[1]The well-known drawing in the Uffizi of an *Angel's head*, ascribed to Verrocchio (*Fig.* 175), is a summary of all these characteristics. The picture in the Florentine Academy [now Uffizi] of the Archangels has an almost exact repetition of the head.

This style disappears with the century and the Cinquecento brings in with it a chastened flow of line: the same model would now have been drawn quite differently, because the artists' eyes saw differently. It now seems that a new sympathy has been aroused for the line in itself, as if it were now conceded that it has a right to live its own life: harsh junctions, violent breaks in continuity and breathless involutions are all avoided. Perugino began the process and Raphael continued it with incomparable sensibility, but even other men of entirely different temperament came to realize the beauty of a noble sweep of line, a rhythmic cadence. It was still possible for Botticelli to make a sharp elbow come right up against the picture frame (*Pietà*, Munich); but now the lines take account of one another and make concessions where necessary, with the result that the eye becomes sensitive to the sharp bisections of the older manner.

2

THE general desire for greater spaciousness necessarily entailed a new relationship between the figures in a painting and the space which surrounded them, a relationship which, in the earlier pictures, was now thought to be cramped. The figures in these earlier works stand right at the front of the stage and thus create an impression of insufficient space which is not dispelled by the halls or landscapes in the background, however extensive they may be. Even Leonardo's *Last Supper* shows some of this Quattrocento limitation, in that the table is brought forward to the very edge of the stage. The portraits of the period show the normal relationship—how uncomfortable life must have been in the little room in which Lorenzo di Credi sets his *Verrocchio* (Uffizi) by comparison with the large airiness of Cinquecento portraits. The new generation wanted air and the possibility of movement, and they obtained these primarily by increasing the amount of the figure depicted—the threequarter-length portrait is a sixteenth-century invention—but, even when they showed only a small part of the body, they were now able to give the impression of spaciousness, and Castiglione seems quite content with his existence inside the boundaries of his frame.

In like fashion, the frescoes of the Quattrocento generally appear cramped and fitted tightly into position. Fra Angelico's frescoes in the Chapel of Nicholas V in the Vatican, have a cramped appearance, and in the chapel of the Medici Palace, where Gozzoli painted the *Procession of the Three Kings*, the spectator cannot quite shake off a feeling of discomfort, in spite of all the ceremonial splendour. Much the same must be said even of Leonardo's *Last Supper*: we expect a frame or border which the picture has not got, and never can have had.

It is characteristic of Raphael that he should have developed during the course of the Stanze, and, if we look at one fresco in the Camera della Segnatura—the

Disputà, for example—by itself, we do not notice anything wrong with its relationship to the wall on which it is painted; but if we look at two pictures together, at the point at which the corners touch, we become conscious of an old-fashioned lack of perception of spatial values. In the second Stanza, the junction of the walls is treated differently and the format of the pictures, in view of the space available, has been made noticeably smaller.

3

IT is no contradiction if, in spite of the desire for spaciousness, the figures gain in size in proportion to the frame.[1] It was felt that they should have a more imposing effect as masses, since there was now a tendency to seek beauty in solidity. Superfluous space was avoided because it was realized that this makes the figures less forceful in appearance, and the means were at hand to give the impression of breadth in spite of limitations of apparent extent.

The tendency was towards compactness, solidity, weightiness. The horizontal gained in importance, and, as a result, the outline of a group was lowered and broadened, making a triangular group with a broad base out of what had been a high pyramid: Raphael's *Madonnas* furnish the best examples of this. The arrangement of two or three standing figures in a closed group is to be interpreted in the same way; and the older pictures which attempt groupings of figures seem thin and fragmentary, and, as wholes, light and almost transparent by comparison with the massive solidity of the new style.

4

FINALLY, as an inevitable result, there was a general increase in absolute size—the figures grew, so to speak, under the artists' hands. It is a well-known fact that Raphael continually increased the scale in the Stanze: Andrea del Sarto surpassed himself with his *Birth of the Virgin* in the court of the Annunziata, and was in turn surpassed by Pontormo. So great was the joy in the powerful that even the newly-awakened sense of unity made no protest. This is equally true of easel pictures and one can observe the change in any Gallery; where the Cinquecento pictures begin, the pictures are larger and so are the figures in them. We shall have to speak again, later on, about the way in which the individual picture was included in the architectural context, and how it was no longer seen for itself alone, but as part of the wall for which it was intended; so that from this point of view alone paintings were bound to increase in size, even if the art had not been moving in this direction of its own accord.

---

[1] Sculptured figures set in niches underwent the same changes.

The style-characteristics just mentioned are of an essentially material nature, and correspond to the expression of a specific emotion; but, as I have already said, other elements, of a formal nature, now come on the scene and they bear no relation to the temper of the new age. These matters cannot be balanced one against the other, with mathematical precision, for 'simplification', in the sense of introducing calm, encounters a simplification which aims at the maximum of lucidity in the picture, while the tendency towards the massive and the comprehensive is countered by a strongly developed will towards ever-increasing richness of the visual image—that will which created groups concentrated into a single major unit, and which first revealed a complete mastery of the third dimension. On the one hand, the intention is to make the act of perception as easy as possible for the eye, and, on the other hand, to pack the maximum amount of content into the picture.

We shall now turn to those things which may be grouped under the headings of simplification and lucidity.

2. Simplification and Lucidity

I

C LASSIC art reverts to the elementary vertical and horizontal for major axes of direction, and to the primitive full-face and pure profile aspects. It was possible to achieve entirely new effects with these means, since the Quattrocento had abandoned such extreme simplicity of axis and aspect in its attempt to render movement at any cost. Even an artist like Perugino, who thought in terms of simplicity, does not have a single pure profile in, for example, his *Pietà* in the Pitti (*Fig.* 54), nor is there ever an absolutely full-face view. Now, when artists possessed the whole range of variety, the primitive suddenly gained a new value: it was not that painters were deliberately archaising, but that they came to realize the effect of simplicity in the midst of riches, since it forms a standard, a norm, which steadies the whole picture. Leonardo appeared as an innovator when he framed his *Last Supper* (*Fig.* 12) between two profiles set on absolutely vertical axes—that, at least, was something he could not possibly have learned from Ghirlandaio.[1] From his earliest beginnings, Michelangelo was aware of the value of simplicity, and Raphael has scarcely a picture, at any rate among his mature works, which does not strike us by its conscious use of simplicity to obtain a strong and emphatic effect. Who among the older generation would have dared to render the Swiss Guards in the *Mass of Bolsena* as he did (*Fig.* 68), three verticals side by side? Yet just this simplicity works wonders here, and in

---

[1] The portrait heads in the Tornabuoni frescoes can hardly be taken into account here, since they are due to social conventions governing bearing and posture and not to formal intentions on the part of the artist. This can be seen from his other compositions.

the most exalted place, the *Sistine Madonna* (*Fig.* 87), he employs a simple vertical with enormous effect, a primitive element in a setting of the most finished art. Fra Bartolommeo's architectonic constructions would be inconceivable without a reversion to these elementary principles.

If we take a single figure, such as Michelangelo's reclining Adam on the Sistine ceiling, which looks so solid and secure, we must admit that the effect could not have been obtained without the placing of the chest in such a way that its full breadth is visible; it is impressive because it is the 'normal' view, obtained under difficulties, and the figure is thus secured in place with a certain inevitability. Another example of the effect of such a tectonic view, as one may call it, is the seated figure of *St. John preaching* by Raphael (Tribuna of the Uffizi; *Fig.* 168). It would have been easy to give him a more striking, or more picturesque, attitude; but as he sits there with head erect and the full width of his chest towards us, it is not only the preacher's mouth which speaks, for his whole form cries out from the picture and this effect could not have been obtained in any other way.

Simple schemes governing the play of light were also sought for in the Cinquecento: we find heads seen in full-face which are divided equally down the line of the nose, that is, with one half dark and the other light, and this type of illumination readily combines with the highest beauty, as in Michelangelo's *Delphic Sibyl* and Andrea del Sarto's idealized *Head of a Youth*. Another method of securing a calm and peaceful effect, when the light fell from high above the figures, was to give an equal amount of shadow to both eye-sockets, as, for example, in the St. John in Fra Bartolommeo's *Pietà* or Leonardo's *Baptist* in the Louvre. All this does not mean that such methods of lighting were always used, any more than simple axes of direction were: it was simply that the effectiveness of simplicity was sensed and its special value realized at its true worth. In Sebastiano's early picture in S. Crisostomo in Venice, there are three female saints standing together at the left, and I must adduce this group as a particularly striking example of the new method of arrangement, although I am not speaking of the bodies but only of the heads (*Fig.* 177). It is an apparently very natural choice: one profile, one—more prominent—in three-quarter view, and the third which is tilted to one side, intrinsically less important and also subordinated in lighting, forming the only inclined line next to two verticals. If we now go through the whole repertory of Quattrocento examples in search of a similar arrangement we shall soon be convinced that the simple was not always the obvious. The feeling for it revived only in the sixteenth century, and yet in 1510, in the very shadow of Sebastiano, Carpaccio could still paint his *Presentation in the Temple* (Venice, Academy) with its three female heads side by side (*Fig.* 176), almost entirely in the older style all three of equal importance, each slightly different

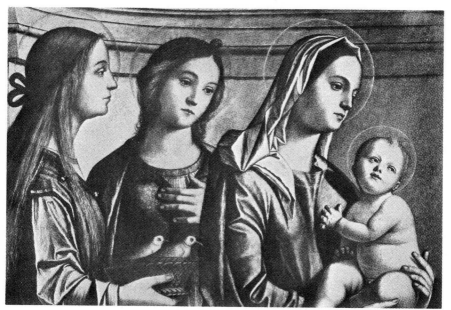

176. CARPACCIO: Detail from the *Presentation in the Temple*. Venice, Academy

in inclination and yet not one of them decisively different, without pre-eminence or subordination and without clear contrast.

2

THE return to elementary methods of arrangement cannot be separated from the invention of composition by contrasts: we may speak of invention in this connection, for it was the classic period which first saw clearly that all values are relative and that every mass or direction can have an effect only when it is related to other masses and directions. Now, for the first time, it was realized that the vertical is necessary because it is a norm by which the variations from the perpendicular can be made perceptible; and now, too, men learned by experience that in the whole realm of the visible, up to the expressive gestures of human beings, any one individual motive can only develop its fullest expressiveness in combination with its opposites. That appears great which is surrounded by small things, whether it be a part of the body or a whole figure; that appears simple which is juxtaposed with complexity, and calm which is opposed to movement, and so on. The principle of effect by contrast is of the greatest importance in the sixteenth century: all classic compositions are founded on it and it is a necessary consequence that, in a work of limited size, each motive may occur only once. Miracles of art like the *Sistine Madonna* are based on the completeness and

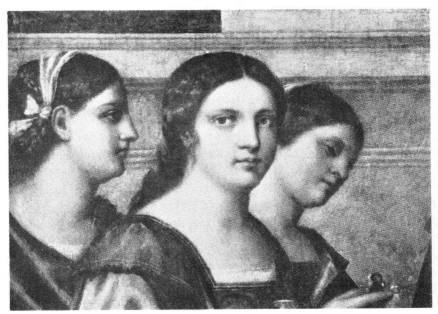

177. SEBASTIANO DEL PIOMBO: Detail from the *St. Chrysostom*. Venice, S. Crisostomo

uniqueness of the contrasts, and this picture, which one might well believe to be less deliberately calculated in its effectiveness than any other, is, in fact, saturated with strong contrasts. To take only one example, it was decided that St. Barbara must be made to look downwards as a parallel figure to the upward-looking Sixtus; this decision was reached long before any thought was given to a special reason for her downward glance. It is characteristic of Raphael's pictures that the spectator does not look beyond the general effect to the individual means which secured the effect, whereas the rather later Andrea del Sarto forces his calculated contrasts on our attention from the first glance, and thus contrasts become meaningless formulae in his hands.

The same principle can also be applied psychologically, so that the expression of any one emotion is not represented near similar emotions, but along with different ones. Fra Bartolommeo's *Pietà* is a model of such psychological economy and Raphael introduced the completely dispassionate Magdalen into the group in his *St. Cecilia*, all of whom are rapt by the celestial music, fully aware of the fact that the degree of their rapture could only be made effective by comparison with this foil. There is no lack of indifferent spectators in the Quattrocento, but such considered deliberations were unknown then. Finally, there is no need to observe how far beyond the horizons of the older art lay such compositions by contrast as the *Heliodorus* or the *Transfiguration*.

THE problem of contrasts is a problem connected with the increased intensity of the emotional effect to be made by a picture, and all the efforts made to simplify the image and increase its significance were but steps in the same direction. All the things then happening in architecture—the process of purification and the exclusion of all detail which played no part in the total effect, the choice of a few large forms, the great increase in plasticity—offer a complete analogy for painting and sculpture.

Pictures were carefully planned so that the great dominant lines should be emphasised. The old method of looking at close range, searching for individual detail and wandering about the picture from part to part, is abandoned, and the composition has to make its effect as a whole, clearly intelligible even from a distance: sixteenth-century pictures have a higher degree of 'readableness', and perception is made extremely easy for the spectator. The essentials emerge at once, there is a decisive division into important and subordinate and the eye is led along specific paths. The composition of the *Heliodorus* serves to show this without need for further examples: our imagination boggles at the thought of the way in which a Quattrocento painter, given such a surface to work on, would have pressed on the spectator a number of things all of equal importance and all obtruding themselves equally on the eye.

The style which informs the whole is equally present in details. Sixteenth-century drapery is distinguished from that of the Quattrocento by the presence of great lines flowing through the whole, by clear contrasts between the simple and ornamental parts, and by the fact that the body, the really essential thing, makes its presence visible below the clothing. Quite a large proportion of the form-fantasy of the Quattrocento consists of the system of folds used in drapery, although people lacking in visual sensibility will overlook these configurations and may even believe that such unimportant details more or less create themselves. One has but to try and make a copy of such a piece of drapery in order to obtain a new respect for it and to perceive a definite style, that is, the expression of a particular will, in these disarrangements of inanimate material; after which one pays attention to all the ripplings and rustlings of the stuff. Every artist has his own style in draperies: Botticelli is among the most cursory, dashing off long simple furrows with customary impetuosity, whereas Filippino, Ghirlandaio and the Pollaiuoli lovingly and devotedly make nests of folds of the greatest formal complexity, as may be seen from Piero Pollaiuolo's seated figure of Prudence with the mantle cast across her lap (*Fig.* 178).[1]

---

[1] The drapery of the Madonna in Ghirlandaio's *Madonna with two Archangels and two kneeling Saints* (Uffizi) is directly related to the famous and often reproduced drapery study by Leonardo in the Louvre (*cf.*, *e.g.* Müntz, p. 240; Müller-Walde, *Pl.* 18). Did Ghirlandaio really copy Leonardo? Or, as Bayersdorfer thought, was the drawing by Ghirlandaio? Berenson rightly upholds Leonardo's authorship.

The fifteenth century strewed its riches prodigally over the whole body, and, if there are no folds to catch the eye, then there are slits, openings, puffs or the pattern of the stuff to do so, and it was thought impossible to allow the eye to remain unoccupied even for a moment. We have already seen the way in which the new interests of the sixteenth century affected the treatment of drapery and it is enough to have seen the women in Leonardo's *Virgin and Child with St. Anne*, Michelangelo's *Madonna* in the Tribune of the Uffizi, or Raphael's *Alba Madonna* (*Figs.* 17, 24, 59), to be able to appreciate the aims of the new style: the essence of the matter is that the clothing must not be allowed to obscure the plastic motive.[1] The drapery is subordinate to the figures and must not obtrude itself as an independent object. Even Andrea del Sarto, who gladly allowed his rustling stuffs to sparkle in broken and picturesque folds, never permitted the drapery to

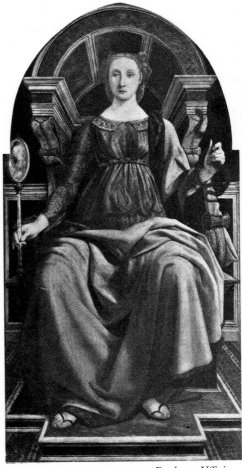

178. PIERO POLLAIUOLO: *Prudence*. Uffizi

become independent of the movement of the figure, whereas in the fifteenth century it often claims attention as an object in itself.

In a piece of drapery, the folds can be arranged more or less at will, and so it is easily comprehensible that the new taste should move away from multiplicity towards simplicity, and seek for strong and leading lines; yet even the fixed forms of the head and body, which cannot be altered at will, were no less subject to the desire for transformation manifested by the new style. Fifteenth-century heads all have in common the characteristic that the main accent is given by the

[1] Leonardo, *Trattato*, Ludwig's Italian-German ed., No. 182: 'Never make your figures so rich in ornament that this interferes with the form and position of the figures.'

gleam of the eye, for the dark pupil and iris have so much greater effect than the pale shadows around them that, inevitably, the first thing we see in the head is the eye, and it may well be that this is usual in real life. The sixteenth century subordinates this effect and damps down the sparkle of the eye, for the leading part is now to be played by the bony structure of the head. The shadows are made darker and give greater vigour to the form and they are no longer split up into small patches, but bound together as large connected masses with the task of connecting, ordering and making the transitions between the parts, so that the earlier collections of disparate details become coherent and unified. Simple lines and firm axes are sought for, and the general swallows up the particular so that no details are allowed to distract the attention. The chief forms must be emphasised to make their effects, and they must tell even at a distance.

It is difficult to discuss such things convincingly without practical demonstration, and even a demonstration would be useless unless accompanied by personal experience of the work of art. Instead of discussing details we will mention only the two parallel portraits by Raphael and Perugino—the *Castiglione* and *Francesco dell' Opera*—and let the reproductions speak for themselves (*Figs.* 77, 78). The spectator will soon be convinced that Perugino uses shadows only in very small doses and without any great depth to them, as part of the elaborate detail of the whole; he uses them, in fact, with such caution that he must have regarded them as a necessary evil whereas Raphael held the opposite view and introduced strong, dark shadows not only to give greater relief but also, and even mainly, in order to reduce the whole to a few large forms. One stroke unites the nose and eye-socket, and the eye itself appears clear and simple in the midst of the encircling masses of shadow. In the Cinquecento this junction of eye-socket and nose is always accentuated because it is of striking physiognomical importance, a centre where many threads of expression meet. It is the secret of the grand style to express much with the fewest means.

We do not intend to follow up these ideas to see how they apply to the body as a whole, nor shall we attempt a detailed account of the way in which the human body is simplified down to its essentials. The decisive factor here is not an increase in anatomical knowledge so much as the visualizing of the figure according to its large forms: the grasp of articulations and of the stages of physical development reflected in the body, itself presupposes a feeling for organic structure which has nothing to do with anatomical learning.

The same development takes place in architecture and one example will suffice here. In the fifteenth century nobody minded if the moulding round the entrance of a niche ran unbroken round the whole arch, but now an impost moulding is required—that is, the important point which marks the spring of the arch must be clearly accented. Just as much clarity came to be required of the articulations of the human body—for example, a new way arose of setting the neck on to the torso. The parts are more clearly distinguished from each other but at the same time the body as a whole acquires a more convincing unity. The important points of attachment were stressed and the lessons which the antique had for so long been trying to teach were learned and understood; so much so that in the long run it became a mere matter of constructing the body according to set schemes, but for this we cannot hold the great masters responsible.

The question now was not only the representation of man in repose, but far more that of human movement, of bodily and spiritual activities, and an incalculable number of completely new problems arose, dealing with emotional states and facial expression. Standing, moving, lifting and carrying, running and flying, all had to be worked out according to the new demands and so did all the expressions of emotion: in every case it seemed both possible and necessary to surpass the Quattrocento in clarity and in the greater force of expression. Signorelli had done the greatest amount of preparatory work in representing the nude in action; independently of the painfully exact studies of details made by the Florentines, he arrived by a surer route at that which is visually important and necessary for the expression of the idea. Yet all his art seems only an intimation and presentiment, when compared with Michelangelo, who first discovered those aspects of muscular functions that force the spectator to understand and share in the action represented. He gets such completely new effects from the material he works with that it would almost seem as if no one had ever attempted such things before. Now that the cartoon of the *Bathing Soldiers* is lost, the seated Slaves of the Sistine Chapel (*Figs.* 40–44) must be called the *Gradus ad Parnassum*, the true School, and if we look at nothing but the drawing of the arms we can still guess at the importance of the whole work. Where the Quattrocento sought for those aspects of any form which are easiest to grasp—as, for example, the profile is the simplest aspect of an elbow—and then repeated these schemes generation after generation, there now came a man who, all at once, broke through these limitations and gave renderings of joints and limbs which must have been an absolute revelation to the spectator. The mighty limbs of these Slaves are no longer taken in their broadest aspects, across the full width of the plane, nor are they bounded by inert parallel contour lines, and as a result they have a life of their own which exceeds the effect of real life. The movement of the line in and out and the contraction and expansion of the forms bring about this effect: later, we shall say something about foreshortening.

Michelangelo remains the great teacher who demonstrated which are the most eloquent aspects. To take a simple example, we may refer to the figures of women carrying burdens by Ghirlandaio and Raphael (*Figs.* 166, 167): when we have seen clearly how Raphael's version of the pendent left arm, which bears the

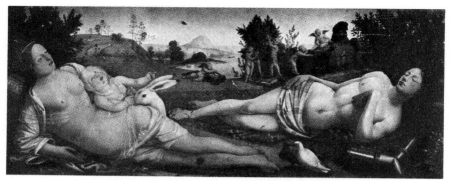

179. PIERO DI COSIMO: *Mars and Venus*. Berlin

weight, excels that of Ghirlandaio, we shall have a standpoint from which to judge of the difference in draughtsmanship in the fifteenth and sixteenth centuries.[1]

As soon as the importance of the joints became clear there naturally arose a desire to make them all visible, and so we find that baring of arms and legs which does not stop short even at saints. Male saints often had their sleeves rolled up in order to display the elbow-joint, but Michelangelo went still further and bared the arm of the Virgin herself, right to the shoulder (*Madonna* in the Tribune); others did not follow him in this, but it became usual to display the shoulder, particularly in angels. Beauty is clarity of articulation.

The principal example of the defective understanding of organic structure, which was typical of the fifteenth century, is probably to be found in the treatment of the loin-cloth of a figure of Christ or St. Sebastian. This piece of drapery is intolerable if it conceals the lines of transition from the torso to the extremities, yet Botticelli and Verrocchio do not seem to have been at all disconcerted at breaking up the body in this way, where the sixteenth century re-arranged the loin-cloth in a way which says clearly that the idea of structure was appreciated and understood, and it was desired to preserve the totality of the image. It is not surprising that Perugino, with his architectonic cast of mind, should thus early have arrived at a similar solution.

To conclude this discussion with a more important example, let us compare the Venus from Piero di Cosimo's *Venus and Mars*, in Berlin, with Titian's recumbent *Venus* in the Uffizi (*Figs.* 179, 180); in this case, Titian must represent the Cinquecento for Central Italy also, since no other equally suitable comparison can be found. We have, therefore, two recumbent female nudes. Now, the obvious

---

[1]Unfortunately, we must reproduce the Raphael figure as a detail from the fresco and not from an original drawing, which, perhaps, would have been still more expressive in line.

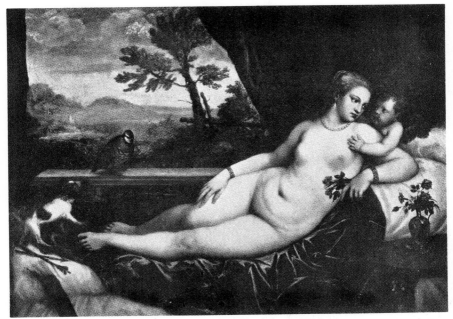

180. TITIAN: *Recumbent Venus*. Uffizi

explanation of the difference in effect would be the difference between the actual bodies; but if it is conceded that here there is a comparison between the articulated beauty of the sixteenth century (such as we have already referred to in connection with Franciabigio, p. 236) and the lack of articulation of the human form which was typical of the fifteenth century, and further conceded that a figure in the taste of the Cinquecento, where the emphasis is put on the permanent and comprehensible underlying forms rather than on the rounded fleshy parts, must necessarily have the advantage of greater clarity; even then, there remain considerable differences in the way in which the form is rendered pictorially. In the one case it is presented imperfectly and piecemeal, and in the other it has been refined into the most perfect clarity. Even a person who knows very little of Italian art will be taken aback when he notices the drawing of the right leg, with its uniform outline parallel to the frame. It is likely enough that the model presented such an appearance, but why was the painter content with it? Why does he make no attempt to render the structure and articulation of the leg? He did not see any need to: the leg is stretched out and would look no different if it were completely stiff; it is compressed by the weight of the other leg, yet it looks withered, and it was against such deformations of the appearance of the object that the new style protested. It is wrong to say that it is simply because Piero was a worse draughtsman than Titian, for in fact we are dealing

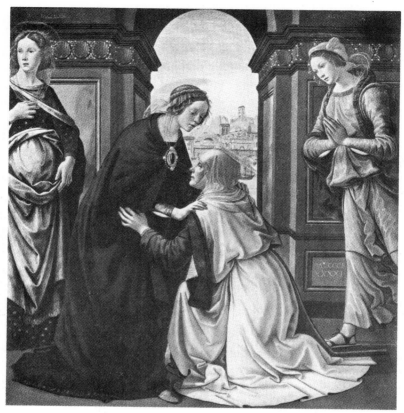

181. GHIRLANDAIO: *The Visitation*. Louvre

with generic differences of style and anyone who goes into the question will be astonished by the number of analogies to be found—it is even possible to find exact parallels for Piero among Dürer's early drawings.

The stomach, distended as always in the fifteenth century, is slumped sideways, which is unlovely in itself, although we might allow the naturalist to gratify himself in this, had he not also cut off all connection between the torso and the legs, so that there is a complete lack of the necessary transitional forms.

In the same way, the left arm suddenly disappears, from the shoulder downwards, without any hint as to how we are to follow it in imagination until we suddenly light on a hand which must belong to it, but which entirely lacks any visual connection with it. If we seek an explanation of the functions, such as the apparent propping action of the arm supporting the body, the twist of the head or the gesture of the wrist, Piero tells us absolutely nothing. Titian renders the structure of the body with perfect clarity, leaving no single detail unexplained and, in addition, he gives the muscular functions, with moderation yet satisfactorily. We need not speak here of the harmony of line and the way in which the contour—particularly on the right side—runs down in an even, rhythmic cadence, but we may make the general observation that even Titian did not compose like this from the beginning: the earlier, simpler *Venus* in the Tribuna, with the little dog, may have the advantage of greater freshness but it is less mature.

What is true of a single figure is still more true of the arrangement of several figures in groups. The Quattrocento made unbelievable demands on the eye, for the spectator has not only to go to the great trouble of

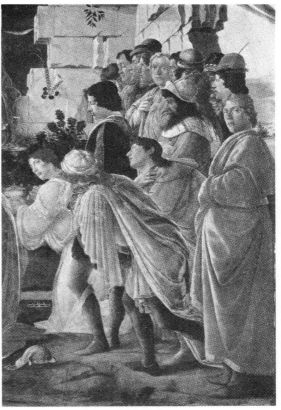

182. BOTTICELLI: *The Adoration of the Kings.* Detail from the Uffizi picture

picking out individual faces from the closely-packed rows of heads, but also finds himself looking at parts of figures which it is almost impossible to imagine as complete forms. It was not yet ascertained how far it was possible to go in the way of overlapping and concealing figures, and I may instance the unpleasing fragments of figures in Ghirlandaio's *Visitation* (Louvre) or Botticelli's *Adoration of the Kings* in the Uffizi (*Figs.* 181, 182), the right half of which the reader is invited to analyse, while advanced students may be recommended to Signorelli's frescoes in Orvieto, with their almost inexplicable tumult. With what a sense of relief the eye turns to Raphael's compositions with their multitudes of figures—I am speaking of his Roman works, for the *Entombment* is still lacking in this kind of clarity.

We find the same defects in the treatment of architectural details: the portico in Ghirlandaio's fresco of *Joachim's Sacrifice* is so arranged that the pilaster capitals exactly reach the upper edge of the picture. Nowadays everyone would say that he should either have included the entablature as well or else cut off the pilasters below the level of the capitals, but we have learned these criteria from the Cinquecento. Perugino was ahead of the others in this respect also, yet we find archaisms of this kind even in him, such as his attempts to indicate the whole span of an arch by the corners of an entablature projecting at the edges of the picture. The spatial calculations of the older Filippo Lippi, however, are truly ludicrous in their effects and form part of the opinion expressed on him in the first chapter of this book.

3. Complexity

THE complete emancipation of bodily movement must head the list of advances in knowledge made in the sixteenth century, for it is this which is the primary condition of the richness of effect made by Cinquecento pictures. The body seems endowed with greater vitality and the spectator's eye is invited to increase its activity. This movement is not to be understood as a change of position in space, for the Quattrocento already has a great deal of running and jumping, although a certain poverty and emptiness is inseparable from it, in so far as a restricted use is made of human articulations and joints, and the possibilities inherent in twists and bends of the major and minor joints were usually explored only to a rather limited degree. The sixteenth century starts from here, with a developed use of the human body and an enrichment of the total image presented by even a motionless figure, so that we realize we are on the threshold of an entirely new epoch. All at once, the axial directions of the body are increased and varied, and what was formerly thought of as merely a plane surface is now thought out in depth as well, becoming a form-complex in which the third dimension plays its part.

It is a widespread error among dilettanti that all things are possible at all times, and that art, as soon as it has acquired any expressive power at all, is capable of rendering all movement equally well; yet, in fact, the real development is exactly like that of a plant slowly putting forth leaf after leaf until it stands rounded and complete, reaching out in all directions. This calm and orderly growth is peculiar to all organic art forms although it is seen at its purest in the antique and in Italian art.

I repeat that this is not a question of movements which aim at some goal or further a specific new expression. It is simply the more or less elaborated representation of a seated, standing or leaning figure, which has the same principal function as before, but which is capable of a very different pattern of limbs and torso, by means of contrasts in the turn of the upper half of the body upon the lower, between head and torso, by the raising up of one foot, by the reaching of the arm across the body or the thrust forward of one shoulder and such-like further possibilities of movement. Immediately, certain laws were formulated and applied to the use of these motives; and *contrapposto* is the name given to inverse correspondences, such as that when the bending of a right leg corresponds to the bending of a left arm or *vice-versa*, yet this concept of *contrapposto* must not be taken to cover the whole phenomenon.

One may imagine a set of tables laying down the differentiations of corresponding parts of the body in this sense—arms and legs, shoulders and hips —which would give an abstract of the newly discovered possibilities of movement in all three dimensions: however, the reader will not expect any such thing here and will be content with a few selected examples, since so much has already been said about plastic variety of form. The workings of the new style can be seen most clearly when the artist had to deal with an absolutely motionless figure, as in the Crucifixion, when it would seem that no variation was possible because the hands and feet were fixed in position. Yet the Cinquecento was able to make something new from this apparently barren motive by subordinating one leg to the other through the placing of one knee over the other, and by twisting the figure as a whole so that there is a contrast of direction between the upper and lower parts—this has already been mentioned in connection with Albertinelli (p. 153). It was Michelangelo who pushed this motive to its ultimate conclusion, and, incidentally, it was he who added emotion, for he created the type of Crucified Christ whose eyes are directed upwards and whose mouth opens to cry out in anguish.[1]

The motive of a bound figure offers greater possibilities—St. Sebastian bound to the stake, the Christ of the Flagellation, or the group of Slaves, with the function of columns, which Michelangelo had in mind for the Julius Tomb. It is possible to trace the effect of these 'Captives' in religious themes quite clearly, and if Michelangelo had executed the whole series for the Tomb there would have been very little else left to discover.

Almost limitless perspectives naturally open up before us when we approach the free-standing figure, and we ask what the sixteenth century would have made of Donatello's bronze *David* (*Fig. 2*)? The general outline of his movement is so close to classic taste and the differentiation of the limbs is so effective, even at this date, that apart from the treatment of form, it might be thought that he would have satisfied even the later generation. The answer is to be found in Benvenuto Cellini's *Perseus*, a late figure—1550—but relatively simply composed and therefore suitable for comparison (*Fig. 183*). Here we can see what was lacking in the *David*, for not only are the contrasts between the limbs sharply intensified, but the figure is taken out of the one single plane and reaches far

---

[1]Vasari (ed. Milanesi, VII, p. 275) interprets it differently—'*alzato la testa raccomanda lo spirito al padre*'. The composition is known only in copies. This is the origin of the seventeenth-century type of Crucified Christ.

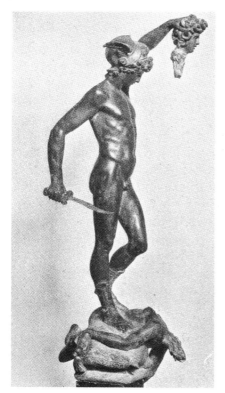

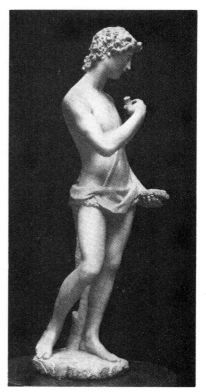

183. CELLINI: *Perseus.*
Bronze Model. Bargello

184. Attributed to MICHELANGELO:
Giovannino. Berlin

forward and back. We may think this ominous and a portent of decay in sculpture; I use this as an example because it is characteristic of the tendency.

It is true that Michelangelo is more varied and yet composes in a closed way, within the limits of the block; but his endeavours to develop his figures in depth at the same time have already been discussed in contrasting the *Apollo* with the flat and relief-like treatment of the *David* (p. 48). The twist which runs through the figure from top to toe serves to stimulate the idea of three dimensions, and the arm reaching across is valuable not only as a contrasting horizontal, but because it possesses a spatial importance as well, since it marks one degree on the scale of the axis in depth and as such already establishes a relationship between the front and back planes. The *Christ* of the Minerva (*Fig.* 143) is conceived in the same way and the Berlin *Giovannino* (*Fig.* 184) also belongs in this context (*cf.* note on p. 46), only Michelangelo would not have approved of the loose massing in it. Anyone who analyses the movement of this figure can profitably take Michelangelo's *Bacchus* into account: the old-fashioned

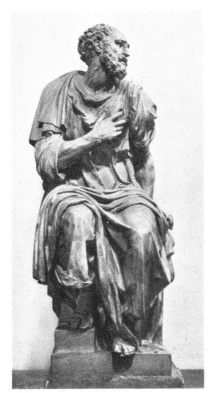 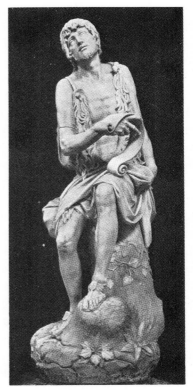

185. MONTORSOLI: *St. Cosmas.*
Florence, S. Lorenzo

186. JACOPO SANSOVINO: *St. John the Baptist.* Venice, S. Maria dei Frari

simplicity and flatness of the formal conception of the genuine early work will appear with complete clarity in opposition to the complicated movement, with its turns in several directions, in the work of a later imitator, and the difference not only between two individuals, but also between two generations, will be apparent to the unprejudiced spectator.[1]

The *St. Cosmas* in the Medici Chapel, sketched by Michelangelo and executed by Montorsoli may be quoted as an example of a Cinquecento seated figure (*Fig.* 185); a noble figure in repose, which might be called a tranquillised *Moses.* There is nothing particularly striking about the motive and yet it is a precise statement of the problem, which the fifteenth century could not have made: if we mentally review the Quattrocento seated figures made for Florence Cathedral we shall recall that not one of these earlier masters even attempted to raise one foot above the level of the other in order to differentiate between the lower

---

[1]The rather elaborate gesture of raising the cup to the lips—a simpler taste would have rendered the actual act of sipping—occurs simultaneously in painting, for example, in the *Giovannino* by Bugiardini in Bologna, Pinacoteca.

limbs, not to mention the bending forward of the torso. Here, in addition, the head gives a new axis of direction and the arms, for all their repose and the unassuming nature of the gesture, form highly effective contrasts in the composition.

Seated figures have the advantage that the form is more compact as a volume and for that reason the contrasts of axial directions clash more vigorously. It is easier to get plastic variety in a seated figure than in a standing one, and it is not to be wondered at that they are more often to be met with in the sixteenth century: the seated type of youthful St. John almost completely ousted the standing one, both in painting and in sculpture, and the late (1556) figure by Jacopo Sansovino in the Frari, Venice (*Fig.* 186), is the more instructive in that it is so exaggerated, since it shows the immense pains incurred by the necessity of appearing interesting.

Recumbent figures offer the greatest of all opportunities for concentrated variety and complexity, and the mere mention of the *Times of Day* in the Medici Chapel (*Figs.* 137–140) must suffice. Not even Titian could withstand their influence and after he had been to Florence he came to feel that the outstretched figure of a beautiful nude woman, as painted in Venice ever since Giorgione, was far too simple; so he sought stronger contrasts of direction in the arrangement of the limbs and painted his *Danae* with her body half-raised and one knee drawn up as she gathers the golden shower in her lap. It is particularly instructive to note that the picture was three times[1] repeated in his studio and in each repetition the pose is more compressed while the contrasts become stronger and stronger in both the principal and secondary figures.

So far, we have chosen examples from sculpture rather than painting, although this was not because painting took a different course—the two developments are absolutely parallel—but because the question of perspective at once occurs in painting, since one and the same movement can have a rich or feeble effect according to the viewpoint adopted by the artist, and, so far, we have dealt only with the increase in actual, objective, movement. As soon as we wish to examine this objective movement in connection with several figures it becomes impossible to relegate painting to the background: it is true that sculpture can treat groups of figures but it soon reaches its natural limits in that direction and the field has to be left to the painter. The tangle of movement which Michelangelo rendered in his ˈ*Iadonna* tondo of the Tribuna has no sculptural analogies even in his work and the *Virgin and Child with St. Anne* of an Andrea Sansovino (Rome, S. Agostino, 1512) seems very meagre beside Leonardo's painted version.

---

[1]The order of the pictures can be exactly determined. As is well known, the first is the one in Naples (1545), followed—with considerable variations—by those in Madrid and the Hermitage while the last and most complete revision of the theme is the Vienna *Danae*.

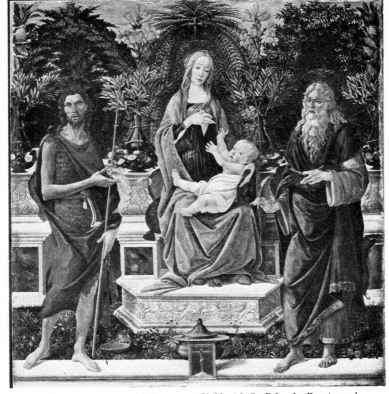

187. BOTTICELLI: *Madonna and Child with St. John the Baptist and St. John the Evangelist*. Berlin

It is a striking fact that, for all the liveliness of the Quattrocento, and even in its most excitable painters—I am thinking of Filippino—a crowd of people never presents a very complex aspect: there is unrest among the details but little movement in the whole, for it lacks divergencies among the main directions. It is possible for Filippino to range five heads side by side with each one inclined in practically the same way as its neighbour; and this, not in a picture of a procession, but in a group of women who are eye-witnesses of the miraculous bringing back to life of the dead Drusiana (Santa Maria Novella, Florence). What a rich variety of axial contrasts there is, to take only one example, in the group of women in Raphael's *Heliodorus*!

When Andrea del Sarto introduces his two handsome Florentine ladies into the room where they visit the mother in bed (Annunziata; *Fig.* XII), he makes them take up positions on two completely opposed axes of direction, with the result that he gives an impression of greater abundance with two figures than Ghirlandaio gives with a whole troupe. The same Sarto can group a number of

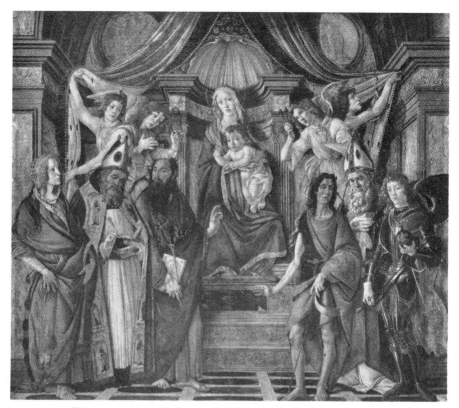

188. BOTTICELLI: *Madonna and Child with Angels and six Saints.* Uffizi

saints standing quietly together in a votive picture and can get a greater variety and richness from simple standing figures (*Madonna delle Arpie*) than a painter like Botticelli can, even when he adds the variation of making the central figure seated, as in the Berlin *Madonna with the two Sts. John* (cf. *Figs.* 125, 187). The determining factor in the difference here is not a matter of greater or less movement in the individual figures: Sarto's advantage lies in the one great contrast between the central figure seen full-face, and the two accompanying figures with their decisively profile positions.[1] The really great increase in the movement contained in a picture is seen only when there is a conjunction of standing, kneeling and seated figures, with the addition of distinctions between front and rear planes and between the upper and lower parts, as in Sarto's *Madonna* of 1524 (Pitti) or the Berlin *Madonna and eight Saints* of 1528, pictures which have their Quattrocento parallel in Botticelli's large composition of the

---

[1]Leonardo may be cited here (*Trattato*, Italian-German ed., No. 187): 'I say again that direct contrasts should be placed close together and intermingled, for they heighten one another and the closer they are together the more they do so.'

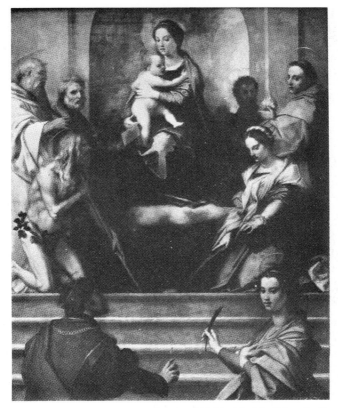

189. ANDREA DEL SARTO: *Madonna and Child with eight Saints*. Berlin

Madonna and six Saints,[1] where the six vertical figures stand side by side almost completely uniform and similar in arrangement (*cf.* Figs. 128, 188, 189).

Finally, if we think of the polyphonic compositions of the Camera della Segnatura, in the presence of this contrapuntal art the comparability of the Quattrocento ceases forthwith; and we are convinced that the human eye had developed new potentialities and powers of perception which made necessary even more complex visual patterns before a picture could really be enjoyed.

2

IF the sixteenth century introduces a new richness in axial directions, it does so in the context of a general opening-up of space. The Quattrocento was still bound by the spell of the flat plane, placing its figures side by side across the

---

[1][Formerly in the Academy, now in the Uffizi.—*Trans.*]. The reproduction given here shows this well-known picture with the upper fifth cut off, since it is an obvious later addition. Only thus do the figures regain their original effect, for a high and empty upper part is quite incompatible with Quattrocento demands for uniform filling of space.

breadth of the picture and composing in strata: in Ghirlandaio's *Birth of St. John the Baptist* (*Fig.* 164) the principal figures are all developed along one plane —the women with the child, the visitors and the maid with the fruit, all stand along one line parallel to the picture plane. In Andrea del Sarto's composition (*Fig.* 106) it is quite different, for the pure curves, the movement in and outwards, give the impression that the space has been vitalized. All the same, such antitheses as 'composition on the plane' and 'space-composition' must be taken with a grain of salt, for the Quattrocentisti themselves made attempts to secure depth, and there are compositions of the *Adoration of the Kings* which employ every means known to them to push the figures back into the middle-distance or the background, away from the front of the stage, but the spectator generally loses track of the thread which was supposed to lead him into depth. In other words, the picture falls apart into disparate strata. The real significance of Raphael's great space-compositions in the Stanze is best taught by Signorelli's frescoes in Orvieto, which the traveller usually sees immediately before he reaches Rome. It seems to me that the contrast between two epochs is completely represented by the difference between Signorelli, whose masses of figures seem to close up at once like a wall in front of us, so that he is only able to show, as it were, the foreground of his vast spaces, and Raphael, who, from the beginning, effortlessly develops all the abundance of his forms outwards from the depths of the picture towards us.

We can go still further and say that the whole conception of form possessed by the fifteenth century is two-dimensional. Not only is the composition stratified but even the individual figures are thought of as silhouettes, though not in the literal sense of the word, yet there is a difference between Early and High Renaissance draughtsmanship which can scarcely be formulated in any other way. Once again I rely on Ghirlandaio's *Birth of St. John*, in particular on the figures of the seated women (*Fig.* 164). Must we not admit that the painter has projected the figures flatly on a plane surface? And then, by contrast, there is the arc of the servant-girls in Sarto's birth-scene, where the principal search is for the effects of salience and recession in the parts—that is, the drawing seeks foreshortened, and not two-dimensional aspects of form. Another example is provided by Botticelli's *Madonna with the two Sts. John*, in Berlin, and Andrea del Sarto's *Madonna delle Arpie* (*Figs.* 187, 125). Why is it that Andrea's St. John the Evangelist is so much more rich and varied in effect? It is true that he is superior in movement, but, more than this, the movement is so rendered that the spectator is led to entertain immediate ideas of plasticity and to experience, in imagination, the projection and recession of the forms. Quite apart from light and shade, there is a different spatial effect because the vertical plane is broken and a tangible three-dimensional image substituted for a flat two-dimensional one. In this three-dimensional image the axis of depth—*i.e.*, precisely the fore-shortened aspect—is given the freest rein. There had been foreshortenings employed before this time, and from the beginning of the Quattrocento we can watch artists grappling with the problem, but now the matter seems to have been settled thoroughly and definitely, so thoroughly that it is permissible to speak of a fundamentally new conception of it. In the *Madonna* by Botticelli already referred to there is also a figure of St. John pointing with his finger in the characteristic attitude of the Baptist, and the placing of the arm in the picture-plane, parallel to the spectator, can be found right through the fifteenth century and has exactly the same form in the preaching St. John as here, where he points to the Christ Child. The fifteenth century was scarcely finished before attempts were made everywhere to work free of this two-dimensional style, and, within the limits of the illustrations in this book, the best evidence for this may be found in a comparison between Ghirlandaio's and Sarto's pictures of *St. John preaching* (*Figs.* 109, 110).

In the sixteenth century foreshortening was reckoned the summit of drawing and all pictures were judged accordingly. Albertinelli finally became so bored with the eternal talk about *scorzi* that he exchanged his easel for the bar of his public-house, and a Venetian dilettante like Ludovico Dolce would have endorsed his opinion—'Foreshortenings are really only a matter for experts, so why give oneself all this trouble over them?'[1] It is likely enough that this was the general opinion in Venice and it must be admitted that Venetian painting already possessed means enough to delight the eye, so that they may have felt it unnecessary to seek information on these attractions of the Tuscan masters. In Florentine and Roman painting, however, all the great masters took up the problem of the third dimension.

Certain motives, such as the arm pointing out of the picture or the bowed head seen full face and foreshortened, occur everywhere almost simultaneously, and it would be not uninteresting to go into the statistics of these cases. Yet it is not so much a matter of single pieces of virtuosity and astounding *scorzi*: what is really important is the universal change in the projection of objects on to a flat plane, the habituation of the eye to three-dimensional images.[2]

3

IT is obvious that light and shade would also have a new part to play in this new art, and one might well believe that an effect of tangible solidity and of circum-ambient space could be obtained much more directly by means of modelling

---

[1]Ludovico Dolce, *L'Aretino* (Viennese 'Quellenschriften' ed. p. 62) [First edition Venice, 1550]. For this reason the experiments of Uccello, among others, need not be mentioned here. Italian [2]landscapes remain remarkably unaffected by problems of perspective and it is no accident that Correggio's art springs from North Italy.

than by foreshortening. In fact, Leonardo made efforts, in theory and practice, towards both goals simultaneously. According to Vasari, Leonardo's ideal as a young artist was '*dar sommo relievo alle figure*' and this remained a lifelong ideal. He began this by using dark backgrounds from which the figures were to emerge, and this is quite a different matter from the earlier practice of employing a mere black foil. He made his shadows much lower in tone and expressly insisted that strong shadows in a picture should occur next to high lights.[1] Even Michelangelo, a draughtsman in the strictest sense of the word, developed in the same way and an ever-increasing strengthening of the shadows can be demonstrated during the course of the work on the Sistine Ceiling; while artists who were more purely painters put their trust, one after another, in dark backgrounds and strongly accented lights. Raphael's *Heliodorus* provides an example (*Fig.* 65) beside which not only his own *Disputà* but also all the frescoes of the earlier Florentines must appear as flat; and what Quattrocento altarpiece could stand the proximity of the strong plastic life of a Fra Bartolommeo? The strength of the impression of physical tangibility in his figures and the weighty solidity of his great niches with their shadowed half-domes must have produced an effect at that time, which we can only reconstruct for ourselves with difficulty.

The general increase in relief naturally involved a change in the form of picture frames, and the flat Quattrocento frame of pilasters with a light entablature was discarded in favour of a tabernacle frame with half or three-quarter columns and a heavy pediment; the playful decorative treatment of such things is dropped in favour of a serious and noble architectural form which could provide material for a chapter in itself.[2]

Light and shade were now employed, not only in the service of modelling, but were very soon generally recognized as extremely valuable aids in enriching the visual image presented by the picture as a whole. When Leonardo lays it down that the light side of a body should appear against a dark foil, and vice-versa, he may still have been thinking in terms of the effect of relief, but light and shade soon became applied universally in a sense analogous to plastic *contrapposto*. Even Michelangelo explored the charms of partial shadow, as the later figures of Slaves on the Ceiling may testify. There are works in which the whole of one half of the body is lost in shadow and this motive can almost be used in place of a plastic differentiation between the parts of the body—the *Venus* by Franciabigio (*Fig.* 170) or the *Young St. John* by Andrea del Sarto (*Fig.* 130) are both of this type. If we look at compositions instead of single figures it becomes even more obvious that these elements are indispensably necessary to this complex art.

---

[1]*Trattato*, Italian-German ed., No. 61.
[2]I do not know what prototypes were employed for the pedimented frames made a few years ago for two well-known Quattrocento pictures in the Pinakothek at Munich (Perugino and Filippino). They seem to me to be rather too heavy and architectonic.

Andrea del Sarto would be lost without his dabs and patches of shadow, which make the whole composition vibrate; and the architectonically-minded Fra Bartolommeo relied heavily on the effect produced by a painterly handling of masses of chiaroscuro. Where they are lacking, as in the sketched-in *Virgin and Child with St. Anne* which is no more than an under-painting, the picture seems to be waiting for the breath of life.

I shall conclude this section with a quotation from Leonardo's treatise on painting[1] in which he says that an artist who paints only for the uncritical crowd will show in his works but little movement, little relief and little foreshortening. In other words, in his view the artistic quality of a picture depends upon the extent to which its author has penetrated into the problems named. Movement, foreshortening, apparent solidity—these are the ideas which we have tried to clarify in their significance for the new style, and, if the analysis is not carried further, the responsibility may be pushed on to Leonardo.

4. Unity and Inevitability

COMPOSITION, as an idea, is of long standing and was a matter for discussion even in the fifteenth century, yet in the strict sense of the word—the correlation of parts, ordered in such a way that they must be seen simultaneously and in relation to one another—it really occurs first in the sixteenth century, and what formerly passed as composition is now seen to be mere aggregation, lacking any special form. The Cinquecento not only grasped a grander kind of co-ordination, replacing the earlier close-up treatment, detail by detail, by an understanding of the function of the detail within the framework of the whole, but it also involves a linking-up of the parts, an inevitability of arrangement, which, in fact, makes all Quattrocento work appear uncoordinated and arbitrary.

The significance of this is made clear by a single example, if we think of the composition of Leonardo's *Last Supper* in comparison with Ghirlandaio's (*Figs. 12, 13*). In the former there is one central figure, dominating and co-ordinating, and a company of men each of whom plays the specific part assigned to him within the general action; it is a building from which no single stone could be removed without upsetting the equilibrium of the whole: in the latter picture there is a number of figures, set side by side, without any law governing the sequence and without inevitability in the actual number of figures represented —there could be more of them, or fewer, and each one could have been posed differently without any really essential change in the appearance of the whole. The symmetrical principle of arrangement was always respected in votive pictures, and there are also secular works, such as Botticelli's *Primavera*, which

[1] *Trattato*, Italian-German ed., No. 59.

hold fast to the principle that there should be one figure in the middle and an equal balance of parts on either side. The sixteenth century, however, could not by any means rest content with this: the figure in the middle was still for the Quattrocento only one among others, and the whole was a collection of parts of approximately equal importance. Instead of a chain of similar links the new desire was for a structure based on decisive pre-eminence or subordination, subordination taking the place of the earlier co-ordination. In proof of this, I may refer to the simplest instance, the votive picture with three figures. In Botticelli's *Madonna with the two Sts. John* (Fig. 187) the three people are placed side by side, each an independent element in the composition, while the three equal niches behind them give additional weight to the idea that the picture could be split up into three parts; an idea which is quite inconceivable in front of the classic version of the theme as we see it in Andrea del Sarto's *Madonna delle Arpie* of 1517 (*Fig.* 125) where the side figures are still elements and indeed have considerable importance in and for themselves, yet the dominance of the central figure is obvious and the links binding them to it are unbreakable.

The transformation to the new style was more difficult in historical pictures than in such votive images, in so far as it was first necessary to establish the centralised scheme of composition in this field, but there was no lack of attempts in the late Quattrocento, and Ghirlandaio showed himself among the most persevering of the experimenters in his frescoes in Santa Maria Novella. There, it is clear that he was no longer quite content with a merely fortuitous arrangement of the figures side by side, and here and there, at any rate, he set himself to tackle the problems of architectonic composition with real seriousness. Nevertheless, Andrea del Sarto's *Scenes from the Life of St. John* in the Scalzo (*Figs.* 108–109; 111–118) come as a complete surprise to the spectator, for he subordinates even the most unpromising and refractory subjects to the centralised scheme, such was his eagerness to obtain an effect of inevitability and his concern to avoid fortuitousness at any cost. No one lagged behind: order and law were imposed even on the crowded chaos of a *Massacre of the Innocents* (Daniele da Volterra, Uffizi), and even a subject like the *Calumny of Apelles*, which so obviously requires continuous narration across the panel, was transposed into the central scheme at the cost of clarity—as in Franciabigio's small-scale version (Pitti) or Girolamo Genga's large one (Pesaro, Villa Imperiale).[1]

This is not the place to describe in detail how the rule was again relaxed, and how the laws governing the presentation of the image were partly abrogated

---

[1]This is the best place to mention one perspective motive. The Quattrocento occasionally sought an attractive effect by an arbitrary placing of the vanishing point towards one side, not actually outside the frame, but close to the edge, as in Filippino's *Madonna* in the Corsini Gallery (*Fig.* 162) or Ghirlandaio's *Visitation* fresco. Such disturbing elements were antipathetic to classic ideals and sensibilities.

in the interests of a more vivid impression: the Vatican frescoes contain well-known examples of symmetry abandoned within the framework of a purely tectonic style, yet it must be emphasised that nobody could use this freedom properly unless he had passed through the discipline of the strictly-ordered composition. It was only against a background of a firmly held conception of form that a partial relaxation of the method of procedure could be effective.

The same thing is true of the composition of single groups, where an analogous striving after tectonic arrangement is traceable from Leonardo onwards. The *Madonna of the Rocks* (*Fig.* 8) can be inscribed in an equilateral triangle, and this geometric proportion of which the spectator is immediately conscious, distinguishes the work sharply and obviously from all its contemporaries. The advantages of a closed composition were perceived where the group as a whole has an appearance of inevitability and yet the individual figures were not restricted in freedom of movement. Perugino worked on the same lines in his *Pietà* of 1495, for which one can find no parallel in either Filippino or Ghirlandaio; and, finally, Raphael in his Florentine *Madonnas* made himself the subtlest of master-builders. Then, even here, the change from regularity to apparent irregularity develops irresistibly; the equilateral triangle becomes a scalene triangle and there are shifts in the symmetry of the axial system, but the kernel of the effect remained unchanged, and the impression of inevitability is retained even in a completely a-tectonic group. In this way, we are brought to the grand-scale composition of the 'free' style. In Raphael, as in Sarto, we find a freely rhythmic type of composition next to a tectonic scheme: in the court of the Annunziata, the *Birth of the Virgin* is placed next to the severe scenes of miracles, and in the tapestries we find an *Ananias* immediately beside the *Miraculous Draught* or the *Charge to Peter*. This is not just the continued tolerance of old-fashioned ideas, for this free style is something entirely different from the former lack of rule, where everything could equally well have been given a different form. Such a strongly-worded expression is permissible, in order to accentuate the contrast, for the fifteenth century can, in fact, show nothing which even approximates to the 'not-to-be-altered' character of groups like Raphael's *Miraculous Draught* (*Fig.* 69). There is no architectonic structure to bind the figures together, and yet they form an absolutely closed group. In the same way, though to a lesser degree, all the figures in Sarto's *Birth of the Virgin* (*Fig.* 106) are subordinated to one sweeping and comprehensive line which possesses a convincing rhythmic inevitability.

In order to make this relationship quite clear it may be permissible to quote a Venetian example which happens to offer very favourable conditions for observing the points in question. I mean the story of the murder of St. Peter Martyr, as depicted, on the one hand, by a Quattrocento painter in the picture

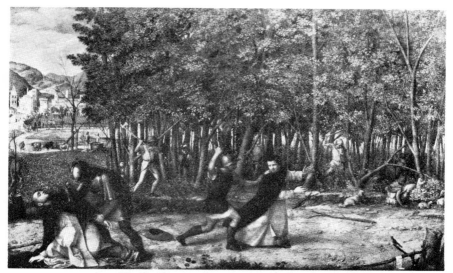

190. BELLINI (?): *The Murder of St. Peter Martyr*. London, National Gallery

in the National Gallery, London[1], and, on the other hand, as shown by Titian in its classic form in the picture, now destroyed, for the church of SS. Giovanni e Paolo (*Figs.* 190–191). The Quattrocento painter spells out the story word by word—there is a wood, with people being attacked, namely, the saint and his companion, and one flees this way and the other that way, and one is stabbed at the right and the other at the left. Titian starts with the assumption that two analogous scenes cannot possibly be represented side by side. The assault on St. Peter must be the principal motive, with which nothing can be allowed to compete, and so he leaves out the second murder, treats the saint's companion simply as a fleeing figure, and at the same time, makes him subordinate to the principal motive by including him in the same context of movement so that he intensifies the impetus of the assault by continuing the direction of the movement. He is hurled off, like a fragment thrown off from the main body, in the same direction as the saint has fallen, and thus an element originally disturbing and distracting becomes an indispensable factor in the effect.

To express this advance in philosophical terms, it might be said that development here, too, means integration and differentiation: each motive must occur only once and the old-fashioned equivalence of the parts must be replaced by absolute differences, and at the same time the distinct parts must fuse together into a whole, no part of which can be deficient without causing the

[1]The ascription to Giovanni Bellini seems nowadays generally abandoned: recently, Jacobsen suggested Basaiti (*Repertorium*, XXIV, p. 341). [The National Gallery Catalogue, 1951, calls it 'ascribed to Giovanni Bellini', but the attribution is accepted by Berenson, *Italian Pictures of the Renaissance*, 1932; Hendy, *Bellini*, 1945, and others.—*Trans.*].

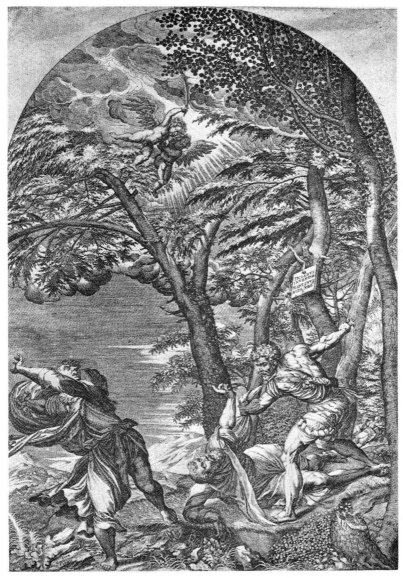

191. TITIAN: *The Murder of St. Peter Martyr*. Engraving

collapse of the whole. This essential character of classic art had already been presaged by Leon Battista Alberti when, in a much-quoted sentence, he defined perfect beauty as a condition in which the slightest alteration would detract from the beauty of the whole. He defined it in words, but here we have the idea made manifest.

The use made of the trees shows how Titian, in a composition of this type, employed all the accessory parts to further the principal effect; for the earlier picture shows the forest existing as an object in itself, where Titian makes the trees share in the movement, accompanying the action and thereby giving an unusual grandeur and energy to the event. When Domenichino retold the story in the seventeenth century, in his well-known picture in the Pinacoteca at Bologna, he leaned heavily on Titian, yet the feeling for all this artistic wisdom was already blunted.

It need hardly be said that landscape backgrounds were combined with figure effects in Cinquecento Roman pictures just

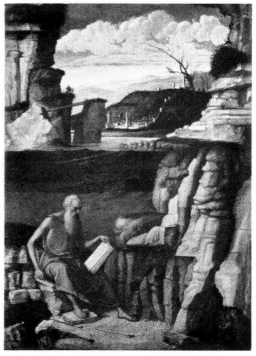

192. BASAITI: *St. Jerome*. London, National Gallery

as much as in Venice. The landscape in Raphael's *Miraculous Draught of Fishes* has this kind of significance, as has already been said, and if we take the next tapestry, the *Charge to Peter*, we find exactly the same thing; for the highest point in the gentle slope of the line of the hill coincides exactly with the caesura in the figure group and thus gently but emphatically helps the Apostles to appear as one clearly distinct group in contrast to the single figure of Christ (*cf. Fig.* 70). If, however, I may be allowed another Venetian example, the *St. Jerome* by Basaiti (London, National Gallery) when compared with Titian's picture of the same saint (in the Brera) shows the difference of outlook between the two epochs as clearly as one could hope for (*Figs.* 192–193). In the former, the landscape is intended to have a meaning of its own and the saint is inserted into it without any essential connection, but in the Titian, on the other hand, the figure and the line of the hill were conceived together from the very first and the steep, wooded slope sharply underlines the upward movement of the penitent, dragging him upwards as it were. It is a landscape setting which is as much adapted to this particular figure as he is to it.

In this way, artists ceased to regard architectural backgrounds as arbitrary enrichments, to be added on the principle of the more the better, but came to look for inevitability in the relationship between figures and buildings. There had always been a feeling that the dignity of human beings could be increased by an architectural accompaniment, but usually the buildings got out of hand and swamped the figures: Ghirlandaio's architectural show-pieces are far too rich to provide a suitable foil for his figures, and, in the simple case of a figure in a niche it is astonishing how rarely the Quattrocento managed to combine them effectively. Filippo Lippi carries the treatment of parts as separate entities so far that his seated *Saints* (in the Academy)[1] never once correspond to the niches in the wall behind them; an exhibition of casual and accidental treatment which must have seemed absolutely intolerable to the Cinquecento, for it is obvious that he was more interested in the charms of waywardness and agitation than

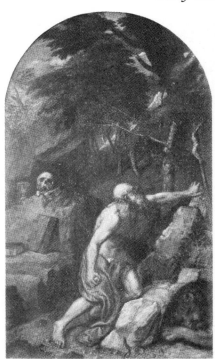

193. TITIAN: *St. Jerome.* Brera

in dignity. Fra Bartolommeo was able to give his heroic figures majesty by the very different method of making them cut across the top of the niche, as his *Resurrected Christ*, in the Pitti, shows. It would be superfluous to refer to all the other Cinquecento examples of effective buildings, where the architecture seems like a potent assertion of the people themselves. However, while we are on the subject of this universal desire to relate the parts of the whole composition one to another we come upon a feature of classic taste which goes beyond painting alone and invites a criticism of the whole of earlier art. Vasari relates an incident which is very typical of this, when he says that the architect of the vestibule to the Sacristy of Santo Spirito in Florence was sharply criticised because the lines dividing the compartments of the barrel vault do not coincide with the axes of the columns[2]—a criticism which might have been made of a hundred other examples.

---

[1][There are now (1950) no seated *Saints* in the Florentine Academy attributed to Filippo Lippi: it seems most probable that Wölfflin is referring to Uffizi 8354, *The Virgin Enthroned, with Sts. Damian, Francis, Cosmas and Anthony of Padua* (*Fig.* 194), which was transferred to the Uffizi from the Academy in 1919.—*Trans.*].

[2]Vasari, Milanesi, IV, p. 513, *Vita di Andrea Contucci* [*Sansovino*], where we may also read with interest how the architect excused himself.

The lack of lines running through the whole composition and the treatment of each part as an end in itself, without reference to a unified total effect, are among the most striking peculiarities of Quattrocento art.

From the moment when architecture cast off its immature and playful flexibility and became mature, measured, and severe it took over the reins for all the arts. The Cinquecento conceived everything *sub specie architecturæ*. The sculptured figures on tombs were assigned their fixed position, framed, enclosed and embedded; nothing can be moved or altered, even in thought, and we know why each part is exactly where it is, and not a trifle higher or lower— I may refer back to the discussion of Rossellino and Sansovino on pp. 67 ff. The same may be said of painting, and where, as wall-decoration, it was related to architecture then it was always architecture which had the last word. What extraordinary liberties Filippino took in his frescoes in Santa Maria Novella! He extends the floor of his stage out beyond the picture-plane so that the figures stand partly on our side of the wall-plane and are thus brought into the most remarkable relationship with the actual elements of the architectural framing. Signorelli did the same thing at Orvieto; Verrocchio's group of *Christ and St. Thomas* provides a sculptural analogy, since the action takes place partly outside the niche. No Cinquecento artist would have done such a thing, and it became an obvious assumption, a premise taken for granted, that painting had to seek its space within the depth of the wall and that the frame must make clear the entrance to the stage.[1]

Architecture having become unified in style, it required, as a corollary, unity in wall paintings, and Leonardo already held the opinion that pictures should not be painted one above the other on a wall, as was the case with Ghirlandaio's choir-decorations, in which we seem to have a view into the different stories of a house, one above the other, and all visible at once.[2] He would scarcely have agreed to the painting of two pictures side by side on the same wall of a choir or chapel, and certainly Ghirlandaio's method is indefensible when it leads him to allow two frescoes to come sharply together—the *Visitation* and the *Rejection of Joachim's Sacrifice*—with the setting apparently continued behind the dividing pilaster; and yet each picture has its own separate perspective scheme, not even consistent with its neighbour.

The tendency to paint in a unifying style on surfaces which had been architecturally unified has become universal since the sixteenth century, but now also the great problem of harmonising the pictorial decoration with its surroundings

---

[1]Although Masaccio had already introduced complete clarity in this respect, during the course of the century it again became so obscured that it was possible to make two frescoes join at a corner without any frame at all. It would be interesting to follow up, in a systematic way, the architectonic treatment of wall paintings.

[2]*Trattato*, Italian-German ed., No. 119. [This passage is translated in McCurdy, *Notebooks of Leonardo*, Vol. II, p. 239–40.—*Trans.*]

was tackled, so that the spatial composition of the picture seemed created precisely for the room or the chapel in which it was situated, and that the one explained itself by reference to the other and in no other way. When this is achieved the result is a kind of spatial music, an impression of harmony, which is among the most potent effects ever attained by the visual arts.

It has already been said that the fifteenth century paid but scant attention to the unified treatment of a room and concerned itself only with each detail in turn, but this observation can be expanded to include larger spaces as well, such as public squares. We may ask, for example, how the great equestrian statues of *Colleoni* and *Gattamelata* came to be placed as they are, and whether anyone nowadays would have the courage to site them so completely without reference to the main axis of the square or the church. Modern opinion is represented by the two equestrian princes by Giovanni da Bologna in Florence, but, even so, there remains a good deal for us to learn. Finally, the unified conception of space asserts itself on the very greatest scale when buildings and landscape are conceived as an effect from one view-point: the lay-out of villas and gardens, the enclosing of whole panoramas, and similar schemes may be called to mind as instances of this. The Baroque took up these planned effects on a still greater scale; yet anyone who has ever looked out from the high terrace of the incomparably magnificently situated Villa Imperiale, near Pesaro, towards the mountains over by Urbino, where the whole countryside is subordinated to the castle, will have received an impression of the noble discernment of the High Renaissance, which even the most colossal arrangements of later times can hardly surpass.

THERE is a conception of art-history which sees nothing more in art than a 'translation of Life' (Taine) into pictorial terms, and which attempts to interpret every style as an expression of the prevailing mood of the age. Who would wish to deny that this is a fruitful way of looking at the matter? Yet it takes us only so far—as far, one might say, as the point at which art begins. Anyone who concerns himself exclusively with the subject-matter of works of art will be completely satisfied with it; yet the moment we want to apply artistic standards of judgement in the criticism of works of art we are forced to try to comprehend formal elements which are unmeaning and inexpressible in themselves and which are developments of a purely optical kind.

Thus, 'Quattrocento' and 'Cinquecento' as style-concepts are not adequately explained by a descriptive analysis of the subject-matter: the phenomenon of 'Quattrocento' and 'Cinquecento' style has a double root and shows a development of artistic vision which is essentially independent of any particular sentiment or any particular ideal of beauty. The noble gestures of the Cinquecento, its

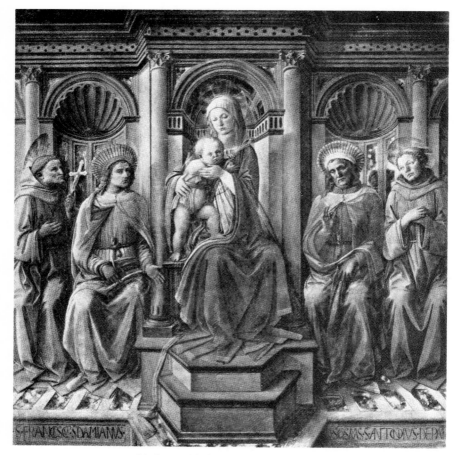

194. FILIPPO LIPPI: *Madonna with Saints Cosmas and Damian and other Saints*. Uffizi

restrained bearing, and its spacious and strong beauty characterize the feelings of that generation; but all the things we have analysed so far—clarity of presentation, the desire of the cultivated eye for ever richer and more significant images, until the point is reached where multiplicity can be seen as a coherent unity and the parts can be fused into an inevitable whole (unity)—these are all formal elements which cannot be deduced from the spirit of the age.

The classic character of Cinquecento art is founded on these formal elements. Here we are dealing with developments which are repeated everywhere; we are dealing with permanent and pervasive art forms, and that which distinguishes Raphael above all the earlier generation is the same as that which, under entirely different circumstances, makes a Ruysdael a classic among the Dutch landscape painters.

In saying this, we have no desire to advocate a formalist type of art criticism: it is indeed the function of light to make the diamond sparkle.

LIST OF ILLUSTRATIONS

LIST OF ILLUSTRATIONS